Glamour Girls of
Sixties Hollywood

ALSO BY TOM LISANTI
AND FROM MCFARLAND

*Pamela Tiffin: Hollywood to Rome, 1961–1974* (2015)

*Hollywood Surf and Beach Movies:
The First Wave, 1959–1969* (2005, paperback 2012)

*Drive-in Dream Girls: A Galaxy of B-Movie
Starlets of the Sixties* (2003, paperback 2012)

*Fantasy Femmes of Sixties Cinema:
Interviews with 20 Actresses from Biker,
Beach, and Elvis Movies* (2001, paperback 2010)

BY TOM LISANTI AND LOUIS PAUL

*Film Fatales: Women in Espionage Films
and Television, 1962–1973* (McFarland, 2002)

ALSO OF INTEREST BY
GAIL GERBER WITH TOM LISANTI

*Trippin' with Terry Southern: What I Think
I Remember* (McFarland, 2009)

# Glamour Girls of Sixties Hollywood

*Seventy-Five Profiles*

TOM LISANTI

McFarland & Company, Inc., Publishers
*Jefferson, North Carolina*

*The present work is a reprint of the illustrated case bound edition of* Glamour Girls of Sixties Hollywood: Seventy-Five profiles, *first published in 2008 by McFarland.*

LIBRARY OF CONGRESS CATALOGUING-IN-PUBLICATION DATA

Lisanti, Tom, 1961–
/ Tom Lisanti.
p.    cm.
Includes bibliographical references and index.

ISBN 978-1-4766-7233-5
softcover : acid free paper

1. Motion picture actors and actresses—United States—Biography—Dictionaries.
2. Actresses—United States—Biography—Dictionaries.    I. Title.

PN1998.2.L574 2017      791.4302′8092273—dc22      [B]      2007027724

BRITISH LIBRARY CATALOGUING DATA ARE AVAILABLE

© 2008 Tom Lisanti. All rights reserved

*No part of this book may be reproduced or transmitted in any form or by any means, electronic or mechanical, including photocopying or recording, or by any information storage and retrieval system, without permission in writing from the publisher.*

On the cover: Carol Wayne; background image © 2017 Shutterstock

Printed in the United States of America

*McFarland & Company, Inc., Publishers
Box 611, Jefferson, North Carolina 28640
www.mcfarlandpub.com*

To Ern, 'cause I know how much you just *love* the sixties glamour girls

# *Acknowledgments*

I would like to thank the following people for all their kind help and contributions in making this book a real pleasure to write—Thordis Brandt, Victoria Carroll, Suzanne Charny, Corinne Cole, Danica d'Hondt, Gail Gerber, Michael Howe, Melodie Johnson, Aron Kincaid, Vicki London, BarBara Luna, Lee Meredith, Ann Morell, Inga Neilsen, Dr. James Platler, Anne Randall, Linda Rogers, Lisa Seagram, Jane Wald, Blair Whipple, and Dr. John Wolberg. Special thanks to C. Robert Rotter, Shaun Chang, David Savage, my web master Jim "JT" McGann, Jeremy Megraw, Michael Moreno, Louis Paul, Adam Phillips, Lee Pfeiffer, Tom Weaver, Peter Riesett, Virgil Stephens, and my friends and family, especially Ernie DeLia and my mom Joan Lisanti.

# Contents

*Acknowledgments* vii
*Introduction* 1

## Profiles
(Interviewees in **bold**)

| | | | |
|---|---|---|---|
| Sivi Aberg | 5 | Linda Foster | 79 |
| Beverly Adams | 8 | Marianne Gaba | 82 |
| Maureen Arthur | 11 | Sue Hamilton | 83 |
| Pamela Austin | 14 | Joy Harmon | 85 |
| **Thordis Brandt** | 16 | Ena Hartman | 88 |
| Bettina Brenna | 22 | Alexandra Hay | 91 |
| Eve Bruce | 24 | Marianna Hill | 93 |
| Michele Carey | 26 | Susan Holloway | 96 |
| **Victoria Carroll** | 29 | Teri Hope | 98 |
| Amedee Chabot | 38 | Mary Hughes | 100 |
| Arlene Charles | 40 | **Melodie Johnson** | 103 |
| **Suzanne Charny** | 42 | Alena Johnston | 107 |
| **Corinne Cole** | 47 | Joi Lansing | 109 |
| Jo Collins | 56 | Anna Lavelle | 113 |
| Yvonne Craig | 58 | China Lee | 115 |
| Pamela Curran | 61 | Lara Lindsay | 117 |
| **Danica d'Hondt** | 64 | **Vicki London** | 119 |
| Phyllis Davis | 70 | Darlene Lucht | 123 |
| Susan Denberg | 72 | Deanna Lund | 125 |
| Lyn Edgington | 74 | Linda Marshall | 128 |
| Dolores Faith | 77 | **Lee Meredith** | 130 |

| | | | |
|---|---|---|---|
| Donna Michelle | 136 | **Lisa Seagram** | 193 |
| **Ann Morell** | 139 | Bobbi Shaw | 201 |
| Cynthia Myers | 144 | Eva Six | 203 |
| **Inga Neilsen** | 146 | Sharon Tate | 205 |
| Alberta Nelson | 154 | Margaret Teele | 208 |
| Warrene Ott | 156 | Marilyn Tindall | 209 |
| Beverly Powers | 158 | Corinna Tsopei | 211 |
| **Anne Randall** | 161 | Victoria Vetri | 213 |
| Jacki Ray | 168 | Jane Wald | 216 |
| Dolly Read | 170 | Jan Watson | 218 |
| Jeannine Riley | 173 | Carol Wayne | 221 |
| Pamela Rodgers | 175 | Nina Wayne | 223 |
| **Linda Rogers** | 178 | Delores Wells | 226 |
| Myrna Ross | 183 | June Wilkinson | 228 |
| Tura Satana | 185 | Edy Williams | 230 |
| Christiane Schmidtmer | 187 | Francine York | 233 |
| Linda Gaye Scott | 190 | | |

*Bibliography* 237
*Index* 239

# Introduction

*Glamour Girls of Sixties Hollywood* pays tribute to 75 "decorative actresses" who for a brief moment were popular pinups during the swinging Sixties. These glamour girls all began their careers cast in minor parts as beauty queens, beach bunnies, call girls, coeds, spy chicks, waitresses, stewardesses, or showgirls in musicals, surf movies, sex comedies, and spy spoofs. On television they played the villain's moll on *Batman*, helpful agents or conniving bad girls on *The Man from U.N.C.L.E.* and *The Wild Wild West*, and fashion models on *Burke's Law*, among others. Despite their small roles, these actresses were definitely noticed by movie and television audiences, especially teenage boys and men. Because of their delicate features, curvaceous figures, and intense sex appeal, they were like fantasy figures come to life on screen and in magazines across the nation.

Being labeled a "glamour girl," of course, had its downside. The gals featured in this book were originally cast not so much for the way they could deliver a line but for their looks and their bra size, which is not surprising since many of them came to Hollywood from the beauty pageant circuit, the modeling world, the pages of *Playboy*, or the stages of Las Vegas. Whatever acting talent they possessed went unappreciated as they were used as eye candy wrapped in a bikini, a towel, a leotard, a low-cut dress, or the shortest of miniskirts. As such, they added glamour to the proceedings, parading scantily-clad across the big and small screens. They were lucky if they got a closeup as the sexist directors of the period often trained the camera on their shapely derrieres or abundant cleavage. They didn't so much act as react to the action going on around them or to the leading players. Their screen time could be so minimal that in some cases if you blinked you missed them. But one would never guess that by the publicity they generated to promote the movies, which assured their pinup status.

The most famous glamour girl of the decade was undoubtedly Raquel Welch, who possessed the beauty, talent, determination, and the luck (which plays a part in every actor's career) to become a movie star. She too began playing bit decorative parts such as a call girl in *A House Is Not a Home* (1964) and a coed in *Roustabout* (1964). On television she appeared briefly as a stewardess on *Bewitched* and a beauty queen on *The Rogues*. After graduating to being the "Billboard Girl" on the TV variety series *The Hollywood Palace*, she landed a lead role in the beach movie *A Swingin' Summer* (1965). It was that film that earned her a contract at 20th Century–Fox. Her first starring movie was *Fantastic Voyage* (1966), followed by *One Million Years, B.C.* (1966), and the rest, as they say, is history.

But unlike Raquel, who became a superstar, the actresses here never made it to the top for one reason or another. It is not surprising that most were as beautiful as Raquel

# Introduction

**All hail Raquel Welch**—*the* **glamour girl of the Sixties.**

Shapely Stella Stevens was the only Sixties Playboy Playmate to become a bona fide movie star.

and had curvaceous bodies to match. What is surprising is that a number of them—including Inga Neilsen, Lisa Seagram, Victoria Carroll, Lee Meredith, Danica d'Hondt, and Suzanne Charny—were professionally trained actors, singers or dancers. Some, particularly Edy Williams and Francine York, had the drive and determination of Welch to become stars but they lacked that certain "it factor" to propel them to superstardom. Even so, a handful of actresses included here had interesting or enviable careers. Like Raquel, a few of these gals had a quality that allowed them to rise through the ranks to leading-lady status in movies (Sharon Tate, Michele Carey, Marianna Hill, Melodie Johnson, Alexandra Hay) and on television (Yvonne Craig, Lisa Seagram, Ena Hartman, Pamela Austin). However, for all of them the star-making projects remained elusive. Only one came close to reaching the heights of Raquel's fame and that was Sharon Tate but in death, not life.

Typecasting was rampant during the Sixties, affecting a good number of the actresses profiled here. It was especially detrimental to young, gorgeous, buxom or statuesque blondes who were usually hired to play "stupid broad" roles. For the most part, no intelligent, pretty blonde characters were written back then. Once an actress was typecast, the die was usually cast, so producers didn't want to take a chance on her in a different type of role. Succumbing to the typecasting-or-no-casting reality of their profession, a number of actresses built moderately successful careers enacting the dumb, sexy blonde (Carol Wayne, Maureen Arthur, Lee Meredith, Joy Harmon, Bobbi Shaw) or the commanding glamazon (Inga Neilsen, Joi Lansing, Thordis Brandt, June Wilkinson). Despite their talent, none of these gals were ever able to break free from these types of roles.

Of the Playboy Playmates who came alive on the silver screen, only Stella Stevens (Miss January 1960) had the voluptuousness of body and acting talent to buck typecasting and become a bona fide movie star beginning with her first-rate comical performance in *The Nutty Professor* (1963). The rest, including Jo Collins, Delores Wells, China Lee, and Donna Michelle, languished in bikini roles, which was a vicious trap. Beach bunnies and spy chicks such as Linda Rogers, Arlene Charles, Mary Hughes, Jan Watson, Marilyn Tindall, and Jacki Ray never broke free from it. Amedee Chabot did but she had to abandon Hollywood for Mexico to do it.

By the late Sixties, roles changed dramatically for actresses with the advent of screen nudity. It was no longer sufficient to see sexy ladies parade across the screen skimpily attired; they were now required to doff their blouses for many a topless scene. Raised on Fifties values, most of the women profiled here refused and saw their careers stall or come to a complete halt. The few who had no qualms about disrobing on camera (Edy Williams, Phyllis Davis, Marianna Hill, Anne Randall, Victoria Vetri, Alexandra Hay) went on to become drive-in trash movie queens during the Seventies but saw their careers fade out during the Eighties. Others who had screen presence (Suzanne Charny, Michele Carey, Melodie Johnson, Lisa Seagram, Lee Meredith, Maureen Arthur) persevered and kept working until they voluntarily stopped or they hit the dreaded age of forty—the death knell for glamour girls in Hollywood who hadn't yet made it to the top. Despite the odds, a handful of actresses (Victoria Carroll, Francine York, Inga Neilsen) have managed to transcend the decades, parlaying their talents from sexpot roles in the Sixties to character parts today.

# *Profiles*

(Interviewees in **bold**)

---

# Sivi Aberg

A Swedish beauty with long blonde hair, blue eyes, and a fresh, wholesome appearance, she toiled in decorative bit roles in film and television during the Sixties but found fame in the Seventies by just looking pretty as a game show model.

**You May Remember Her Most From:** TV's *The Gong Show* as the glamourous assistant to wacky host Chuck Barris.

**Her Groovy '60s Credits:** Comedian Bob Hope spotted beauty queen Sivi Aberg at the 1964 Miss Universe pageant and offered her a minor role in the comedy *I'll Take Sweden* (1965). Surprisingly, Aberg doesn't appear as a Swede but instead is the pretty coed who canoodles up to Frankie Avalon at a bonfire and offers to take his mind off of his absent girlfriend Tuesday Weld. In *That Funny Feeling* (1965), Aberg's role is even smaller as she is lost amongst the dozens of bodacious beauties who surround playboy editor Bobby Darin, who amazingly prefers the scrawny Sandra Dee. Another bit role followed in *Easy Come, Easy Go* (1967) as an amorous party guest who hugs and caresses Elvis Presley, mistaking him for her friend as he tries to navigate across a crowded dance floor to find Dodie Marshall. Television offered the curvaceous Swede with the much touted figure (37-24-37) more screen time including multiple episodes of *Batman* where she joined Marilyn Hanold and Edy Williams as the bagpipe-playing molls to Liberace's evil piano-playing Chandell, who kidnaps sweet Aunt Harriet in "The Devil's Fingers" and "The Dead Ringers," and a bikini-clad surfer girl who aides the nefarious Joker in "Surf's Up! The Joker's Under!" On *I Spy*, Sivi emerged from the Moroccan desert like a beautiful fair-haired mirage as a German tourist who gives a lift to camel-riding agents Robert Culp and Bill Cosby in "The Honorable Assassins." At the 1967 Hollywood Deb Star Ball, Sivi beat out, among others, Celeste Yarnall, Ann Morell, Debbie Watson, and E.J. Peaker to be named "The Hollywood Star of Tomorrow," probably more so for her looks than her body

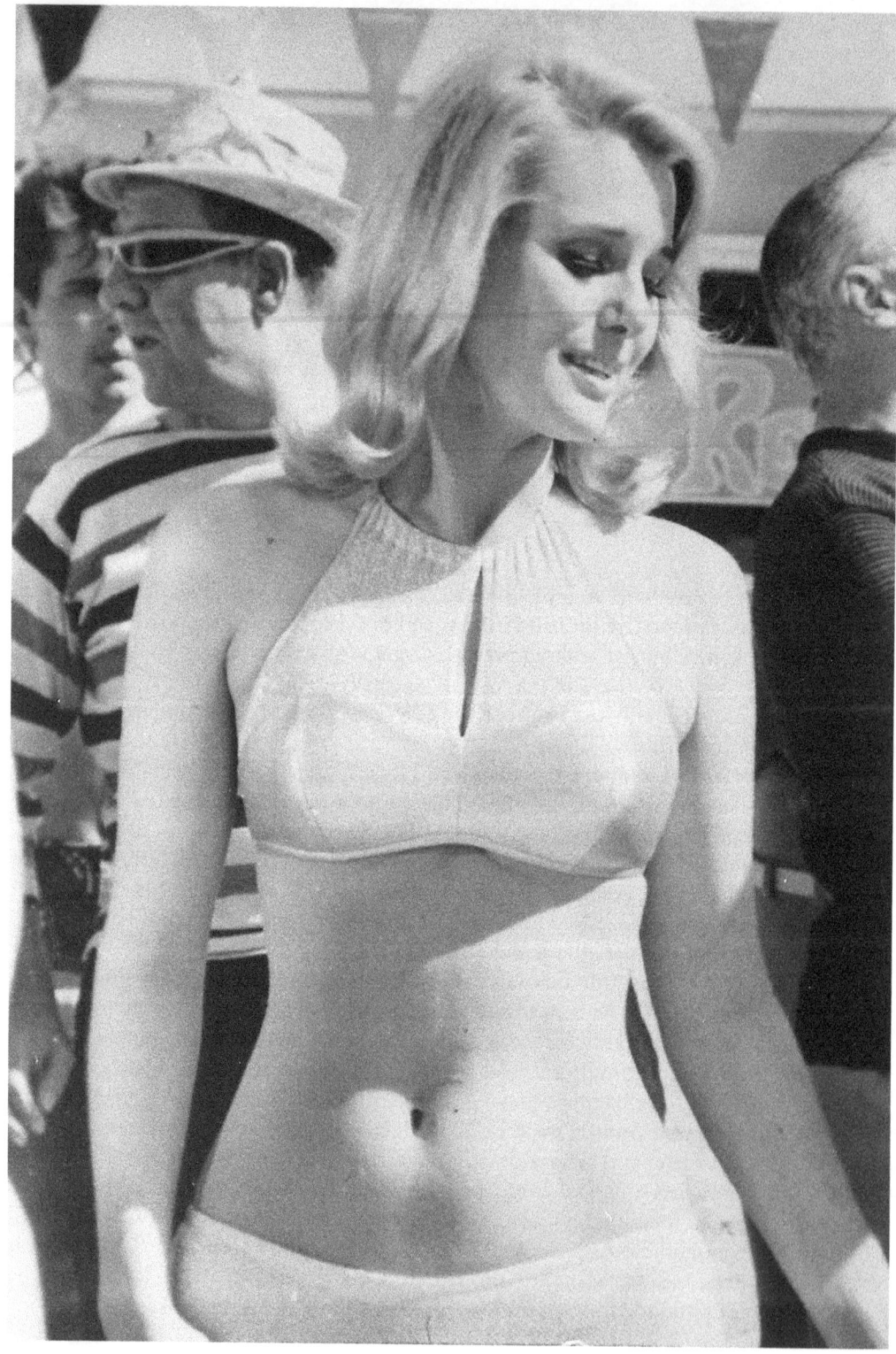

Sivi Aberg (1967).

of work (her height, 5-foot-8 without heels, lost her a number of roles). She next took a big career risk for a Sixties starlet and played a sexy lesbian in *The Killing of Sister George* (1968). Director Robert Aldrich's groundbreaking drama was one of the first movies to openly deal with lesbianism and one of the first to be slapped with an X rating. Beryl Reid played the paranoid, alcoholic, overwrought star of a BBC soap opera and Susannah York played her waif-like younger lover. The gorgeous Aberg with her long blonde hair parted in the middle pops up in a bar scene, standing out like a Swedish goddess amongst a slew of unattractive butch lesbians all seeming to sport short cropped hair. Aberg played Diana, the miffed girlfriend of one of Reid's catty friends who abandons her to dance with York. She offers to teach Reid to dance but the bemused older woman would rather drink at the bar. When Reid comments that the dancers resemble something out of Edgar Allan Poe, the dim-witted Aberg asks, "Edgar *who?*" Not surprisingly, the movie did nothing for Sivi's career and she returned to television, making guest appearances on a few series including three cameos on *Rowan and Martin's Laugh-In*, *Hogan's Heroes* (in "LeBeau and the Little Old Lady" in a one-line role as a shapely resistance fighter), and two episodes of *Mannix*. She then worked as a regular, one of the original "Operation Entertainment Girls," on the USO-type TV variety show *Operation: Entertainment* in 1968. Performing for and meeting the troops around the world, Aberg became a favorite pinup amongst military men. Sivi would be joined by Thordis Brandt in the second season.

**The Beginning:** Sivi Aberg was born Siv Marta Aberg on May 7, 1944, in Gavle, Sweden. A natural blonde, she blossomed into a luscious beauty with a tantalizing figure. After graduating school with a degree in cosmetology, the statuesque blonde decided it was time to flaunt her physical assets. She entered and won the Miss Stockholm pageant, which led to her being crowned Miss Sweden. At the 1964 Miss Universe contest held in Miami, Florida, Sivi placed fourth runner-up to Miss Greece Corinna Tsopei, who took the title that year.

**The '70s & Beyond:** Sivi followed the pattern of a number of her Sixties contemporaries by appearing in low-budget exploitation movies in the Seventies. In *Dr. Death: Seeker of Souls* (1973) she played a murder victim brought back to life by 1,000-year-old magician John Considine, who is able to transfer another woman's soul into her shapely body. Later she literally gets the axe and her decapitated head is delivered to her boyfriend Barry Coe. In 1973 the statuesque beauty became a regular on the TV game show *The New Treasure Hunt* as an anonymous model who fetched for the show's contestants decorated boxes containing anything from booby prizes to $25,000. This wasn't her first game show gig. During the Sixties she was a guest on *The Dating Game* and an assistant on *Dream Girl*. On the big screen, she turned up briefly in *The Teacher* (1974) starring Jay *Dennis the Menace* North as a teenager seduced by neighbor Angel Tompkins; Aberg was featured in another lesbian role. Sivi has nothing more to do than to show off her extremely curvaceous bikini-clad body as she takes a leisurely swim while her bitchy girlfriend Quinn O'Hara argues with Tompkins at a pool party. Another minor decorative role as a bountiful blonde bakery customer ogled by zany Marty Feldman followed in the comedy *Silent Movie* (1976). More prominent was her role on the hilarious amateur talent show *The Gong Show* as she and host Chuck Barris, who produced *Dream Girl*, would playfully banter as she revealed contestants' scores if they were lucky enough *not* to get gonged by the celebrity panel. The show was a huge hit. Television viewers may not have remembered her name but she was instantly recognized and played herself in "Sanford and Gong" on *Sanford and*

*Son* in 1976. Aberg's game show career came to a halt in 1978, the same year she appeared as herself in the celebrity athletic competition *US Against the World II* as part of the world team along with William Shatner, Britt Ekland, Jane Seymour, and Dudley Moore. After playing a small role as every man's fantasy housekeeper in the TV-movie *Drop-Out Father* (1982), Sivi Aberg too dropped out and reportedly went into the real estate business.

# Beverly Adams

A curvaceous, sultry, green-eyed brunette, she was the definitive Sixties chick, appearing in Elvis Presley musicals, beach flicks, spy spoofs, and biker movies. She gained even more notoriety when she began sporting the "in" Vidal Sassoon short haircut made famous by Mia Farrow and then married the famous stylist.

**You May Remember Her Most From:** her role as sexy Lovey Kravezit, the Miss Moneypenny of the Matt Helm spy movies starring Dean Martin.

**Her Groovy '60s Credits:** Beverly Adams made her TV debut on *The Adventures of Ozzie and Harriet*. This led to more minor roles on *Channing*, *The Red Skelton Show*, three appearances playing a model on *Burke's Law*, and *Dr. Kildare* (as a nurse). She made her film debut in a bit part as a student nurse clad in only a bra and slip in *The New Interns* (1964) followed by roles as a sexy young thing who flirts with Elvis in *Roustabout* (1964) and a coed in *Girl Happy* (1965), also starring the King. She then entered Columbia Studios' New Talent program; when she completed it, she was offered a contract due to her screen test where she played the Billie Dawn character from *Born Yesterday*. However, unlike that part, her subsequent movie roles did not require much acting ability. She was loaned to American International Pictures to play the sexy mantrap Cassandra, a beach beauty conjured up by witch doctor Buster Keaton to distract the surfer boys from hitting on sailor Frankie Avalon's girlfriend Annette Funicello, in *How to Stuff a Wild Bikini* (1965). Even though she was saddled with long red wig, Adams looked terrific stuffed in her wild leopard bikini and instilled some joviality into the role as klutzy Cassandra falls for Harvey Lembeck's biker leader Eric Von Zipper instead of ad man Dwayne Hickman, who is pursuing Annette. Her next movie was the enjoyable *Winter a-Go-Go* (1965), a beach party in the snow with Adams this time in "the Annette Funicello role" as the marriage-minded good girl vying with sophisticated rich bitch Jill Donohue for handsome ski lodge owner William Wellman, Jr. Adams won the guy but lost in the acting department as costars Donohue, Linda Rogers, and Nancy Czar upstaged her. Amongst her television roles at this time were the aptly named D. D. "Danger" O'Riley, the sweetly naïve model and house sitter who is spending a bit too much time with neighbor Darrin to his wife's chagrin in "George the Warlock" on *Bewitched*, and one of Gidget's overly developed high school friends in "In God, and Nobody Else, We Trust" on *Gidget*. In the international spy movie *Kiss the Girls and Make Them Die* (1966) starring Mike Connors, Adams appears briefly as Karin, one of a bevy of beauties with whom mad industrialist Raf Vallone plans

Beverly Adams, best known as Dean Martin's amorous secretary Lovey Kravezit in the Matt Helm spy adventures beginning in 1966.

to repopulate the U.S. after his satellite emitting ultrasonic waves has destroyed the sex drive of the world's population. She meets a grisly end when suffocated by a boa constrictor hidden inside a frilly white boa given to her by Vallone after she decides to marry another man.

Adams next began playing her most memorable role, that of agent Matt Helm's secretary, Lovey Kravezit, starting with *The Silencers* (1966) starring Dean Martin as the wisecracking secret agent who poses as a fashion photographer. Though she only appears briefly at the beginning of the movie (awaiting her boss in his huge bubble bath), she left an indelible impression on movie audiences, especially of the male kind, when after emerging from the bath she is covered only with a towel. Adams had more to do in the sequel *Murderers' Row* (1966). Clad in a see-through mini-dress with yellow stripes tactfully placed, she trades double-entendres and kisses with Martin while taking dictation, and later joins the black-clad Slaymates for a memorial at a pub when he is presumed dead. Movie theater owners took notice of Adams and voted her one of the Top Ten "Stars of Tomorrow" in the *Motion Picture Herald*'s annual poll in 1966. In *The Ambushers* (1967) Beverly only makes a cameo appearance at the training center where ICE has planted a voice message in the clip of her bra, knowing Martin's amorous spy would try to undo it, which he does in the steam room. The horror anthology *Torture Garden* (1967) starred the hammy Burgess Meredith as a carnival sideshow mystic who reveals to customers their future. In one of the segments, Adams stiffly played a Hollywood starlet who foresees herself sabotaging her roommate and (due to her ambitions) becoming a robot or "living doll" to retain her youthful beauty. Beverly next played John Cassavetes' thrill-seeking motorcycle mama in the biker flick *The Devil's Angels* (1967). Part of an outlaw gang on the run from an accidental hit-and-run, they are seeking a place where they can live without being hassled by the Man. When one of the members is falsely accused of raping a local girl, the gang goes on a rampage. Having a chance to ride off with her man, Adams decides to stay with the rebellious biker gang hellbent on destroying the town. Though it seems she is having fun in the part, Adams was a bit too glamourous and lacked a toughness to pull off playing a biker chick. She gave perhaps her finest performance in her last Sixties movie, the James Bond imitation *Hammerhead* (1968) starring Vince Edwards as stoic American secret agent Charlie Hood who poses as a dealer of pornographic art to infiltrate the realm of collector Hammerhead (Peter Vaughn), who is also after NATO's nuclear secrets. She portrayed Ivory, one of Hammerhead's mistreated mistresses, who escapes her predicament by drinking and dancing. She escapes his clutches, falls in with a group of hippies and at the finale she delivers a spear through the villain's heart. As his body plunges into the ocean, she coos, "Bye, baby... and thanks for everything!"

While filming *Torture Garden* in London, Adams visited a hair salon owned by Vidal Sassoon. She not only wound up with his trademark short hairstyle, she nabbed a husband as well. She dropped out of show business after giving birth to daughter Catya Sassoon (who died of a heart attack in 2002) and son Oley Sassoon, now a director.

**The Beginning:** Beverly Adams was born on November 7, 1945, in Edmonton, Alberta, Canada, to Tillie and Wayne Adams. Her father was in the U.S. Army so the family moved around a lot, eventually settling in Burbank, California. A very bright and popular child, she was student body president and cheerleader in high school. While attending Valley State College she worked as a secretary for a judge and began modeling. While hosting a teenage fair, she was spotted by a talent scout who arranged an interview with Ozzie Nelson, who hired her for his TV series.

**The '70s & Beyond:** Beverly Adams, now Beverly Sassoon, spent the decade helping her husband promote his line of hair products and gave birth to two more children, Elan and Eden. In 1980, Beverly divorced Vidal and resumed her acting career. She played a doctor in "New Blood" on *Quincy, M.E.* and appeared on *CHiPs* and in the telemovie *No Place Like Home* (1983). She took a respite once again from show business to concentrate on her own line of beauty products and later authored the books *A Year of Beauty and Health* (1975), *Beverly Sassoon's Beauty for Always* (1982), and the fiction novel *Fantasies* (1991). In the Nineties, she briefly resumed her acting career appearing in episodes of *Silk Stalkings* and *The Profiler*, and in the TV-movie *Mind Games* (1996). In 1996, she was a regular on the short-lived series *The Guilt*. Today she is a spokeswoman for the business that bears her name, Beverly Sassoon and Company.

# Maureen Arthur

Similar in looks to Sue Ane Langdon, for a short period during the late Sixties this buxom light leading lady with the kewpie doll voice was the popular choice to play kooky gold diggers and dumb bimbos.

**You May Remember Her Most From:** the musical *How to Succeed in Business Without Really Trying* (1967) as the daft but conniving sexpot who thinks she has a head for business.

**Her Groovy '60s Credits:** Maureen Arthur began the decade as a regular on the daytime game show *The Jan Murray Show* (she "served as a combination model, singer, and comedienne") from 1960 to 1962. After a stint on the short-lived Wayne and Schuster summer sitcom *Holiday Lodge*, Arthur appeared in the touring production of the Tony-winning musical *How to Succeed in Business Without Really Trying* as conniving Hedy La Rue. Returning to Hollywood in 1965, she guest starred on a number of popular series including *I Spy* as an inebriated party gal who craves green olives in "Tigers of Heaven," *Get Smart* as a zaftig contessa in "Hoo Done It," and *The Monkees* as a gangster's moll in "Alias Mickey Dolenz." She then reprised her stage role in the movie version of *How to Succeed in Business Without Really Trying* (1967), for which she received a Star of the Future Award from theatre owners and a Laurel Award nomination for Best Female New Face. With her curvaceous body measuring 38-24-36 (accentuated in the tightest of dresses), plunging necklines, and orange hair, Arthur is sensational as the bubble-headed Hedy La Rue, the overly ambitious former Copacabana head cigarette girl who as company president Rudy Vallee's mistress demands an executive position despite her incompetence in the business world. Instead, she is given the role of Treasure Girl on the company's TV game show *Wide World Wicket Treasure Hunt* by Robert Morse, who has climbed the company ladder from window washer to vice-president of advertising due to help from a book. Arthur causes a company panic when she reveals the location of the hidden stocks. Despite her muck-up, she winds up wife of the chairman of the board. One of the film's funniest running gags is that every time Arthur enters or exits a room with her trademark exaggerated wiggle, she is accompanied by "a va-va-voom drum beat." Typecast as the dumb sexpot, Maureen played a ditzy dragstrip groupie named Babe in *Thunder Alley* (1967) starring Fabian and Annette Funicello, and a worker at a beauty farm run by Sue Ane Langdon in the spy adventure *A Man Called Dagger* (1967); she also sang the film's theme song. In the Cold War comedy *The Wicked Dreams of Paula Shultz* (1968) starring Elke Sommer and some of the cast from *Hogan's Heroes*, Arthur sports a black wig; she then played a moonshine-loving vixen in the violent B-movie *Killers Three* (1968), which was produced by Dick Clark who also had a leading role. In the trying-to-be-with-it comedy *How to Commit Marriage* (1969) Arthur is wasted in the bland role of a demure divorcee who romances Bob Hope and in the satire *The Love God?* (1969) she played the dumb *Nude & Naughty* cover girl and wife of smut peddler Edmond O'Brien who takes over Don Knotts' bird-watching magazine and transforms it into a nudie rag. At this time she was also a featured regular in the TV variety show misfire *What's It All About, World?*, ABC's answer to NBC's popular *Rowan and Martin's Laugh-In*.

**The Beginning:** Maureen Arthur was born in San Jose, California, on April 15, 1934, but grew up in St. Louis, Missouri, where her father accepted a job as a theater operator running Arthur Enterprises, one of the Midwest's largest movie chains. When her family introduced a vaudeville night, the vivacious teenager got the chance to come out from behind the concession stand and strut her stuff. This led to work as a radio disc jockey and some local TV appearances. A gifted vocalist, she was discovered by a talent scout who spotted her performing on television in St. Louis. While studying theatre arts at Northwestern University, she entered and won a nationwide talent contest on *The Garry Moore Show*. Top prize was a week's gig at the Palace Theatre and the opportunity to compete on *Chance of a Lifetime*, which she won six weeks in a row. She then became a favorite guest star on all the New York-based TV talk and variety shows programs such as *The Tonight Show* and *The Ernie Kovacs Show*, usually doing her dead-on impersonation of Marilyn Monroe. Heading to Hollywood, her film debut in the juvenile delinquent film *Hot Rod Gang* (1958) went unnoticed but she continued landing dramatic roles in episodes of *Bourbon Street Beat*, *Richard Diamond, Private Eye*, and *Perry Mason*. On December 5, 1959, she became Mrs. George Wilder.

**The '70s & Beyond:** Maureen Arthur's last big screen sexpot-type role was in the soapy *The Love Machine* (1971), based on Jacqueline Susann's bestselling novel. Arthur played the office tramp, and the only woman in town who can't bed womanizing newscaster John Philip Law, and vigorously competes with her castmates to see who can deliver the worst performance. None of her latter films were successful so Arthur looked to television for roles. She remained active throughout the Seventies mainly playing worldly blondes or blowsy working gals in failed pilots and sitcoms such as *Love, American Style*; *Sanford and Son*; *Alice*; and *Laverne and Shirley*. Her only movie appearance during this time was the small role of a bankrupt, prim and proper widow who is taken advantage of by amorous banker Charles Durning who makes her trade her body for a loan extension in the turn-of-the-century heist comedy *Harry and Walter Go to New York* (1976) starring James Caan and Elliott Gould. The Eighties found her in another short-lived series (1984's *Empire*) and guest star roles on *Mork and Mindy*; *Murder, She Wrote*; *Matlock*; and two episodes of *Empty Nest*. Her last big screen appearance was as herself in the documentary

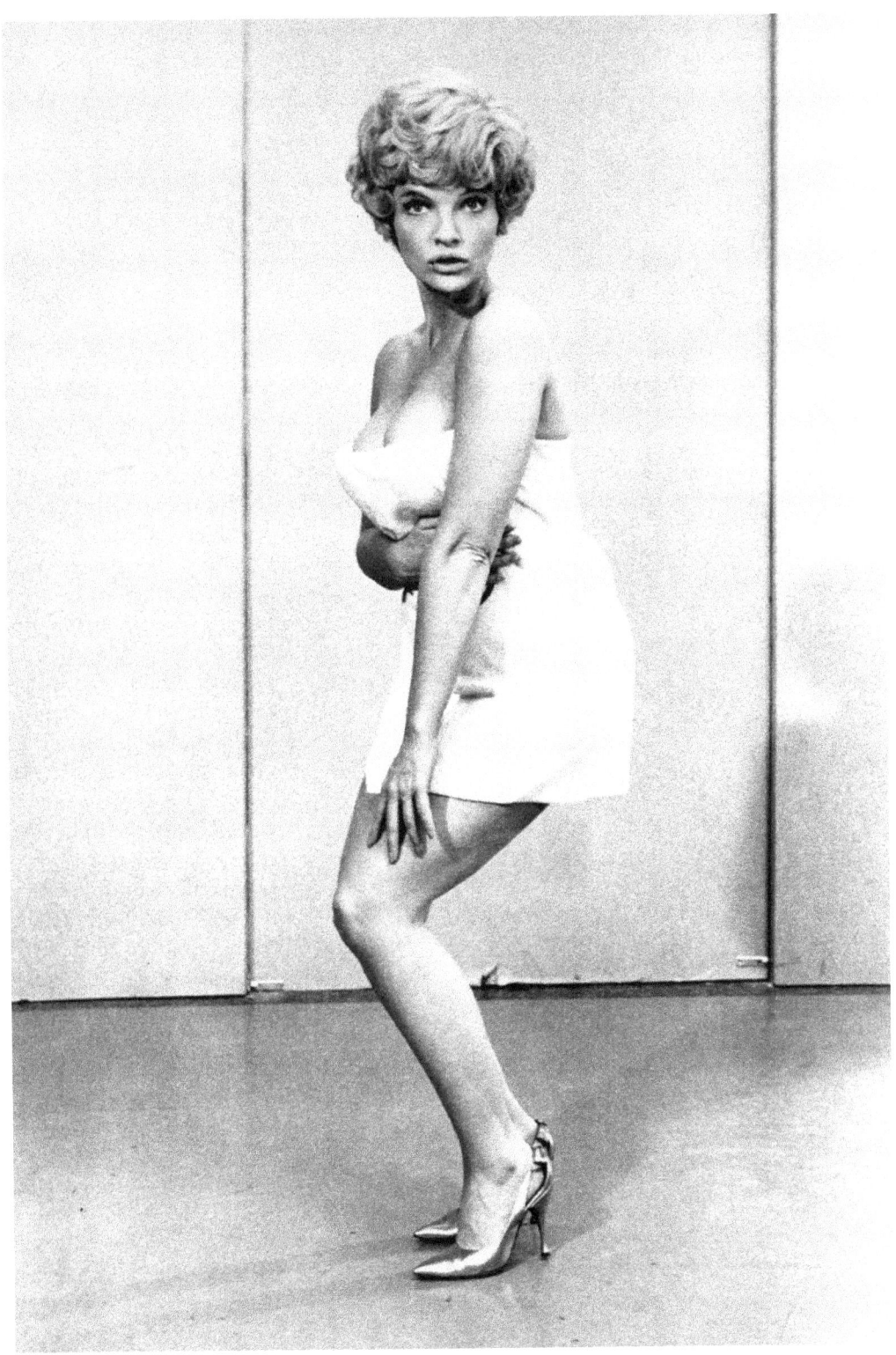

Maureen Arthur (1967).

*Off the Menu: The Last Days of Chasen's* (1997). Retired from acting, Maureen devotes her time to Variety Club, a charity where she serves on the national board.

---

# Pamela Austin

A spunky, wholesome, All-American blonde beauty from the Midwest, she abandoned her teenage ingénue roles to play the sex kitten, culminating with her brief fame from a series of TV commercials for Dodge Rebellion.

**You May Remember Her Most From:** *Kissin' Cousins* (1964) as a shotgun-toting hillbilly honey who wants to be more than just kissing cousins with distant relative Elvis Presley.

**Her Groovy '60s Credits:** Using her real name of Pamlea Akert, Pamela Austin made her film debut playing one of the high school girls whom tourist agent Elvis Presley guides around the island of Oahu in *Blue Hawaii* (1961). Signed to a contract with Warner Bros., Pamela changed her name and, looking like a cross between Sandra Dee and Diane McBain, played small teenage roles in *The Chapman Report* (1962) and more notably *Rome Adventure* (1962), as a bratty adolescent tourist enamored of expatriate Troy Donahue who is romancing librarian Suzanne Pleshette and the sophisticated older Angie Dickinson. Austin played yet another teenager in the Bob Hope–Lucille Ball comedy *Critic's Choice* (1963) in between guest starring on numerous TV shows

Pamela Austin (ca. 1964).

including multiple appearances on *77 Sunset Strip*, *My Three Sons*, and *The Adventures of Ozzie and Harriet*. A sexier, more vibrant Pamela first emerged in the youth-oriented hoedown *Hootenanny Hoot* (1963) where she energetically played an aspiring dancer of a touring folk group who falls in love with slick agent Joby Baker amidst their plans to "put on a show." After appearing in the memorable *Twilight Zone* episode "Number Twelve Looks Just Like You" where at age nineteen all women are required to undergo an operation to become identical and emerge looking like the beautiful and physically flawless Austin (whose measurements were touted as 35-22-35), she was cast as serviceman Elvis Presley's sexy hillbilly cousin, vying with her own sister Yvonne Craig for his attention in *Kissin' Cousins* (1964). The shapely Austin never looked sexier in her Daisy Mae–type outfits. When she finally gets Elvis to kiss her, she instructs him to do it "mountain style" and plants a long kiss on his mouth, sending herself into a tizzy. Later she realizes that the King doesn't prefer blondes and works her charms on a sergeant. Though these movies made Pamela known to the Clearasil set, she still was not a household name. That changed when she was spotted on *My Three Sons* playing a chorus girl and selected to become TV's Dodge Rebellion Girl in 1966 due to her All-American blonde wholesomeness. In a series of commercials for the automaker, the game starlet can be seen "falling off cliffs, shooting out of cannons, and cracking up airplanes" a la Pearl White, all to get the audience to "Join the Dodge rebellion!" Austin was an immediate hit and fan clubs sprung up all across college campuses. Her impact was huge. She took advantage of the publicity and starred as the ultimate damsel-in-distress orphan Pauline in the projected TV series *The Perils of Pauline* opposite Pat Boone as her star-crossed lover. The pilot was reworked three times before being rejected by the network and wound up being re-edited for a theatrical release in 1967. Pamela next became a recurring player on the new variety series *Rowan and Martin's Laugh-In* as the resident dumb blonde sex kitten during its first season beginning in January 1968. The producers wanted to sign her as a regular cast member but Austin's handlers had bigger plans for her and foolishly rejected the offer. Audiences stayed away from "Pauline" and the critics roasted Pamela while Goldie Hawn who replaced her on *Laugh-In* became a megastar. Austin ended the decade with guest TV roles on *It Takes a Thief* as a general's daughter who masquerades as spy Robert Wagner's wife in "Hans Across the Border" and *Love, American Style* as the pretty date of shy country boy Dwayne Hickman in "Love and the Phone Booth."

**The Beginning:** Pamela Austin was born on December 20, 1941, in Omaha, Nebraska, the daughter of an Air Force major, and spent most of her youth abroad. As a child Pamela's passion was ballet but in college she studied drama and dance before dropping out after two semesters at Sacramento State College. She left school when offered a chance to dance with vocalist Tony Martin on a six-month nationwide tour. When it finished, she headed for Hollywood to try her luck as an actress, and roomed at the Studio Club.

**The '70s & Beyond:** By 1970, this blonde beauty was already married and divorced twice. Austin took a brief respite from acting, possibly to concentrate on raising her son Beau from her first marriage to football player Charles Britt of the Los Angeles Rams; she had married Britt in 1963 and divorced him the following year. Husband number two was press agent Guy McElwaine (from 1965 to 1968). Austin returned to acting in 1972 appearing on *Columbo* in "Blueprint for Murder" and starring in the juvenile but hilarious made-for-TV movie, *Evil Roy Slade*. Austin is fetching as a schoolmarm who so charms wicked gunslinger John Astin that he tries to give up his life of crime while trying to avoid capture by singing lawman Dick Shawn. This film was Pamela's swan song. Her whereabouts today are unknown.

# Thordis Brandt

A striking, statuesque blonde, this Nordic beauty possessed acting talent but could never break free from larger-than-life Glamazon roles and was usually relegated to decorative supporting roles in spy spoofs and comedies.

**You May Remember Her Most From:** *In Like Flint* (1967) as one of the Amazonian guards who tangle with suave secret agent Derek Flint (James Coburn).

**Her Groovy '60s Credits:** Thordis Brandt's first TV credit was *Ben Casey* as a nurse. This led to a few other TV roles including *Hogan's Heroes* playing a sexy German girl who fawns over Leon Askin's slovenly general in "Top Hat, White Tie and Bomb Sights" in

Publicity photo of Thordis Brandt in *Live a Little, Love a Little* (MGM, 1968).

1965. Bit roles in films followed, starting with *Nevada Smith* (1966) as a saloon girl who is pulled by a Wrangler-clad stud into his room for some off-screen poking—cowboy-style. Later she can be seen briefly in the background when cowpoke Steve McQueen accuses gambler Martin Landau of killing his parents. After playing decorative walk-ons in *The Oscar* (1966) and *Way...Way Out* (1966), Brandt danced in the Elvis film *Spinout* (1966) where MGM touted her and five others (including Arlene Charles) as "the most beautiful girls in the world." She also glided in the background as a *Playboy*-type model in the mod comedy, *The Swinger* (1966). Her first role of note was that of spy Fred Johnson, a man disguised as a seductive buxom woman, in the spy spoof *The Last of the Secret Agents?* (1966); her lines were dubbed by a male actor. Television finally connected Brandt's voluptuous body to her speaking voice beginning with five appearances on *The Girl from U.N.C.L.E.* in small parts such as a helpful U.N.C.L.E. agent, a flirtatious diner, and a sexy nurse. Keeping with the good girl roles, she played a pretty blonde hired by agent Robert Culp to distract impish Pentagon clerk Wally Cox from the wicked wiles of Leticia Roman, whose mission is to entice Cox to defect, in "Casanova from Canarsie" on *I Spy*. Thordis finally got to play the vixen on *The Green Hornet* as the actress moll of racketeer Victor Jory in "The Frog Is a Deadly Weapon" and on *The Man from U.N.C.L.E.* in the highly entertaining two-part episode "The Prince of Darkness Affair" as the miniskirted Miss Zalamar, assistant to Bradford Dillman's maniac Luther Sebastian bent on world domination. The episode was later edited into the feature film *The Helicopter Spies* (1968). Continuing in the spy genre, Brandt was cast as one of the Fabulous Face Amazons plotting to take over the world despite opposition from James Coburn's debonair agent Derek Flint in *In Like Flint* (1967). With her blonde tresses hidden under a powder blue cap with matching uniform, it is difficult to distinguish Thordis from the rest of the gals. Brandt's Amazon is the one who discovers that their brainwashing technique hasn't been working on Flint's female assistants and tips off her boss Jean Hale, who orders Brandt to freeze the girls in the crynology lab. Later, when the bad girls turn good, she and Amazon Inga Neilsen lead the ladies in Operation Smooch.

That same year the Nordic beauty was voted a Hollywood Deb Star and vied for its Star of Tomorrow award. She lost to Swedish bombshell, Sivi Aberg. More minor roles followed as a police clerk in the Jim Brown heist flick *The Split* (1968) and a fashion model in *Live a Little, Love a Little* (1968) starring Elvis Presley as a photographer juggling jobs between one racy and one staid men's magazine. In *Funny Girl* (1968) Thordis was cast as one of the stunning Ziegfeld Girls. Brandt is the one wearing a black dress during the rehearsal scenes prior to the sumptuous production number "His Love Makes You Beautiful" where she and Inga Neilsen were beautifully costumed as Winter Brides. To help promote the movie, Brandt posed for the *Playboy* pictorial "The Girls of *Funny Girl*." However, unsure what her folks might think, she wore a dark wig, used the alias Barbara Stevens and provided a fake bio. Thordis played yet another unbilled role as a Las Vegas cocktail waitress in *Where's It At?* (1969) before finally offered the chance to strut her stuff in a meaty role as Tasha, a beautiful psychic who joins a team investigating a series of bizarre murders linked to a witch's coven in the swamps of Louisiana in the low-budget horror film *The Witchmaker* (1969). In the height of idiocy, her character decides to sunbathe in a skimpy bikini, making her the prime target of warlock John Lodge, who needs her to become his thirteenth witch for a hideous blood ritual. Under his spell the helpless Brandt lures members of her party into the swamp to be slaughtered for their needed blood. Thordis does well in her role and even doffs her bikini top—alas for the European version only.

**Thordis Brandt (1970).** *Courtesy of Thordis Brandt.*

**The Beginning:** Thordis Brandt was born in Germany and moved to British Columbia, Canada, at age ten in 1953 with her Norwegian mother. After completing her degree in nursing (which she financed by modeling), the statuesque blonde relocated to Santa Monica with two classmates. She began working at the UCLA Hospital where one of her patients was actor-director Jackie Cooper, who was working on the hit series *Ben Casey*. He hired her to be a consultant on *Ben Casey*, which led to an acting career.

**The '70s & Beyond:** Thordis Brandt gave a fine account of herself in *The Witchmaker* and it should have led her to leading roles in Roger Corman–type exploitation movies in the Seventies a la Phyllis Davis. But it was back to bit roles such as drama school owner John Huston's Swedish masseuse who threatens to whip him in the disastrous comedy *Myra Breckenridge* (1970) starring Raquel Welch as a transsexual. Thordis was so embarrassed about her part that she had her name removed from the credits. Her last brief screen appearance was in the no-budget comedy *Up Your Teddy Bear* (1970). Clad in a flowing blue gown, she was one of a number of sexy women hired by Victor Buono's overage juvenile lackey to seduce nerdish voyeuristic toymaker Wally Cox and trick him into signing a contract with Julie Newmar's toy company. On the beach, Brandt slips out of her dress and in her black bra and panties begins making out with Cox on the sand a la *From Here to Eternity*. However, a huge wave rushes over them, washing Brandt and her movie career out to sea. An on-and-off again romance with *Gunsmoke* star James Arness sidelined Thordis from acting. After their final breakup in 1972, Thordis was sidetracked by another relationship with a writer who would travel to prisons teaching writing techniques to the inmates. After that relationship ended, Thordis decided to have a child. Her son Christopher Brandt was born in 1983 and studied law. Throughout the years, Brandt continued working in the nursing profession. She still resides in the Beverly Hills home she bought in the mid–Sixties and continues working as a private duty nurse.

## *Thordis Brandt speaks out on...*

**Going from nursing to acting:** While at UCLA I was assigned to be the private duty nurse for Jackie Cooper. He was the sweetest man alive on this Earth. He said to me once he recovered that I was going to go with him to Columbia Studios to work as a nurse advisor on *Ben Casey*. I began working there and one day an actress who played a nurse didn't show up. They asked me to take her place. I had lines to speak and got my Screen Actors Guild card from this. I loved acting so much. I still worked as a nurse to pay my bills but began taking acting classes on the Columbia lot and I also studied with the great Jeff Corey.

**Her agent:** His name was Fred Ishimoto and he owned the Shipley-Ishimoto Agency. I walked into his office by mistake and he signed me. Fred was a dear man and always treated me with total respect. His clients included Irene Tsu and many other Asian actors. I was his only Caucasian one. He was very close to the writer James Clavell. I had the pleasure to meet him and the three of us spent endless hours together in Freddy's office drinking Plum Saki and out-besting each other with cleverness!

**The Men and Girl from U.N.C.L.E.:** Stefanie Powers and Noel Harrison were wonderful. Noel was such a sweet man. This show was a lot of fun to work on. The producers told me that they could use me in the background a lot if I could change the way I look. I was a real chameleon so I was able to pull it off. On *The Man from U.N.C.L.E.* Robert Vaughn and David McCallum kept to themselves. Neither one socialized with me on the set.

**The Green Hornet:** I walked into the interview and the casting director asked me if I could breathe. I replied, "Of course I can." He said, "Okay, you've got the part." I played an older woman who was supposed to be a European actress about 35 years old and the girlfriend of Victor Jory. I had long blonde hair but they tucked it in and put this God-awful wig on me so I would look older. My agent warned me that I was Van Williams' type. I walked onto the set and Van, who was so handsome, came over to say hello. I saw

Bruce Lee standing off very shyly in the shadows. I walked over and introduced myself because I was really attracted to him. He told me I looked like a goddess. I was dumbstruck because Bruce was absolutely gorgeous!

**Bruce Lee**: Bruce Lee was very quiet and shy but could also be very aggressive if he wanted to be. He was a show-off and always wanted to flaunt his body. He had a magnetism that was indescribable. We began dating but he was married, which I didn't know. Of course he didn't tell me—why ruin a good thing?—but when I found out I was heartbroken and stopped seeing him. Apparently, he and his wife had an "understanding."

*In Like Flint*: Jean Hale was adorable and very friendly. James Coburn kept very much to himself. The director was Gordon Douglas, who was such a sweetheart. I had so much fun working on this even though I got sick and wasn't in the scene with the boats. Peter Finch had a house in Montego Bay where we filmed this and was always bragging to Gordie [Gordon Douglas] about all the girls he got. Gordie had this huge bed and rounded up about ten of us to play a joke on Peter. We put on bikinis and got into bed with Gordie with our bare legs or shoulders exposed. Peter walked into the room and Gordie exclaimed, "See, Finch, I get around too!" Peter laughed and almost dropped to the floor.

*Funny Girl*: I did the movie even though I didn't have a speaking part. But Ray Stark chose Inga Neilsen and me to represent the film and we went on tour with Walter Pidgeon. What a god! I loved that man so much. He was such a class act and always had a limerick for every occasion. Afterwards, Barbra Streisand called me to thank me for doing a good job and for saying such nice things about her. I didn't get to know her well but I heard about her clashes with William Wyler, who was such a nice man.

**Inga Neilsen**: Inga is a sweetheart. We've stayed friends all these years. We worked a lot together and went on location to Montego Bay for *In Like Flint*. She sang recently at a local club and all her old friends showed up.

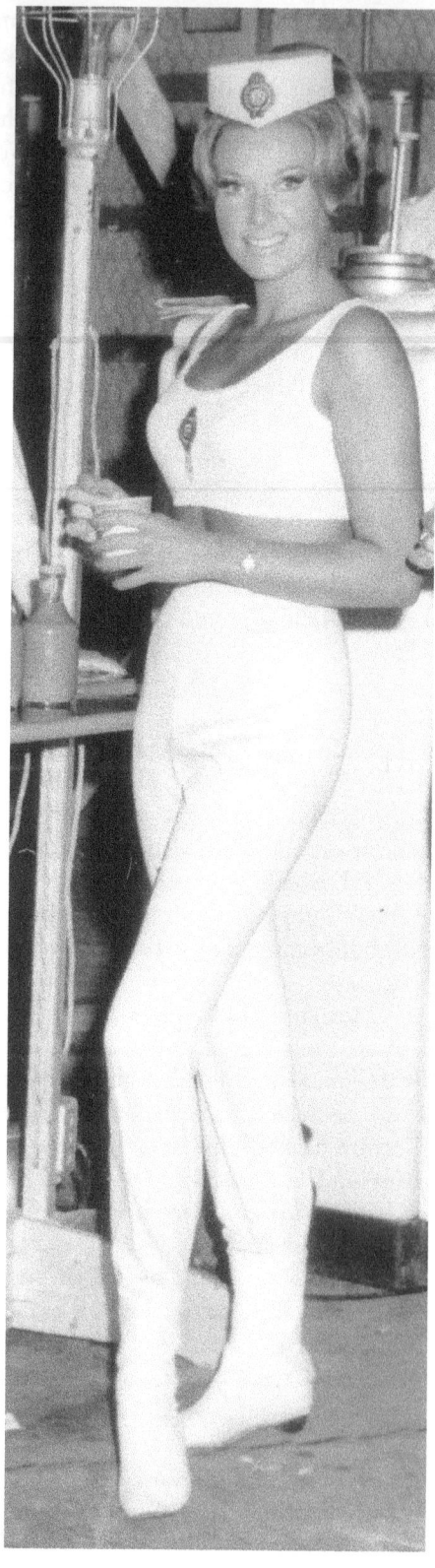

**Thordis Brandt as an Amazonian guard in** *In Like Flint* **(20th Century–Fox, 1967).**

**"The Girls of *Funny Girl*" pictorial in *Playboy*:** In those days, good girls from respectable families just did not do *Playboy*. My family would have never lived that down. They thought it was too much that I was prancing around in a bikini. However, *Playboy* offered me $500, which in those days was a lot of money. I posed using a false name and wearing a black wig.

**Elvis Presley:** Elvis was absolutely adorable but, boy, was he a flirt! He just loved women. I played a model in *Live a Little, Love a Little* and he was the photographer. He flirted with me through the camera. During the break he asked me to have lunch with him but I was dating Jim Arness so I shook my head no. He was kind of taken aback that somebody was turning him down.

**Typecasting:** Yes, most of my roles were typecasting. I would get sent out on the calls looking for women who were sexy but classy. I'd asked my agent what they meant by that and he would tell me, "A cross between Martha Hyer and Grace Kelly." I would spend hours in front of the mirror to try to achieve this look. I was a beauty but didn't know what I had. Jim Arness once said to me, "Thordis, Ursula Andress doesn't have anything on you. Neither does Raquel Welch. You're as beautiful if not more." But I always considered myself a nurse first and worked as an actor for the fun of it.

***The Witchmaker*:** Lynda Day George was supposed to play my part but she had a lot of exposure and I think wanted too much money. The format for this film was actually very good except that it was made so cheaply. We shot the interiors in Hollywood in an old studio built in the 1920s and the rest on location mostly in the swamps outside of Shreveport, Louisiana. It was winter and it got pretty nippy out there at night. I must have gained about ten pounds because we stayed in this motel that served biscuits with gravy every day.

I had to do several scenes pretending to get swallowed up by quicksand, which was actually just good old swamp mud. I noticed that there was always a guy standing around with a hand gun at the ready and I thought to myself, "Will they shoot me if I do a lousy job?" Anyhow, after all the mud (oops, quicksand) scenes were done, I finally asked the guy about the gun since he didn't shoot me. He explained to me that in the winter the poisonous snakes like to crawl about four feet down in the mud to hibernate there. So if there should be a snake down there getting ready to bite our feet, he would shoot it before it could strike us. Tony Eisley and I spent hours of relieved laughter about this, trying to figure out how this guy would have seen a snake four feet down.

**Co-star Warrene Ott:** I have many fond memories of Warrene. She was of course very beautiful and could have been the new Elizabeth Taylor but there was always a great sadness about her "aura" which seemed to keep her from pursuing her happiness. We drifted apart after *The Witchmaker* and years later I learned that she had died! I was in shock as she was still so young. Apparently she had gained a lot of weight and was wheelchair-bound. It was a sad ending for a beautiful soul.

**Her nude scene:** For the European version of *The Witchmaker*, there was a scene where I am running away topless. For the American version I told them I wouldn't do that so I covered my breasts with my hands, which of course was extremely awkward.

**James Arness:** I met Jim Arness in 1965. He saw me at the commissary at Columbia Studios and asked to meet me. I was introduced to him on the set of *Gunsmoke* and he totally flipped over me. Jim was an extremely quiet and private person. We began dating and had a lot of fun. But I would go out of town for acting jobs and he would stop talking to me. Time would go by and then he'd finally call me and we would start seeing each other again. This went on for years. Finally, he told me that he loved me and wanted to marry me. But he wanted to live together first so I could see what his life was like. I had a house in Laurel Canyon that I bought in 1968 but I agreed to give it a try and moved into his home in the Pacific Palisades.

After awhile Jim proposed with the condition that I had to stop working as an actress. I asked why and he said, "You don't need to. I have plenty of money." I told him I'd be bored not working so he suggested I work as a volunteer at a hospital. I was young and wanted to experience life and wasn't ready for volunteer work. I was still acting but when I would come back from work he would move all of my things out of the house. He played this game that if I didn't do what he wanted me to do, I was out. I'd apologize and we'd get back together but after awhile I would get the acting bug and we'd go through the same thing all over again. I loved the man and wanted to be with him but I wanted to have it both ways. We stayed together to about 1972.

**Post–James Arness:** What broke Jim and me up completely was that I met someone else. I went back to nursing. The fellow I met was a writer. He was very dedicated to helping others and would travel to prisons teaching writing techniques to the inmates. I devoted a lot of time and energy to that relationship and I never went back to acting. We broke up in 1979. My biological clock was ticking so in 1982 I decided to have a child. My son Christopher Brandt was born the following year.

**Her life today:** I still work as a private duty nurse. A lot of actors that I worked with wound up being patients of mine years later when they got sick. My son is gorgeous! For a long time I tried to get him interested in acting but he is studying to be a lawyer. I think it is wonderful how people are still interested in actors from the Sixties. It was a wonderful time in Hollywood.

# Bettina Brenna

Another extremely statuesque Glamazon, this former showgirl didn't amass many credits but in whatever movie or TV show she appeared in, she could not but help stand out due to her physical attributes.

**You May Remember Her Most From:** *Funny Girl* (1968) as one of the glamourous Springtime Brides.

**Her Groovy '60s Credits:** The towering dark-haired Bettina Brenna made her first television appearance joining glamour girl Phyllis Davis as sexy showgirls ("Kitty Kats") who lunkhead Jethro tries to entice into his new love nest, which is actually a beat-up old caravan, in "Jethro's Pad" on *The Beverly Hillbillies* in 1966. Her movie debut was in the Italian movie *Un Italiano in America* (1967), directed by and starring Alberto Sordi as a gas station attendant summoned to the States by his con man father Vittorio De Sica, who tries to use his son to attain wealth while on the lam from his creditors. Brenna popped up in the Las Vegas scenes. *Funny Girl* (1968) featured Brenna as the second tallest

Ziegfeld Girl after Inga Neilsen. Her standout moment is during the lavish production number "His Love Makes You Beautiful" where Brenna was one of the starry-eyed Springtime Brides. She is the one with the nasal voice. The part where Barbra Streisand is standing between the soaring Brenna and Neilsen, eye-to-eye with their breasts, is quite amusing. To help promote the movie, Brenna was one of the many gals who played Ziegfeld Girls to appear in the pictorial "The Girls of *Funny Girl*" in *Playboy* and one of the few to appear topless. It was back to being a showgirl for Bettina after this; she had a successful run in the show *Bottoms Up* at Caesar's Palace in Las Vegas. She once again decorated the pages of *Playboy* in a Woody Allen pictorial satire on Japanese pillow fighting entitled "Shindai!" in the February 1969 issue. Seen as a geisha girl, Brenna is clothed throughout the shoot until the final picture where she bares one large-size breast for the camera. Returning to Hollywood, she then landed a recurring role on *The Beverly Hillbillies* from 1969 to 1970 as Miss Gloria Buckles, the statuesque gold-digging secretary of Mr. Drysdale; she falls in love with the much smaller and older hillbilly Shorty Kellems played by Shug Fisher. Everyone thinks Shorty is worth millions so all the nubile girls at the bank including Brenna's Gloria put the moves on him but when they learn he is worth a couple of thousand dollars they dump him in the "cement pond." In "Shorty Go Home" Brenna has a funny line when she describes Jed Clampett to another secretary as "the funny old geezer with a torn hat and raunchy clothes and talks with a hillbilly drawl." When

The lavish production number "His Love Makes You Beautiful" from *Funny Girl* (Columbia, 1968) with (*left to right*) Virginia Ann Ford, Mary Jane Mangler, Bettina Brenna, Barbra Streisand, and (*second from right*) Thordis Brandt.

Jane Hathaway reminds her that he is worth 90 million dollars, she changes her tune and says, "He's that distinguished looking gentleman with the casual wardrobe and *darling* rural accent." In "What Happened to Shorty," the rascal returns with plans to marry Granny's rival Elverna Bradshaw but when he sees his favorite secretary Gloria Buckles he professes his love. Though she almost drowned him in the pool previously, Gloria has a change of heart—but when she learns of Elverna she dumps him again. Eventually, the odd pair marries. Brenna really shines in "Annul That Marriage" where the Clampetts try to give Gloria a lesson in farm living but the poor city gal can't tell the difference between a donkey and a cow. Surprisingly, *The Beverly Hillbillies* was Bettina Brenna's Hollywood swan song.

**The Beginning:** Bettina Brenna grew up in Woodland Hills, California, where she graduated from University High School. While majoring in theatre at USC, she became a professional skin diver and was chosen to host the 1965 Underwater Film Festival at the Santa Monica Civic Auditorium, where she narrated two undersea documentaries including Jordan Klein's *Behind the Scenes of Thunderball*. That same year she was a contestant in the Miss Tarzana beauty pageant. After earning her degree, the 6-foot-2 brunette began working as a showgirl at Nevada's Sahara-Tahoe Hotel.

**The '70s & Beyond:** After appearing on *Love, American Style*, Bettina married talent manager Dick Linke in March 1972 and may be currently residing in Hawaii.

# Eve Bruce

A towering Glamazon in the tradition of Thordis Brandt and Inga Neilsen, this buxom blonde was relegated to adorning the backgrounds of Elvis movies, spy spoofs, and sex comedies. She rarely had more than a few lines though with her imposing curvy stature this 6-foot-2 beauty couldn't help but stand out.

**You May Remember Her Most From:** *Cactus Flower* (1969) as the ding-a-ling girlfriend of actor Jack Warden.

**Her Groovy '60s Credits:** Eve Bruce's luscious body (42-25-37) should have made its first Sixties appearance in the slapstick comedy *It's a Mad Mad Mad Mad World* in 1963 but her brief scene (with Mickey Rooney and Buddy Hackett slathering sun tan lotion on her) was cut from the final print. Instead, her first decorative role was as an anonymous harem girl in *John Goldfarb, Please Come Home* (1965). Next she was one of the many spa denizens who fawn over ranch hand Elvis Presley in *Tickle Me* (1965) and she had a silent bit as a swimsuit-clad fashion model seen lounging on the floor while manic photographer Jerry Lewis tries to shoot a cereal ad in *The Family Jewels* (1965). Her early TV roles mirrored her movie characters and included "showgirl" in "Kentucky's Vacation" on *Kentucky Jones* and "Amazon" in "Consider Her Ways" on *The Alfred Hitchcock Hour*. Back on the big screen, Bruce got to act opposite James Coburn in the spy spoof *In Like Flint* (1967) though she doesn't get as many close-ups or lines as Glamazons Thordis Brandt and Inga

Dr. Peter Sellers and nurse Eve Bruce confer in a scene from *Where Does It Hurt?* (Cinerama Releasing, 1973).

Neilsen. Eve actually is barely noticeable as one of the myriad of Amazonian guards who work for the three most powerful women in the fashion industry, hell bent on taking over the world. The most screen time she gets is in the scene where she is standing silently to the right of Marilyn Hanold in the ladies' headquarters as Coburn's Derek Flint learns of the dastardly plan and is taken aback by the idea of women ruling the world. In *Yours, Mine and Ours* (1968) Bruce was cast in the minor role of one of two sexy young ladies out to trap themselves a man at an overcrowded bar where Henry Fonda brings nurse Lucille Ball on their first date. Fonda twice has to slither past the amorous mini-skirted Amazon and friend to get to the bar. Eve only has one line so it is not surprising that she did not receive screen credit. After making two appearances on the sitcom *Hey Landlord* and playing a sexy masseuse named Helga who gives agent Robert Wagner a rubdown in "When Good Friends Get Together" on *It Takes a Thief*, she was cast as one of the beautiful Azati Girls, hookers all, in the comedy *How Sweet It Is* (1968). She followed this with another minor role as burlesque dancer "Miss USA," who is chided by the manager for having varicose veins, in the Andy Griffith comedy *Angel in My Pocket* (1969). Bruce finally landed a nice-sized supporting role in the comedy *Cactus Flower* (1969), which plays like a dated, elongated episode of TV's *Love, American Style*. Walter Matthau is a dentist pretending to be married and having an affair with free-spirited hippie chick Goldie Hawn while his long-suffering nurse Ingrid Bergman pines for him. When Matthau proposes and Hawn demands to meet his wife, Bergman masquerades as the missus with Matthau's actor friend Jack Weston pretending to be her boyfriend as the couples rendezvous at a swinging dance club. Enter Eve Bruce, giving an amusing performance as the bubble-headed Georgia, the buxom girlfriend of Weston who (after catching him with Bergman) believes his ruse of being a CIA agent. A few nights later, at the same club, Bruce is a knockout wearing a low-cut gold lame mini-dress as the date of Weston. After Matthau apologizes to a miffed Weston for treating him so badly, the blonde asks Weston naively, "If you work for the CIA, why do you hang around with dentists?" Later she becomes even more befuddled when he explains the mixed-up pairings. Bruce plays her part very well and elicits the laughs.

**The Beginning:** Eve Bruce was born in Alexandria, Virginia, to one of that state's most prominent families. After graduating high school, she attended UCLA, taking pre-med courses, but dropped out after esteemed actor Rod Steiger, her drama teacher, convinced her to become an actress. She did some movie extra work, appearing in a few films including *Until They Sail* (1957) and *Rally 'Round the Flag, Boys* (1959). Her desire to learn her craft took the blonde beauty to New York where she studied at the Actor's Studio with Lee Strasberg. Standing 5-feet-11½ and measuring 42-24-37, it is no surprise that she landed the role of Stupefyin' Jones in the touring production of *Li'l Abner* or that she posed for a few girlie magazines including *Spree*. Back in New York, she also appeared in the off–Broadway production *Ladies Night in the Turkish Bath*.

**The '70s & Beyond:** While Eve Bruce began the Sixties being caressed in suntan oil, the Seventies began much harsher when she was cast as a Times Square hooker who picks up drunken newscaster John Philip Law in *The Love Machine* (1971). When her blonde locks are revealed under her dark wig, Law immediately thinks of his former girlfriend and changes his mind. When Bruce questions his sexuality, he flies into a rage and beats her up. She lost out on a role in *Diamonds Are Forever*, but was cast as a nurse in the mindless slapstick comedy *Where Does It Hurt?* (1972), a send-up of the medical industry starring Peter Sellers as a corrupt hospital administrator. The role brought her lots of publicity but alas not many roles. Her last film appearance was playing a bar patron in the low-budget roller derby movie *Unholy Rollers* (1972) starring Claudia Jennings. In between, she turned up in episodes of *The Young Lawyers*, *The Name of the Game*, the James Garner series *Nichols*, and of course *Love, American Style*, which seem to employ every Sixties sexpot still working in the early Seventies. Eve Bruce's final acting role was that of Amazonian Princess Latana in two episodes of the Sid and Marty Krofft Saturday morning TV show *Far Out Space Nuts* (1975); the series starred Bob Denver and Chuck McCann as NASA dockworkers accidentally launched into space. Soon after, Eve retired from show business.

# Michele Carey

An earthy, smoky-voiced, blue-eyed brunette, she had the versatility to go from playing a tomboy to a sex kitten to a vengeful vixen while still looking glamourous. Along with Marianna Hill, they were the two most promising actresses discovered by legendary director Howard Hawks in the Sixties.

**You May Remember Her Most From:** playing a Malibu Beach denizen in *The Sweet Ride* (1968) and as a free-spirited artist attracted to photographer Elvis Presley in that same year's *Live a Little, Love a Little*.

**Her Groovy '60s Credits:** Michele Carey arrived in Hollywood in 1964 with her young son in tow and quickly snagged decorative minor roles on TV as an U.N.C.L.E. agent in "The Double Affair" on *The Man from U.N.C.L.E.* and the sexy girlfriend of James Callahan in a few episodes of the George Burns-Connie Stevens sitcom *Wendy and Me*. Her first movie role was a minor one as a kimono-clad beauty (a jealous Annette Funicello finds her with Dwayne Hickman at his bachelor pad and chases her away) in *How to Stuff a Wild Bikini* (1965). Howard Hawks, who previously rejected Carey for a role in his race car drama *Red Line 7000* (1965), handed her a leading role in his entertaining western *El Dorado* (1967), a remake of his own *Rio Bravo*. With her wild mane of uncombed, sun-streaked hair and husky voice, Carey was perfectly cast as the rebellious Joey, a young woman who wears buckskin pants, rides a horse bareback, and carries a rifle. During the course of the movie she shoots hired gun John Wayne, mistakenly thinking he killed her brother, and tussles with him (the Duke trips her and then smears her shirt with blood from his gunshot wound) and his young sidekick, James Caan. Fans got to see Carey's gorgeous set of gams in *The Sweet Ride* (1968), about aimless young people ensconced in the Southern California beach culture. Michele played Thumper Stevens, an adult film star longing to get pregnant by her beatnik boyfriend Bob Denver, who shares a Malibu beach house with surfer Michael Sarrazin and tennis hustler Tony Franciosa. She more than held her own in both senses of the word opposite the film's female lead Jacqueline Bisset. It was back to Malibu for Carey in *Live a Little, Love a Little* (1968), one of Elvis Presley's hippest films of the Sixties despite a scene in which he sleeps with the sexy brunette with a bed board between them. Carey was cast as a mini-skirted free spirit who keeps changing her name and can't decide between playboy photographer Elvis (whom she slips a pill, causing him to have a psychedelic freak-out scene) and her staid boyfriend Dick Sargent. Guess who wins out? In *Changes* (1969), a coming-of-age flick, Carey is simply charming as a swinging carnival chick who beds college student Kent Lane and wants to settle down with him, but the aimless youth abandons her. Keeping her face familiar to TV audiences, Carey turned up playing a dancer and murder suspect in "The Ring of Anasis" on *T.H.E. Cat*, a bad girl who meets a golden end as she tries to steal a stone that can turn minerals into gold in "The Night of the Feathered Fury" on *The Wild Wild West*, and an IMF agent in "The Brothers" on *Mission: Impossible*.

**The Beginning:** Michele Carey was born in Annapolis, Maryland, on February 26, 1943. At the time her father was a wrestling coach at the Naval Academy. He relocated the family to Rochester, Minnesota to continue his medical studies. His daughter Michele was a child prodigy at the piano, winning the national contest at the Chicago Music Festival at age thirteen; she also played with the Rochester Symphony Orchestra. When her family moved to Colorado, the blossoming teenager lost interest in her music studies and began modeling. A short disastrous marriage while still in high school left her with a son to support. She became a highly successful Powers model but acting was her desire.

**The '70s & Beyond:** Michele Carey returned to the gritty and dusty western genre

**Michele Carey (1968).**

for her next two movies but still managed to look fantastic in each. *The Animals* (1970) was a violent revenge tale about a young schoolteacher who with the help of an Apache tracks down the three varmints who brutally raped her and left her for dead. *Dirty Dingus Magee* (1970) was more lighthearted as Carey gives an amusingly silly performance speaking a mixture of pidgin English and baby talk ("What we do now? Make bimbam?") as a sex-obsessed mini-skirted Indian squaw named Anna Hot Water, the love interest of fleeing con man Frank Sinatra. In the modern western *Scandalous John* (1971) Carey was cast as the watchful granddaughter of Brian Keith, a boisterous old rancher who goes on a one-cow cattle drive. None of these films performed well at the box office so the sexy brunette retreated to the small screen, which she disliked as she stated in many interviews at the time. She was in the made-for-TV walking-dead movie *The Norliss Tapes* (1973), *It Takes a Thief* as the roommate of a murdered girl in "Nice Girls Marry Stockbrokers," *Gunsmoke* as a woman with a shady past in "Tara," and *Love, American Style* as a chick who falls for a mimic in "Love and the Impressionist." Carey's big-screen comeback was as a hooker in *The Choirboys* (1977), the highly anticipated movie version of the bestselling novel; the offensive drama (which was disowned by author Joseph Wambaugh) was skewered by the critics and deservedly died at the box office. By 1979, Carey had sunk to providing the voice for Effie, a computer, in the short-lived TV series *A Man Called Sloane* starring Robert Conrad. Her last movie was *In the Shadow of Kilimanjaro* (1986) where she was hunted by starving wild baboons in Africa. This was no *Planet of the Apes* as Carey and her career were chased into the bush, never to materialize again.

# Victoria Carroll

An attractive blonde, this talented, versatile actress had comedic skills that weren't tapped into much during the Sixties where she played mostly minor decorative roles. Those skills were revealed during the Seventies as a founding member of the improvisational comedy troupe The Groundlings. She is still acting and going strong today.

**You May Remember Her Most From:** *Nightmare in Wax* (1969) as the mini-skirted, go-go dancing starlet with a attitude problem who meets a nasty waxy end.

**Her Groovy '60s Credits:** Dancer Victoria Carroll began to get chorus work in movies such as *Robin and the 7 Hoods* (1964) before accompanying a friend to a drama class where the director offered her a role in a play; this led to the start of her acting career. She made her TV debut playing a shapely nurse in "McHale and His Jet Set" on *McHale's Navy* in 1964 followed by a small role in "The Jack Jones Show" on *The Jack Benny Program* as a schoolteacher moonlighting as a stripper. Her dancing prowess won her minor roles in *My Fair Lady* (1964) as a magpie in the Ascot races scene. Impressed, director George Cukor then gave her a bit with Rex Harrison during the scene in the Embassy ballroom. *The Art of Love* (1964) offered her a bigger role as a sexy dancer who performs (in a very long red wig) as Lady Godiva at a dance hall run by Ethel Merman in this funny comedy about artist Dick Van Dyke who fakes his death in cahoots with friend James Garner to increase the value of his paintings.

A string of minor decorative roles followed for Carroll. She was a sexy shoeshine girl who buffs ad man Brian Donlevy's loafers in the beach party movie *How to Stuff a Wild Bikini* (1965); a lady of the evening who is holding an umbrella and mistaken for a spy by recently recruited agent Marty Allen in *The Last of the Secret Agents?* (1966); and a racetrack cutie more interested in kissing winning driver Elvis Presley than presenting him with his trophy in *Spinout* (1966). None of these roles offered Victoria much to do other than show off her anatomy. It was left to television to display her comedy talents. On *The Beverly Hillbillies* she was Mr. Drysdale's niece who runs off with a penniless king after he is rebuffed by Elly May in "His Royal Highness"; on *Green Acres* she was a coat check girl who mistakes Eddie Albert's Oliver for a two-timing playboy in "Oliver's Jaded Past"; and on *Get Smart* she used a dialect as a Russian swimmer who calls Don Adams' Maxwell Smart looking to defect in "Last One in Is a Rotten Spy." This led to six appearances on the TV series *Hogan's Heroes* playing various roles including a fraulein Resistance fighter in "Klink vs. the Gonculator" and a German nurse who rejects the advances of Werner Klemperer's Col. Klink in "Up in Klink's Room." Back on the big screen, Carroll was able to land bigger roles but, as with Francine York, they were in low-budget productions. She played a dance hall girl in the Civil War musical *The Fastest Guitar Alive* (1967) starring a miscast Roy Orbison as a Confederate spy masquerading as a singer-guitar instructor whose mission is to steal a gold shipment and bring it back to the South. In the hillbilly action flick *The Road Hustlers* (1968) Victoria has nothing more to do than fill a bikini as a sexy playgirl of syndicate crime boss Scott Brady, who learns that she has been two-timing him with rival bootlegger Robert Dix. Though her role was incidental to the plot, the producers wisely used an image of her on the poster ads and lobby cards.

During this period, Carroll also worked steady in a number of variety series including over a half-dozen appearances on *The Red Skelton Show* and a regular stint on the short-lived *The Jerry Lewis Show* playing a character named Samantha Portnoy. But Victoria's nadir Sixties role was as a bitchy starlet who makes demands of the studio boss before becoming one of the victims of wax museum artist Cameron Mitchell in *Nightmare in Wax*. Though released in 1969, the movie was completed in 1966 and sat on the shelf for a time. Disfigured in an accident at the studio, the mad Mitchell mounts his revenge by injecting studio contract players and bosses with a serum that turns them into barely living exhibits in the wax museum. He uses Carroll to lure the studio head to his lair. She meets a grisly end and then is carted around town by Mitchell as he strokes the hair of her cold dead body. One reviewer snidely remarked, "Victoria does her best acting as a corpse." Despite the naysayer, whose review Carroll laughingly quotes to this day, the movie was a big boost for her career and she stayed very active on television, finishing off the decade with roles on *Family Affair*, *Mannix*, and *Marcus Welby, M.D.*, among others.

**The Beginning:** Victoria Carroll was born Mary Carol Lee Ford on January 21, 1941, in Southern California. Her parents Oscar and Lillian Ford were in vaudeville and she and her two older brothers became part of the act where little Carol Lee was billed as "The World's Youngest Mind Reader." Her father eventually abandoned performing to work in publicity at 20th Century–Fox, and Carol Lee concentrated on her goal of becoming an artist. In high school she acted in a few plays and developed a love for dancing, which led to a stint at the Moulin Rouge.

**The '70s & Beyond:** Victoria Carroll continued playing supporting roles on television, turning up in episodes of *The Immortal*; *Love, American Style*; and *The Rookies*. In 1973 she played a small role in the lesbian drama *A Gemini Affair* (1973) starring Marta Kristen and the following year she became one of the original members of The Groundlings founded by Gary Austin in his garage. This became a hugely popular improvisation comedy troupe (members have included Laraine Newman, Jon Lovitz, Chris Katan, and Will Ferrell) that performed on stage, eventually getting their own permanent space on

**Victoria Carroll as a go-go-dancing starlet in** *Nightmare in Wax* **(Crown International Pictures, 1969).** *Courtesy of Victoria Carroll.*

the famous Melrose Avenue. Among Carroll's standout characters were atomic blonde bombshell Carmen Pluto, starlet-authoress Lureen Sue Franchot, and Jenny DePronto of Jerry and Jenny De Pronto's World 'O' Dance. She interacted with many now-famous comics including Phil Hartman and Paul Reubens a.k.a. Pee-wee Herman. Victoria proved not only to be a talented comedienne but a talented seamstress as well and won the LA Critics Circle Award for Outstanding Costume Design for *A Flea in Her Ear* in 1974.

Carroll's success as a Groundling led to a few film appearances including *Hustle* (1975) with Burt Reynolds, *The Billionaire Dollar Hobo* (1977) with Tim Conway, *The Kentucky Fried Movie* (1977) in a skit with George Lazenby, and *The Lucifer Complex* (1978), a Grade-Z production about agent Robert Vaughn uncovering a Nazi's cloning plot to revise the Third Reich, co-starring former Playboy Playmate Corinne Cole. *Pandemonium* (1982) was a spoof on slasher movies with Carroll as the mother of a nubile teenager being stalked by a psycho at cheerleading camp and Tom Smothers as the Canadian Mountie who comes to their rescue. Television fans may recall Victoria from her recurring role as blustery diner owner Mel's girlfriend Marie on *Alice* from 1978 to 1983. Later she was a regular in the forgettable blink-and-you-missed-them comedy series *No Soap, Radio* (1982) starring Steve Guttenberg as the third-generation owner of a seedy Atlantic City hotel complete with "wacky" sitcom residents and *Small & Frye* (1983) about a private eye who could shrink to six inches in height. It was on the former where she met actor and animal activist Michael Bell, godfather to actor Steve Guttenberg. They soon wed and in 1986 had a daughter named Ashley. Carroll also played the amusingly named character Bubbles Sincere in the 1984 unsold pilot *W*A*L*T*E*R* starring Gary Burghoff; it was a spin-off from *M*A*S*H*, directed by Bill Bixby. During this time Carroll and her husband founded The West End Playhouse. Up until 1990, they wrote, produced, directed, and acted in various stage productions. Highly successful, she won Dramalogue Awards for acting in and producing *Perfect Timing* in 1985 and *Ladies of the Camillias* in 1988. Despite her busy stage career, Victoria also found time in the Eighties to appear on *The Love Boat; Too Close for Comfort; Days of Our Lives* (as Mrs. Roberta Neely in 1984); *Murder, She Wrote; Night Court; Highway to Heaven; Sledge Hammer!; Hunter;* and *Coach* before devoting most of the Nineties to voiceover work on the animated series *TaleSpin, Darkwing Duck, The Incredible Hulk, The Smurfs,* and *Batman*. Still married to Michael Bell, Victoria retired from acting a few years ago to concentrate on her family and award-winning artwork under the name Victoria K. Bell. In 2004, she reunited with the Groundlings for a series of 30th anniversary shows, which led to a role in "Valerie Demands Dignity" on the HBO series *The Comeback* starring Groundlings alumni Lisa Kudrow in 2005. And she and her husband Michael appear as themselves in the eye-opening feature film documentary *Pets on Your Plate* (2007), about how domestic animals are being used for both cosmetic products and food.

## *Victoria Carroll speaks out on...*

**Her early artistic and dancing aspirations:** I didn't know what I wanted to be. I've always loved dancing and still take ballet class. There are a great many artists in my family. My parents and my brothers were all very gifted artists so I grew up with a lot of art and loved it. But I also liked dance. When I graduated high school I started working as an artist and found myself sitting all day long over a drawing board. I decided to take a dance class again for the exercise. My dance teacher was Rudy Richards, who told me about an audition at Hollywood's Moulin Rouge. He taught me a few steps and I went in to audition for Don Arden. I got the job and began making more money dancing than I was doing my art work.

*My Fair Lady*: I danced professionally for about four years and that is how I landed a role in this classic film. I auditioned as a dancer and when George Cukor took an interest in me I didn't know what to do. I was just so overwhelmed by his celebrity and his

Victoria Carroll (ca. 1968). *Courtesy of Victoria Carroll.*

reputation. He was a kind and gentle man who introduced me to his agent. When I told the agent I had no acting credits, he wasn't interested despite Mr. Cukor's recommendation. We worked quite a long time with Rex Harrison and Audrey Hepburn. They were just lovely people. Rex Harrison recorded his songs live. The other actors' voices were pre-recorded. Mr. Harrison insisted on not lip-synching. They played the music and he sang live to the playback, which was very impressive.

**What she thought made her stand out for George Cukor to notice her:** Honestly,

I don't know. I do know that my career eventually led me to do comedy. I think I've always had that tilt and have been a little bit off-center. That may have been what it was. Playing the magpie in the Ascot races scene, I had just a little touch of whimsy, which Mr. Cukor may have noticed.

**Her stage name:** When I went to register at SAG after being cast on *McHale's Navy* I was told that the names Mary Ford and Carol Lee Ford were already registered. I called my agent and he suggested I use the first name of Victoria. I paired it with Carroll to keep some portion of my real name.

**Ethel Merman:** I had a small part in *The Art of Love* as one of the dance girls in this club, which I think was hinted as being a bordello, and she was the owner. Three of us—Miiko Taka, Dawn Villere, and myself—went on a publicity tour with Ethel Merman, Ross Hunter, and Cy Coleman. I heard lots of *colorful* Hollywood stories from them. At that time I was very young so it *singed* my innocent, pink, shell-like ears. But Ethel Merman was terrific. Everyone everywhere we went requested her to sing "There's No Business Like Show Business." I asked her one night if she got tired of singing that song. She said, "Never. Every time I sing it, it's like the first time." I thought to myself, "There's a pro." She just loved it.

*How to Stuff a Wild Bikini*: What I remember most is the body makeup. The bikini girls would answer a 5 or 6 a.m. makeup call. Standing buck naked in a roomful of nubile nymphets was very humbling. We stood shivering in a cold room while we were sloshed with a big sponge and Sea Breeze, which is an astringent that was mixed with the pancake makeup. That was applied over every inch of our bodies. Even inside our ears. It was *just* torture. I will never forget the scent of Sea Breeze. When filming in Technicolor, you had to have a certain pigment of color in the makeup so your skin would look normal on film. Thank God they have made advances in lighting and makeup. Those were the horse-and-buggy days!

**Elvis Presley:** He was very much a Southern gentleman but always surrounded by his entourage. I didn't get much of a chance to talk to him or get to know him. I got the impression that he was uncomfortable in his own skin and maybe not comfortable doing movies. I don't know why but it felt this way to me. In all fairness, it is impossible to get a realistic character evaluation of someone in three or four days.

**Her favorite TV work:** I loved doing *Hogan's Heroes* because I got to do accents. I played a Russian, a French museum curator, and a German double agent. It was a lot of fun. But I barely spoke with Bob Crane. He was very distant. I would hang out with Robert Clary who was very friendly and Richard Dawson who was so much fun and such a hoot.

I also did a couple of episodes of *The Incredible Hulk* ["Mystery Man" in March 1979; "Fast Lane" in January 1981] with Bill Bixby. It was such a wonderful experience because he was fabulous. He was also a terrific director. We developed a friendship and I worked with him for years after that. If he was directing something, I usually acted in it. My husband and I had a theatre called the West End Playhouse. I would invite Bill to come and see our shows. He would always attend and I'd tell him which actors he had to see. I thought I was starting to take advantage but he said to me, "Victoria, if you find me a good actor you are doing *me* the favor." He was a fine human being and working with him was always a lot of fun. I miss him a lot.

**Why she was stuck in minor roles during the Sixties:** I think it was just a matter of building a career. Demonstrating to the industry that you had talent or at least possibilities and that you could work hard and progress. I've talked with other people who worked as long as I, and when you first start out you count lines. *I've got two lines—I've got three lines.* Then you work your way up to co-starring and guest starring and you are working a lot and having huge chunks of dialogue. I was on *Days of Our Lives* where you have thirty pages of dialogue to learn at night. Then after you've been in the business awhile making a living you want to do other things and not work as hard any more. You start counting your lines again. *Oh great, I only have three lines in this show. I could relax.*

**Raquel Welch's determination to become a star:** Her drive and her manager certainly helped Raquel but I think of that line from *The Red Shoes.* Somebody says to Anton Walbrook, "You've worked miracles in three weeks. Look what you've done." He replies, "My dear friend, even the greatest magician can't pull a rabbit out of a hat unless there's a rabbit in there to begin with." Raquel Welch was an extremely beautiful woman—and still is—and had a tremendous amount of charisma. You can push someone until you're blue in the face but unless they catch on with the public, nothing happens. It's that X factor that you can't really define but everyone is aware of its power. I think there were a lot of actors and actresses who had her drive and were pushed by heavyweight agents and managers but nothing happened.

*The Fastest Guitar Alive*: This was my dance hall girl period. I played a lot of them. Elvis Presley was supposed to star in this but he backed out, because of a contract dispute or because he just didn't want to do the picture. You'd know why when you watch it! Roy Orbison, who was a very sweet man, took his place. I think it was his first acting role and they did everything to make him attractive. And he was pretty on the inside but I do not think he was what you would call a Hollywood leading man. But what a dear, kind, and talented man he was.

*Nightmare in Wax*: I had to audition for this. Most parts that I played I read for. You had to in those days—actually still do. Cameron Mitchell kept re-writing the script. I wanted to be loyal to the producers and the director. I was just a fledgling actress. I thought, "I can't call the producers and say, 'Cameron Mitchell just called me and he wants me to change all the lines and rewrite the scene, is that okay?'" I was caught between a rock and a hard place. In one particular scene at the Whiskey a-Go-Go I didn't have time to learn the new lines that Cameron had re-written. So with the director's approval of the new lines I had minutes to look at them before shooting the scene. When I didn't remember a line I would pull on my hair and the script girl would read me my line off camera. I would wait a beat so I didn't overlap the sound and then I would say the line. It was also the scene where Cameron decided he wanted me to be a little bit dumber and have an accent. It was probably the best scene in the movie! It certainly was fresh. But the movie is a little bit uneven, to say the least.

**Cameron Mitchell**: Cameron was a little bit crazy, I think. But he was very passionate about doing a good job and making the picture as fine a piece of work as he could. I think he did improve the film with his changes but in the process the director [Bud Townsend] was probably getting an ulcer and having a mini-nervous breakdown.

*The Road Hustlers*: We filmed this in South Carolina. It was an extremely low-budget movie. It gets a bit scary when you don't have a ticket home and your paycheck doesn't come through. Some of us banded together and threatened not to come to work until we had our return plane tickets. They finally came up with them so we finished the film. I had a relatively small role so I was surprised when they used a full-length image of me on the poster ads. I've done other things but I am always interviewed about this movie and

*Nightmare in Wax*. I think because if you are still alive or the picture is bad enough, you become camp.

**Nudity:** This was just starting to come in when I started working in the mid–Sixties. Almost every interview I went on they'd tell you that there is a nude or topless scene. I would say, "No, thank you." They then name the star of the movie and say, "She's doing a nude scene." I'd respond, "Yes, but she is probably getting paid a million bucks and has a lot more lines!" I was not going to take my top off for a part that had two or three lines. That's when I really wanted to go into comedy. Nudity just wasn't my thing. I just wasn't comfortable doing that.

**Why her comedic talent was ignored during the Sixties:** I think the image of women was a little different at that time. I think as we got into the Seventies, the opportunities arose a lot more for comedic actresses. I just really concentrated on doing comedy. But I always wanted Mariette Hartley's career. She is a friend now and a fantastic human being. For me, my career began with The Groundlings. When I am asked about all this early stuff, my memory is sort of hazy.

**Her favorite Groundlings' character:** I liked Lureen Sue Franchot. She was a composite of all those supposedly sexy, decorative parts that I played during the Sixties. I got to satirize myself and that was such great fun. Lureen was the ultimate dumb blonde though she was an authoress and actress. She'd say things like, "I just finished another film. It's called *Bang! Bang! You're Dead* and it's about an Avon Lady who travels door-to-door and kills people a lot. Ooh. Ooh. And then I did *The Man with the Velcro Tongue*. It's about a salamander in the Brazilian rain forest who gets radiated. He comes to Los Angeles and kills buxom ladies. Ooh. Ooh." This would go on and on an on and we would do this in improv on a panel. We'd introduce ourselves and then take questions from the audience in character. So over the years you build up this incredible character. She was my alter ego of sorts because I got to make fun of all the sexist stuff and stupid things I had to do in the Sixties.

**Improvisation:** Paul Reubens and Phil Hartman joined The Groundlings a few years before I left. We all worked together. Phil improvised a character named Chick Hazard. It was a film noir-style detective story and we'd do that for the second half of the show. We all had our characters and we'd take all the suggestions such as the murder weapon, the place of the murder, etc., from the audience. Phil would always amazingly tie it up, put it all together, and solve the crime. It is difficult doing improv but it is also the highest high I've ever had. I don't know if it is more difficult than doing theater or film as they all have their own special set of difficulties. But when you work with such wonderful minds and get used to each other's rhythms and patterns, it can be wonderful. There are rules in improvisation and once they are ingrained in you it is the most wonderful feeling. Things come out of your mind that you didn't even know were there. It is really exhilarating and so much fun.

**Her departure from the improvisational group:** I stayed with The Groundlings for about seven years. After I married Michael Bell in 1984 we opened the West End Playhouse. We wrote, directed, produced and acted. We did some wonderful productions there and launched a few directorial and writing careers. And we received many honors including Dramalogue and LA Critics Circle Awards.

**TV's *Alice*:** This something I am very proud of! It was great. I had worked previously with Vic Tayback [Mel] in a theater company called The Company of Angels. We were very comfortable with each other. The whole cast was lovely and I was thrilled to

Max Baer, Jr., as Jethro dresses up as royalty to try to win the love of Victoria Carroll (playing Mr. Drysdale's niece) on *The Beverly Hillbillies* (CBS Television, 1967).

work with Bob Carroll, Jr., and Madelyn Davis. They created *I Love Lucy*. I felt very lucky to be in that brilliantly creative company.

**Her best work:** It has to be the last play that I did, *The Ladies of the Camellias*. My husband and I produced it and starred in it at our theater seventeen years ago. My dear friend Lillian Groag wrote and directed it. The show has since played all around the world. Cut to seventeen years later and Lillian asked me to once again play Sarah Bernhardt in *The Ladies of the Camellias*. We performed at the beautiful Colony Theatre in Burbank, California, and I am extremely proud of this. This production was the highlight of my professional career.

**Lisa Kudrow:** She was a Groundling. I had seen her at some of the shows and my best friend Phyllis Katz taught her when she was a member. The casting people from *The Comeback* came to see our 30th Anniversary Show and they asked me to appear in an episode. I thought it was so wonderful to be asked to work with a Groundling who was starring in the show. Lisa Kudrow is just a beautiful young woman and sharp as a tack. The show was scripted but they did allow us to improvise and we did. I played Mary Murphy, a *TV Guide* columnist interviewing Lisa.

**Her current activities:** Jeremy Rowley is writing and producing a show for Comedy Central. It is a satire on all the forensic shows like *CSI*. I will be acting on the show. And in 2007 my artwork will be featured in a gallery show.

# Amedee Chabot

An effervescent blue-eyed blonde with a voluptuous figure a la Anita Ekberg, she was only hired for her gorgeous looks and how well she stuffed a wild bikini. Although her screen time was usually brief, audiences could not help but notice this beauty. Fed up with the minor roles Hollywood offered, she went to Mexico and became a star.

**You May Remember Her Most From:** *Muscle Beach Party* (1964) as a leotard-clad health nut and groupie who hangs around muscleman Peter Lupus and his bodybuilder pals.

**Her Groovy '60s Credits:** In 1963 Amedee Chabot, a former beauty queen, made her first TV appearance on *The Joey Bishop Show* and was chosen as one of the year's Hollywood Deb Stars. After brightening up two episodes of *The Beverly Hillbillies* just with her smile, Chabot made her film debut with much fanfare as one of the two female muscle girls who train with the bodybuilders who tangle with Frankie Avalon and the surfer crowd in *Muscle Beach Party* (1964). Seen throughout the movie clad in a blue leotard, Chabot has no lines and is used for decorative purposes only. Observing her curvaceous figure (36-21-36), the producers must have felt there was no reason for her to utter a word and let her body do the talking. During the film's wild finale, Amedee repeatedly punches out a beach boy in the melee between the muscle men and the surfers. AIP promoted Amedee and the movie heavily so it is surprising that she never worked for the company again. In the *Beach Party* knock-off *For Those Who Think Young* (1964) Chabot saunters over to lothario James Darren on the sand and thanks him for the skimpy bikini he gifted her, angering his date Pamela Tiffin. After playing one of the call girls in *A House Is Not a Home* (1964), she landed a very minor role in the Dean Martin hit *The Silencers* (1966). Another bit role followed in the Jerry Lewis comedy *Three on a Couch* (1966) before she was upped to Slaymate in *Murderers' Row* (1966). Chabot was used only as window dressing, as were all the girls, first appearing on screen in a black trenchcoat along with the other Slaymates mourning the supposed death of Dean Martin's super spy at his favorite watering hole. As Miss November, Chabot reappears at the fadeout, clad in a gold bikini, along with the other Slaymates; they surround Helm's indoor pool after Martin and Ann-Margret take the plunge from his circular bed into the water. Chabot's last Hollywood appearance was in *The Gnome-Mobile* (1967) starring Walter Brennan in a dual role. She turns up at the finish, after a long and tedious romp through gnome-dom, playing a happily married gnome who is being transported by the Gnome-Mobile to a new place to live.

**Amedee Chabot in costume as Agente 00 Sexy (1968).**

Floundering in Hollywood, Chabot jumped at the chance to play lead roles, usually cast as the bubble-headed blonde gringo, in Mexican cinema (even though she did not speak a word of Spanish). Between 1966 and 1968 Chabot appeared in approximately 23 movies, most of which were never distributed in the U.S. She seemed to always be bikini-clad in her films beginning with *El tesoro de Montezuma* (1966) where she was cast as a sexy Interpol agent opposite Mexican wrestling star Santo, and in the horror comedy *Autopsia de un fantasma* (1966) with John Carradine and Basil Rathbone. In the sex comedy *El día de la boda* (1966) she is used only as decoration as her dress is torn off, leaving her standing in her underwear at her attorney's office. Chabot was clad for her next role as the most beautiful sight on the range in the Mexican-style spaghetti western *El hombre de negro* (1967), pitting cattle ranchers vs. sheep herders. In *Los asesinos* (1967), another violent western, Chabot co-starred opposite Nick Adams' cigar-smoking, poncho-wearing lone gunfighter (a la Clint Eastwood) in his last film appearance. Her most notable role was as the cat suit-wearing *Agente 00 Sexy* (1967). Masquerading as a mobster's moll, she helps protect a naive schnook who is forced to double as the gang's leader. In some of Chabot's later movies she was cast as the bad girl: the James Bond rip-off *Peligro!...mujeres en acción!* (1967) and the black comedy *Las sicodélicas* (1968), one of Chabot's last features, where she co-starred with Mexico's top leading ladies (Maura Monti, Elizabeth Campbell, and Isela Vega) as a team of sexy assassins who use a funeral home as their cover. Despite her immense popularity with the Mexican moviegoing public, Chabot returned to the States in 1969, never to appear on the silver screen again.

**The Beginning:** Amedee Chabot was born in Chicago in 1945 and raised in Northridge, California. She developed into a stunning young woman and in 1962 she was crowned Miss California before winning the Miss USA title. Chabot represented the country in the Miss World contest and made it into the finals, placing eighth. Impressing Bob Hope, one of the pageant's judges, that year, she was invited to join him on one of his U.S.O. tours, which led to an acting career.

**The '70s & Beyond:** Returning to the U.S. after abandoning her Mexican movie career, Amedee Chabot moved to Merced, California, where she concentrated on being a wife and mother for many years. In the early Nineties she decided to sell off several properties she owned in Mexico. Realizing that she had a flair for real estate, she embarked on a new career. Chabot has since become one of the most successful brokers in central California and was featured on the cover of *Broker Agent* magazine.

# Arlene Charles

A statuesque curvy blonde indistinguishable from most other Sixties glamour girls, she never progressed from playing bikini roles in movies, including three with Elvis Presley.

**You May Remember Her Most From:** *Clambake* (1967) as the girl with the deep cleavage who goes for a boat ride with conceited playboy Bill Bixby.

**Her Groovy '60s Credits:** Standing 5-foot-9 and sporting a shapely 36-25-36 figure, Arlene Charles made her film debut in *Winter a-Go-Go* (1965) playing one of the scantily clad Winter a-Go-Go girls who are hired by ski lodge owners William Wellman, Jr., and James Stacy to waitress and entertain their young clientele. The role required nothing more of her than to prance around the ski lodge in super-tight ski clothes or even less. She next played a bikini-clad robot in the spy spoof *Dr. Goldfoot and the Bikini Machine* (1965) starring Vincent Price as the mad doctor who plans on taking over the world by having his army of fembots marry and then slay wealthy men; his plans are thwarted by naïve secret agent Frankie Avalon. As No. 9, Charles' assignment was to sink her claws into a Swiss banker, killing him for his dough.

After sharing the screen, albeit in a minor role, with those buxom powerhouses Jayne Mansfield and Mamie Van Doren in *Las Vegas Hillbillys* (1966), Charles could be seen but not heard as a "friendly" gal in the western *Alvarez Kelly* (1966) but that didn't stop the studio from promoting the film with photos of Charles and co-star Jan Watson with full cleavage prominently displayed. In *Spinout* (1966) she was one of a myriad of beauties (six of them, including Charles and Thordis Brandt, were touted by MGM as "the most beautiful girls in the world") who populate the background of this colorful Elvis musical. Though she had no lines, Arlene gets lots of close-ups with the King, especially at the indoor mansion party where she stands out wiggling up a storm in her pink and orange outfit as Elvis rocks out to the title tune. Television offered Charles more of a chance to shine in episodes of *Love on a Rooftop*, *The Wild Wild West* (as one of three blondes scamming townspeople by pretending to be green-skinned aliens needing gold to repair their spaceship in "The Night of the Flying Pie Plate"), two episodes of *Occasional Wife* (as a beauty vying for playboy office worker Michael Callan in "Alias Peter Paterson" and as a secretary in "The Soft Spot") and *The Monkees* (in a cameo as a genie a la Barbara Eden in "The Spy Who Came in from the Cool"). Charles played another decorative role on *The Flying Nun* as Alejandro Rey's bikini-clad paramour who declines his weekend invitation when interrupted by Sally Field's Sister Bertrille in the

**Arlene Charles made a fetching robotic assassin in** *Dr. Goldfoot and the Bikini Machine* **(AIP, 1965).**

series' pilot episode. Back on the big screen, Charles got lines to speak in the minor role of Olive in *Clambake* (1967), her second Elvis movie. In a low-cut lime blouse and yellow slacks, the full-lipped blonde with the big bouffant hairdo is introduced when Bill Bixby's rich playboy accidentally flips an olive into her cleavage while enthralling a bevy of beauties with his stories about speedboat racing. After scoring a second bull's-eye straight down her blouse, he asks the gals if one of them would like to "squeeze in" with him while he tests out his new boat. Just as he is about to choose salivating gold-digger Shelley Fabares, Charles coos, "Mr. Jamison, I just *love* to squeeze." He chooses the busty gal and they go off. On the lake, to Charles' dismay, Bixby is distracted by the skillful waterskiing antics of Fabares, who has purposely followed them. Arlene appeared in one last Elvis movie, *Speedway* (1968), though you'd be hard-pressed to pick her out from all the gyrating go-go dancers at the club where racecar driver Elvis hangs out. She played a prudish intellectual who, with some buxom beauties (including Edy Williams), aids sailor Gardner McKay in a boat race in her last movie, an obscure comedy with one of the great camp titles of all time, *I Sailed to Tahiti with an All-Girl Crew* (1969). To get her name mentioned in various newspaper columns, Charles played the publicity game, Sixties starlet-style, making numerous publicity appearances. For example, she was "Girl of the Golden West" at the opening of autumn racing season at Hollywood Park in 1964, "Miss Liberty Belle" at the Rose Bowl's Annual Circus and Fire Show in 1965, and she accompanied Johnny Grant on one of his many Christmas goodwill tours through Vietnam, helping to boost the morale of the GIs in 1969.

**The Beginning:** Arlene Charles was born Arlene Gorek in Merrillville, Indiana. A local beauty queen, she was crowned Miss Indiana and represented the state in the 1964 Miss America pageant before relocating to Hollywood.

**The '70s & Beyond:** Arlene Charles was *Parade* magazine's cover girl in May 1970 and was still getting press even though her acting career had petered out. She abandoned Hollywood when she married heavyweight boxer Jerry Quarry in August 1973. They divorced a few years later. In 1999, she was reunited with pop star Mike Smith, lead singer of the Dave Clark Five, whom she dated briefly during the Sixties. They wed two years later in Spain, where they settled down. The newlyweds planned to move to the U.S. in 2003 when Smith broke his neck in a tragic accident, leaving him paralyzed from the waist down. Today, they reside in the London area where Smith undergoes physiotherapy in a medical facility.

# Suzanne Charny

A lithesome, dark-haired beauty, her dancing prowess led her to movie and TV appearances in the Sixties before she went dramatic in the Seventies.

**You May Remember Her Most From:** *Sweet Charity* (1969) as the "Lead Frug Girl" who, clad in a black mini-dress, leads a group of mods in a variety of dances.

Suzanne Charny as the "Lead Frug Girl" in *Sweet Charity* (Universal, 1969). *Courtesy of Suzanne Charny.*

**Her Groovy '60s Credits:** Suzanne Charny was one of the original gyrating, miniskirted go-go dancers on NBC's teenage music program *Hullabaloo*. Similar to ABC's *Shindig*, *Hullabaloo* featured a different celebrity host each week to introduce the musical performers. The show received most of its press not for the rock groups or vocalists that guest-starred but for its dancers who bumped, grinded and twisted. Charny quit the TV

In *Sweet Charity*, Suzanne Charny (*far right*) leads a group of mod dancers doing "The Boxer." *Courtesy of Suzanne Charny.*

series to perform at the 1964 World's Fair, which led to the Broadway musical *Sweet Charity* (playing the naïve Rosie, the virgin of the Fandango Ballroom) and then to the Las Vegas production of it.

In 1967, Suzanne Charny copped her first Hollywood acting role, playing a beautiful model, matched up with Ted Bessell's Donald via a computer dating service much to Marlo Thomas' chagrin, in "To Each Her Own" on *That Girl*. Her big-screen debut was in the film version of *Sweet Charity* (1969), which featured her as the lead dancer in the number "The Rich Man's Frug." Clad in a black sequined mini-dress and long white gloves, Charny takes center stage, dancing up a storm with her long ponytail swinging in all directions, and stops the show in this elaborate production number set at an exclusive discothèque where the elite frolic and play. As Shirley MacLaine, Ricardo Montalban, and others look on, Charny leads a group of stylishly attired hoofers in dances such as the "Aloof," the "Heavyweight," and the "Big Finish." Despite *Sweet Charity*'s mixed reviews and failure at the box office, Charny became an overnight sensation; one critic raved that Suzanne was "outstanding." A hot property, she danced on all the top TV talk and variety shows of the day including a number of appearances on *The Tonight Show Starring Johnny Carson*, and toured Vietnam as part of Bob Hope's entourage.

**The Beginning:** Raised in Brooklyn, Suzanne Charny (not "Charney" as she was billed incorrectly a number of times) attended the High School for the Performing Arts in New York City. More interested in dancing than her studies, she cut school one day at age fifteen to go on an audition and was chosen by the esteemed choreographer Jerome Robbins to play one of the Shark Girls in the Australian touring production of *West Side Story*.

**The '70s & Beyond:** Deciding to concentrate on being a dramatic actress, Suzanne Charny let the dancing drift and played an ambitious back-stabbing starlet in "A Preview in Smarakand" on *Bracken's World* in 1970. On the big screen, Charny played a free-spirited flight attendant in the irreverent comedy *The Steagle* (1971) starring Richard Benjamin as a bored married English professor who decides to live out all his fantasies during the time of the Cuban Missile Crisis. Strangely, she followed this with the no-budget horror schlockfest *Garden of the Dead* (1972), playing an overwrought trailer trash waitress menaced by zombies on a prison farm where her boyfriend is incarcerated. Much better was the gripping TV disaster movie *Short Walk to Daylight* (1972), which contains arguably her best performance as a feisty yet vulnerable mini-skirted New York City chick who is trapped in the subway system along with other passengers and crew (including James Brolin, Abby Lincoln, Don Mitchell, and Brooke Bundy) when an earthquake hits early on a Sunday morning. The small band of survivors then has to find a way out of the rubble before the river waters from the broken tunnels reach them. Throughout the rest of the decade, Charny was off the big screen but made many TV guest appearances on *Kojak*, *The Six Million Dollar Man*, *The Rockford Files*, and *Quincy*, among others. Her varied roles included playing an Italian mother terrified of letting a surgeon operate on her daughter in "Blood Kin" (*Marcus Welby, M.D.*), a vampire-high class call girl in "The Vampire" (*Kolchak: The Night Stalker*), and a prostitute working for Ina Balin in "The Madam" (*Toma*). Charny also kept busy in local theatre, founding the Group Repertory Theatre (now the Lonny Chapman Theatre), and she received the LA Drama Critics Award for her performance in *Trip Back Down*. In the Eighties, she briefly returned to the big screen playing supporting roles in *Hollywood Harry* (1986) and *Vasectomy: A Delicate Matter* (1986). Her TV swan song was playing the short-term role of attorney Sherry Rogers on the TV soap opera *Capitol* in 1986. Currently working as a graphic designer, Suzanne Charny was awarded a 2004 LA Gypsy Robe in honor of her contributions to the world of dance.

## *Suzanne Charny speaks out on...*

*Hullabaloo*: I had been visiting my sister in Florida so I had a dark tan and very long hair down to my waist. I looked like a beatnik going into the *Hullabaloo* audition not knowing it was an all–American show. I danced rings around everybody and David Winters (who was a *wonderful* choreographer) pulled me aside and said, "The producers don't know it yet but you've got the job. Just make sure you look different when you come to the first day of rehearsal." I was living with my parents at the time so they kept giving me milk baths to lighten my skin and we cut my hair and put it in a bun.

**Bob Fosse**: I know Bob Fosse's reputation but to me he was wonderful. I became very close to him and Gwen Verdon. They believed in me so much and I became sort of like their protégé. I was originally the understudy for the part of Rosie in the Broadway production of *Sweet Charity* but I did the previews because Barbara Sharma, who had the part, was—*sort of resting*. The day before opening night, Gwen Verdon announced, "I want Suzanne to do it. I want to be sure of the reviews and I want Suzanne in the part." I had an understudy's dream getting to open in the show.

When I heard they were mounting a Las Vegas production, I said to Bobby, "Please let me go to Vegas. It is a step closer to Hollywood." Gwen didn't want me to leave but *I wanna to be in pictures*.

*Sweet Charity*: Universal wanted Barrie Chase to play the Lead Frug Girl in the film.

Billboard touting Suzanne Charny's success in *Sweet Charity*. Courtesy of Suzanne Charny.

But Bob Fosse and Gwen Verdon said, "We want Suzanne and that's it." They really went out on a limb for me. The choreography pretty much stayed the same from the stage show so I was comfortable going into this. We rehearsed for a month and it took a few weeks to shoot the entire number. That was not my real hair as I wore a fake piece. It was so heavy that when I did my head rolls the weight pulled the top of my head, giving me what they call a pull burn. I looked like a conehead under the hair with all the pins they stuck in it. My scalp got infected. Bobby wanted me to wear these certain shoes that only came a half a size too small. So between my head and feet I was in agony! But it is better to look *marvelous* than to be comfortable.

They had a big red-carpet premiere for the movie. I'm embarrassed to reveal this but I had Universal make me the same headband that held my hair up in the number but in rhinestones to match my outfit. I wanted to wear my hair like I did in the movie so people would recognize me. It worked! The film was originally shown with an intermission right after the Frug number. Cary Grant came up to me in the lobby and said, "You were wonderful!" That made my night. I loved the movie—*of course, I was in it*—and I thought the critics were very unfair.

*That Girl*: I had an horrendous experience in my first acting job on *That Girl* but the second one on *Bracken's World* made up for it. *That Girl* was the nightmare of my life all due to Marlo Thomas. *I can write a book on that one!* Everything you can do to ruin someone starting out as an actress in the business, that's what happened to me on *That Girl*. I cried and was ready to go back to New York and my father said to me, "That's not a Charny!" Working on *Bracken's World* made me realize that I wasn't bad on *That Girl* and everything done to me was to screw me up.

**Obtaining a role in** *Short Walk to Daylight*: I had guts then. It was done at Universal and they wanted a name for the part—typical. I was just starting out as a dramatic actress but couldn't get an interview. I went to the office and just sat there all day. When the director Barry Shear came out with the network people, I said to them, "I've been here all day. My name is Suzanne Charny. *Please* let me read for this role." They looked at each other and said, "Come on in." I got the part. I related to Sylvia because I am a girl from Brooklyn who rode the subways. The character carried a rape whistle and when I used to live in New York I always had a hat pin in my purse to protect myself.

**Making the TV disaster movie:** During filming, I got *so* into the character that, in the scene where I start to lose it, blowing the whistle and beating my head on the door, I cracked my skull. Barry Shear exclaimed, "That was great!" I had a feeling that was going to be a cut to a commercial because it reached a certain height. We actually shot part of this movie in a deserted subway stop in New York City where they told us to pretend that the third rail [which carries the electricity for the trains] was live. Afterward, they said, "Now we'll tell you—the third rail *was* live." When we returned to LA they found out that the dirt on our clothes and faces in New York didn't match the fake dirt they supplied in LA. We had to re-shoot a few scenes due to this. The entire cast [James Brolin, Don Mitchell, Abby Lincoln, Brooke Bundy, Laurette Spang, James McEachin] was wonderful to work with. We all had to do our own stunts. They had lifeguards on the set during the scene when the tunnel starts to flood and they had to jump in and pull some of us out because the current was so strong.

*Garden of the Dead*: This truly was a *horror* movie! It was just terrible. They kept writing the dialogue as we were filming it. All I had to do was scream like Fay Wray. I also got hit on the head with the barrel of a shotgun that one of the extras threw over his shoulder during a break. He didn't have a clue I was behind him. I went out cold like a fighter in the ring and ended up getting a brain scan. It was one of those jobs that you take the money and run. I never saw the movie nor have I ever told anybody about it. I buried it in the garden of the dead!

*Kolchak: The Night Stalker*: This was a good job too because at the time I was doing the play *Born Yesterday* and I didn't want to be loaded down with dialogue to memorize. But I had an accident on that set. They designed fangs for me and I had to do my own stunts. In the scene where I am about to bite the quarterback and the football team rushes in, one of them was in a harness and after I hit him the crew had to pull him up. Their timing was off and the actor hit me under the chin. The fangs flew out and my two front teeth chipped apart. They had to shoot everything else from that point on focusing on just my eyes because the crack in my teeth was too noticeable. I had to have my teeth bonded.

**Her favorite TV show appearance:** *Toma* was my favorite. I got it on my 30th birthday but I didn't know whether to laugh or cry because they cast me as an over-the-hill hooker! I loved working on this show. After I did my big scene, the whole crew stopped and applauded while Susan Strasberg, who played Tony Musante's wife, gave me a hug. It made me feel so good. I loved the part and sort of went over the top with it but everything worked out well.

**Why she stopped acting on screen**: I didn't give acting up. It kind of gives you up. The parts got less and less. I either guest starred or co-starred and didn't want to do small roles that only required one- or two-day shoots so I returned to the theatre. It is difficult when an actress gets older and there are not many parts.

# Corinne Cole

A sexy, curvaceous blonde, this former Playboy Playmate had comedic talent which she demonstrated in sex comedies and spy spoofs but her personal life constantly interfered with her acting career.

Playmate to Slaymate Corinne Cole in *Murderers' Row* (Columbia, 1966).

**You May Remember Her Most From:** *Murderers' Row* (1966) as the treacherous Slaymate Miss January who tries to assassinate Dean Martin's Matt Helm.

**Her Groovy '60s Credits:** Corinne Cole's first notable movie role was in the epic comedy *North to Alaska* (1960) in which, using the name Lari Laine, she played one of four "working girls" who flirt with rich gold adventurer John Wayne at the Hen House. Cole had nothing more to do than fawn over the strapping Wayne but, being the only blonde and clad in a white frilly dance hall girl outfit, she could not help but stand out amongst the other gals. On television, she popped up in minor roles on *Bachelor Father* and *Cain's Hundred* in 1962. Soon after Lari Laine morphed into Corinne Cole and became enamored with internationally known Las Vegas impresario Jack Entratter, who founded the Rat Pack. This relationship sidelined her acting career until 1964. Cole reappeared on the big screen in a bit role in *That Funny Feeling* (1965), a lame romantic comedy starring Sandra Dee and Bobby Darin. With her hair darkened, Corinne (in a tight orange dress) played an aspiring actress who gets a part in a show coveted by maid-thespian Dee. A larger, amusing role followed when she was cast as the harried secretary to Robert Coote's Sir Hubert, publisher of *Girl-Lure* magazine, in the Ann-Margret comedy *The Swinger* (1966). The exhausted blonde is constantly being chased around the old letch's desk and in one scene she emerges from his office tucking in her blouse and says proudly, "I got a draw." In *Murderers' Row* (1966) Cole brought new meaning to the term Slaymate as a seductive "Miss January." Wearing a body stocking and two pink muffs on her hands, the pinup poses in front of a map of Minnesota for the Slaymate calendar. After the shoot, the seductive beauty sneaks into Helm's bed and snuggles up to him. Tired, he asks her to leave and "to go out like a lamb" to which she retorts, "That's March. I want to wish you a Happy New Year" and begins kissing him. But this slinky, seductive Slaymate has murder on her mind, not romance. Alas, her nefarious plan goes awry and ends not with a bang but a boom. After playing minor roles in *Made in Paris* (1966) as fashion buyer Ann-Margret's assistant, *The Big Mouth* (1967) with Jerry Lewis and *Who's Minding the Mint?* (1967) as Jim Hutton's sexy neighbor, Cole landed a part in *The Party* (1968) starring Peter Sellers as an inept Indian actor mistakenly invited to a producer's dinner soiree. Cole, looking smashing in a tight-fitting purple evening gown, gave a funny performance as a booze-swigging party guest and unhappy wife. In one scene she keeps insisting to Sellers that there is something in her martini glass when it is obviously empty. Later she is "peed on" by a statue after Sellers starts playing with the switches on a wall panel. As the party goes on, the drunker Cole gets, and at the end she is literally chugging vodka straight from the bottle and hooks up with Steve Franken's equally inebriated waiter as she ditches her disapproving husband. Her good notices led to guest starring roles on *Ironside* and *The FBI*. In *The Monkees'* "Wild Monkees," she played the leader of some biker chicks who have swapped the leather for mini-dresses and just want to settle down. Thinking the gals "like 'em tough," The Monkees pretend to be members of a rival motorcycle gang and have to face the gals' peeved ex-boyfriends in a road race. In 1968, Cole once again stopped working to concentrate on her romance with Jack Entratter.

**The Beginning:** Corinne Cole was born Corinne Elaine Kegley in Brentwood, California, on May 13, 1937. Her father, Carl S. Kegley, was a Stanford-educated deputy attorney general for the state of California for nine years and later a prominent criminal trial attorney in private practice. Her mother, Alice Polk, was a descendant of President James Knox Polk and was a former Ziegfeld Girl and contract player at Paramount Studios. Corinne's childhood consisted of singing, ballet, horseback riding, and art lessons between days spent at the country club. After boarding school and graduating from public high school, the intelligent blonde enrolled in the University of California at Berkeley to study journalism. Transferring to UCLA, Corinne was spotted by a RKO Studio talent scout who entered her in a beauty contest, which led to the Miss U.S.A. pageant where she placed first runner-up. Resembling Carroll Baker, Cole was a successful model before she became Playboy's Miss May 1958 using the name Lari Laine. Hollywood took notice of her and she made her film debut in a tiny role in *The Journey* (1959) before playing a secretary in the low-budget potboiler *Arson for Hire* (1959) starring B-movie star Steve Brodie. She also began a professional relationship with Ozzie and Harriet Nelson who cast her in various roles in 23 episodes of their successful sitcom, *The Adventures of Ozzie and Harriet*. In between she appeared as a regular on *The Del Moore Show* and made guest appearances on *The Steve Allen Show*, *The Jack Benny Show*, and *Shower of Stars*.

**The '70s & Beyond:** Corinne Cole never took advantage of the notoriety her roles brought her as her on-again, off-again marriage with Vegas bigwig Jack Entratter took precedence. After his death in 1971, Corinne returned to acting, playing a pregnant biker chick kidnapped by vicious punk Ted Cassidy in the obscure action film *The Limit* (1972), directed by Yaphet Kotto, and a Nazi prison warden in the Grade-Z production *The Lucifer Complex* (1978). She made headlines when she was kidnapped at gunpoint and stuffed into a trunk of a car while married to Robert Heffron, a wealthy businessman with whom she had a son, Benjamin. She was rescued unharmed by the Beverly Hills police department. By the Eighties, a newly divorced Cole returned to her journalism roots and began writing the internationally syndicated newspaper column "Real to Reel" about Hollywood goings-on. In 1991, Cole married good friend and widower George Sidney and for a time co-hosted a weekly *Real to Reel* TV show. The couple remained together until his passing on May 5, 2002. Today, Corinne Cole Sidney resides in Las Vegas. She is chairman of the Fine Arts Committee at the University of Nevada at Las Vegas and teaches two days a week.

## *Corinne Cole speaks out on...*

**How she began modeling:** I was walking on the campus at UCLA while wearing a red cashmere sweater set. A man came up to me and asked, "How would you like to be in the Miss USA contest? RKO Pictures is looking for someone to sponsor." I agreed and I placed first runner-up. I always kidded I didn't win because "I didn't know one judge." That led me to modeling and I appeared on 29 national magazine covers in one year while going to college. More and more I drifted away from school to show business.

*Playboy:* They had seen me on magazine covers and a lot of photographers I worked with kept telling me that *Playboy* wanted me to be a centerfold. I kept refusing because of my family's background; my father was running for the U.S. Congress at the time. I had a "California girl" look—sort of pre–Cheryl Tiegs, who came ten years after me. That's what Hugh Hefner wanted—a natural, all-American-looking girl. I was working with a talented photographer named Ron Vogel and his wife, who was pregnant. Ron submitted my pictures to *Playboy* without telling me. He said he needed the money to support his new family. I finally agreed to a semi-nude layout and that I would select the photos to be used. After all, I grew up with Degas on the walls so nudes were art to me. I know I was the first Playmate who had picture approval and had the first to have her full face on the cover of the magazine.

*Playboy* actually helped my acting career. I got a lot of jobs after publication. When you come out in *Playboy* you are like a spaceship blasting off into outer space. It doesn't last that long. I ordered 500 advance copies before it was out on the newsstand. I had my *Playboy* on every casting director's desk in town.

**Hugh Hefner:** I never knew Hugh Hefner before I was a centerfold. He has always been appreciative, gracious, and supportive of me. I'm fond of him to this day.

*North to Alaska*: John Wayne was terrific to work with. He was very friendly and nice—not lecherous at all. The director Henry Hathaway intimidated me so much because I was in awe of him. While we were filming they told me that Mr. Darryl Zanuck [the head of 20th Century-Fox] wanted to see me. I replied, "Great! Have Mr. Zanuck come down to the set. I'll be glad to talk to him." Well, he never showed. My agent dropped me and said I was the dumbest actress in Hollywood because Zanuck could have made me a big star. I just laughed and got another agent. The best thing I had was a great drama coach and friend, Jeff Corey. I wasn't a Meryl Streep but I was a natural "straight woman" for comics. I am very proud of going through Hollywood the way I did because everything I did was always on my terms—not on my back.

**Ozzie and Harriet Nelson:** Ozzie was such a wonderful mentor of mine and so interested in helping me. Harriet Nelson was encouraging too. They were just so kind. Every time I needed help to pay my rent, I would call Ozzie and he would give me a part. I became sort of a semi-regular on that show [*The Adventures of Ozzie and Harriet*]. He gave me so many ranges in the varied parts I played on this, it was unbelievable. Ozzie was an amazingly kind person. I loved him, Harriet, and David. Ricky was so young then that I hardly knew him.

**Why she changed her stage name from Lari Laine to Corinne Cole:** I didn't like the name Lari Laine. I hated it. Ozzie Nelson suggested we change it. I wanted to use my real name, Corinne Kegley, but Ozzie said, "You can't use Kegley because that's too hard for people to remember." So Ozzie came up with Cole.

**Why she briefly stopped acting in the early Sixties:** After my mother died in May of 1959, I wasn't so excited about show business—it was a job. Jack Entratter became my focus after my "love at first sight." The day you fall in love with the most powerful man in Las Vegas, and Hollywood gets wind of it, your career is more or less over.

**The Rat Pack:** Frank Sinatra was a lot of fun, contrary to what people who didn't know him or understand him have said. He was a great guy and beyond talented. Jack actually put the Rat Pack together because Frank wanted to have more fun on stage. So Jack sent for Sammy Davis, Jr., and Dean Martin to come help make Frank happy. Jack added Joey Bishop as emcee and Frank pulled in Peter Lawford. It was like New Year's Eve every night, sixteen weeks a year. As a side note, these shows didn't just happen out of spontaneity, they were all rehearsed in the Sands' steam bath before the eight o'clock show. And as all great performers can attest to, the boys switched parts, improvised, and knew exactly where the applause and laughs would come. Frank, Dean, and Sammy were possibly the greatest living talents of the 20th century. No one can imitate these shows to this day.

I basked in the reflective glory of Jack Entratter. I became disillusioned with the trappings of fame after seeing what really famous people like Frank Sinatra and Mia Farrow went through with the paparazzi and demanding fans—it was not for me. One opening night, fans even tore my dress and pulled out my hair just to get to Frank and Mia. Still, it was a magical time and Jack produced those shows.

**Dean Martin:** Dean Martin was always professional and fun too. He was sober and just played "Drunkie" as Frank tagged him. He never stayed up late. During the midnight second show he would take a sleeping pill in about the middle of the performance to make sure he got enough sleep before his golf game the next day.

**Meeting with director George Sidney:** I was living in Las Vegas with Jack Entratter and he told me that his friend George Sidney was doing a movie and wanted to meet with me about being in it. I flew to LA and had to go through three of Mr. Sidney's secretaries before I finally got to George's office. I had met him at the Sands many times while watching the Rat Pack but I never asked him for a job. I sat down to talk with him and after a while I said, "Well, I guess the interview is over. Do I have the job or not, Mr. Sidney?" He said, "Oh, yes you've got the job." I was excited and asked, "What's the part?" He replied, "I haven't written it yet."

*The Swinger*: This movie was a take-off of *Playboy*. It was a big break to work in a picture directed by George Sidney because he was a very famous director then. The role was a bit different for me because at that time I was not interested in just being another sexpot in Hollywood. Ann-Margret was just great to work with. She is endearing and sweet. I am still friends with Annie. She reminded me recently that we worked together five times. What she didn't say was that she was the star five times, and I was a supporting player at best.

*Murderers' Row*: Nancy Kovack was in the first movie [*The Silencers*] and she was scheduled to play Miss January in this. In between movies she married the great musician Zubin Mehta and passed on the film at the last second. My agent called me and I went to Columbia Studios to read for the part. I did not tell anybody that I knew Dean Martin socially. I had to audition for this role five times until director Henry Levin finally offered me the part.

When I got on the set for the first day of shooting, which was our love scene in bed, Dean Martin said to me, "This is a hell of a way to miss my best friend's wedding." Frank Sinatra was marrying Mia Farrow that day at the Sands in my apartment. I said to Dean, "Yes, we are missing a big day." Nobody outside the Rat Pack knew they were getting married. It was very funny to us. I had a body stocking on because I was supposed to be nude but we couldn't get the shot because my bra was showing. Finally I said, "Frig it! I'm taking off the body stocking!" They closed set for me and we got the take. Dean said, "What a way to spend the day—being in bed with one of my best friend's fiancée."

*The Big Mouth*: I went down to San Diego where this was being filmed and I waited there a week. Every day I would go to the set and they would tell me I was not scheduled for the day. I would sit there watching Jerry Lewis throwing baseballs back and forth with the crew or I'd go back to my room and read a book. It was the slowest film I ever worked on in my life. I like to *work* when I work. Jack Entratter called me and, stealing a quote from Bette Davis, I said, "Who do I have to fuck to get *off* this picture?" I really wanted to go to Europe with Jack. He called Jerry and I was on my way to London. I'm still very fond of Jerry Lewis and his wife Samantha. He is another enormous talent on both sides of the camera.

**Blake Edwards**: Blake Edwards was a wonderful director. He treats all actors like stars. He had just directed *Days of Wine and Roses*. When I walked into his office to meet with him about a role in *The Party*, I sat down and he asked me how I would play a drunk. I said, "Mr. Edwards, you're asking me how to play a drunk after you made one of the greatest films of all time about drunks?" He replied, "Yes. This is a part of a woman who goes from a little tipsy to plastered." He repeated, "How would you play a drunk?" I looked at him and said, "As if I thought I was cold sober." He said, "Lady, you just got the part." I must have been over the hundredth unknown to go in for it because every actress in town wanted that part. It was based on a very famous comedian's wife who was always three sheets to the wind at parties.

What most people don't know is that *The Party* was all improvisational. We had no

Corinne Cole as model Miss January takes direction from Dean Martin as spy/photographer Matt Helm in *Murderers' Row* (Columbia, 1966).

script! The cast didn't know from one day to the next day what we were going to shoot. Blake Edwards said, "This is what we have in mind to do. I want you and Steve Franken to fall into the swimming pool together." In one take we did our drunken slide into the pool (full of toxic foam used to put out runway airplane fires). It was unbelievable. Steve was just marvelous to work with. We rehearsed that scene between takes every day for a week and waited to see when it would come up on the call sheet. Together we planned out how we were going to survive for three minutes. I was a good swimmer and so was he. Nowadays, stunt doubles would take that dive.

**Peter Sellers and Claudine Longet:** I was costumed in an elegant silk one-shoulder (no bra) purple gown. They made three exactly alike for me. I asked why I couldn't be in white or beige because I had a fantastic figure [38-24-34]. The costumer said, "Oh, no. Mr. Sellers only likes purple so that is what you have to wear." Peter was extremely preoccupied and seemingly aloof yet very sweet to me. He was a terrific craftsman and reminded me of the silent comedians Charles Chaplin, Buster Keaton, and Harold Lloyd, all rolled up into one genius. He knew exactly how every joke would play out.

I was supposed to sing a solo in this as I studied with a vocal coach named Harriet Lee for years. About three weeks into the shoot, Blake asked me if I minded if they gave the song to Claudine Longet. What could I say? Claudine scared me from the first day of the picture. [Years later she was tried and acquitted for murdering her lover, skier Spider Sabich.] I gracefully bowed out and got paid the same money—song or no song.

**The party-like atmosphere on *The Party*:** This was the greatest film to work on. I'd say, "We should pay the director to work on this set." There were more affairs going on off the set than on any film I had ever been in. I mean, those trailers were rocking! Everybody was shtupping everybody. It was hysterically funny and decadent. Danielle De Metz and Denny Miller were the life of the party literally. They didn't have an affair together because Danielle was romancing some other guy on the set. There were several divorces resulting from this movie. Blake Edwards was courting Julie Andrews at this time after going through a horrendous divorce.

**Carol Wayne:** Carol Wayne had real talent and was very droll. We didn't become bosom buddies but I liked her a lot. Frank Sinatra always called me "a great dame." I'm always happier being with the guys than with the girls. I liked women very much but I seem to get along better with men.

*The Party* **aftermath:** A gaffer came up to me at the wrap party and said, "I've been watching you for nine weeks. I never saw you take a drink from a cup or bottle but I bet the crew you've been drunk on the set the whole time." I was so flattered and said, "That is the nicest compliment I ever had because I was stone cold sober." I never got out of character the whole nine weeks. I ate, slept, and drove like I was higher than a kite. We had to come back for re-shoots because they enlarged my part about two months later and I had to go through the whole bombed-tipsy process again. I was ready for an AA meeting!

**Stardom:** I really didn't have much of an interest in acting as my relationship with Jack Entratter flourished. Who needed to be a star when I lived better than stars did? Also, I didn't have aspirations after my mom died. I always said, "Behind every young actress there is a mother." It is usually the daughter trying to fulfill the mother's lost wishes. I am sure I was doing the same thing for my sweet mother, whom I miss to this day.

*The Monkees*: I remember at my wedding dinner [in 1967] with Jack Entratter I got up from the table and said, "You'll have to excuse me. I am starring on *The Monkees* and have to be on the set tomorrow morning at five o'clock." I left on a private jet and got to the set on time. I did a lot of comedies and worked with all the greats. Years later I learned from George Sidney that Columbia Studios was interested in starring me in a sitcom but when George called Jack about it (they were friends), Jack responded, "Absolutely not!" Actually, I consider that a blessing. I might have awakened at forty and started screaming like other people I have known.

**The Monkees:** They were completely professional with me but they were running all over the place. Who was here, who was there. It was like Ollie Ollie Oxen Free, where are you? The assistant directors were constantly trying to round up these guys. Our director Bruce Kessler was fabulous—Mr. Cool.

**Her hiatus from acting in the late Sixties:** I married and divorced Jack Entratter twice and lived with him until he died. His two adult daughters were the wicked witches of the West to me. Perhaps I wasn't old enough to know how to handle them. *They* wanted to be Mrs. Jack Entratter. I was dizzy from turning the other cheek. They lied and told cruel jokes about me. However, Jack called me his magnificent obsession. We couldn't stay apart. We traveled the world—presidential suites, yachts, private planes, and limousines. We had staffed homes in Palm Springs, Los Angeles, and Las Vegas. We were happy once he realized how selfish his children were with him.

When Jack mysteriously died from a fall off his bicycle at fifty-six years of age in 1971, I left town the day of his funeral even though I loved the *laissez faire* attitude of Vegas. George Sidney flew up and told me to come back to Los Angeles, otherwise I'd be found dead in the desert because I knew too much. Every wife knows the truth from "pillow talk." I listened to my friend George. Jack's daughters cruelly had the homes I was living in with Jack sealed while he was dying in the hospital. I was not married out of my choice to Jack at the time of his death; [he died] because of what his daughters put his blood pressure through. I had charge accounts. I had everything a wife could want. Thanks to his daughters, I couldn't get my own dog, courtier clothes, jewelry, or my grandmother's linens out of our homes. I was in Jack's will but his daughters got the executor to use the will Jack had before their mother died, nine years earlier. My will was "lost." That was a hard blow for twenty years. I didn't fight them because I didn't want to sully Jack's reputation. I walked away like the lady I am. Thank God I still owned a house in Bel Air, California. I decided to go back into the only thing I thought I knew how to do—acting.

*The Limit*: I got this starring part as a pregnant motorcycle queen opposite Ted Cassidy of *The Addams Family*. The movie was put together as a tax reduction for some wealthy investors. Yaphet Kotto was a wonderful director and a marvelous professional. He rehearsed us for two weeks before filming began. I even rode a motorcycle. When I was a child of ten, my Austrian uncle would take me for rides on his motorcycle and let me drive it. We shot this film right on schedule. I was known as the "one-take Charlie girl." I loved doing movies spontaneously and especially live television, which was very fast-moving.

*The Lucifer Complex:* Actress Merrie Lynn Ross had a studio contract to produce and star in six movies. We were friends because she was dating director Mark L. Lester [who went on to direct *Firestarter* and *Commando*, among many others] and he offered me the lead in *Truck Stop Women*. I didn't like the idea of being a truck driver and I thought it was too big a stretch for a girl with a forty dollar Vidal Sassoon haircut. I didn't like the part and passed on it. Mark was stunned, "*How could you turn this down*!?!" How come someone like me who wasn't famous (though I was known within the industry) turn down a lead in his movie?

Merrie Lynn and I became pals (still are). Back then she called me and said, "Corinne, how would you like to play against type? There is a lead role of a Nazi prison warden." I said, "I could do that—*that part I'd like*!" And I tucked my hair in a Nazi cap. It was high camp. I loved working on this movie. Merrie Lynn and I would sit in her fancy trailer and had fun with Aldo Ray who was always drunk on the set but a darling. I had great respect for Robert Vaughn as an actor but I really didn't get to know him. He was professionally cold. Other than Dyan Cannon, Merrie Lynn was the only actress who was a friend of mine who asked me to be in every movie she was working on.

**Why she stopped acting a final time:** In 1973 I married a "civilian" named Robert Heffron and adopted an infant son in 1977. Robert was a tire distributor and a really nice guy. I was interested in motherhood at that time. Sitting in a hot studio with full makeup on my face is a bore. There is no fun place in show business if you are not at the top of the heap. If you are not a star, it's hard work. The minute you get a job, you have to be looking for another gig. Robert was successful and having a son was my joy in life. Unfortunately, I was not the best wife to Robert and let the marriage go downhill. It was one of my big mistakes.

**George Sidney:** I had many affairs and infatuations but never a love in my life like George. He was the greatest husband any woman could ask for and the greatest love of my life. Our marriage was a loving 24/7 of togetherness. We never argued or had a fight.

And that was because of him. I married George Sidney two and a half months after his wife passed away in 1991. We had always been friends but I was surprised to learn how much he had loved me secretly all those years. He never made a pass, how did I know? We moved from Beverly Hills to Las Vegas in 1998, five years before he died. We both had accumulated huge art collections and found the perfect home to house them. After he passed away I established the George Sidney Student Scholarship at the University of Las Vegas and George's memorabilia is in the Smithsonian for all to enjoy.

**Her career overall:** I really wasn't impressed with anything that I did. I had an over-privileged background. But I was not ambitious—I've got to say that. I was professional and probably one of the *most* professional actresses on the set because anything I undertook, I wanted it to be my best. Still, I didn't have the drive like Raquel Welch, Dyan Cannon, and Ann-Margret, which you really need to make it in Hollywood. God gave me great beauty. I was smart and married the best men. I'd rather live like a star than be one—lucky me.

**Her life today:** I didn't realize how infamous I was in Las Vegas due to my years with Jack Entratter, until I returned. I have so many friends from then and now—I feel truly blessed. I am involved in civic duty in Las Vegas and am chairman of the Fine Arts committee at the University of Las Vegas.

# Jo Collins

A fresh-faced, green-eyed, raven-haired beauty, she was one of the most celebrated Playboy Playmates of the Sixties, becoming the pinup *du jour* of GIs stationed in Vietnam due to her many visits to that war-torn country. Despite her popularity, she was never able to rise above minor roles on the big screen.

**You May Remember Her Most From:** *Lord Love a Duck* (1966) as a sexy bikini-clad starlet whose producer boyfriend replaces her with high school student Tuesday Weld as the star of his next beach movie.

**Her Groovy '60s Credits:** Jo Collins was *Playboy*'s Miss December 1964 and was selected as Playmate of the Year in 1965 though she listed some head-scratching answers in her profile. Her turn-on was "furniture" and her favorite novel was "*Fannie Hill*." Collins became a favorite pinup of servicemen worldwide and to show her support she traveled to Vietnam a number of times to help boost morale, resulting in her being nicknamed "G.I. Jo." She made her film debut in *Ski Party* (1965) as one of the beach girls who don ski clothes for a party in the snow. Of course there is an occasion for the gals to doff their bulky sweaters and slacks and slip into their bikinis as Frankie Avalon croons "Lots Lots More" poolside. Collins is featured very prominently in this production number as she dances and gyrates to the catchy pop tune. She also competes with ski bunnies Patti Chandler, Salli Sachse, and Mikki Jamison for pompous ladies man Aron Kincaid's attention but he only has eyes for Dwayne Hickman, dressed in drag as a feisty English lass. Despite

*Playboy*'s 1965 Playmate of the Year Jo Collins (*center in black bikini bottom*) as one of the myriad of beach girls in *How to Stuff a Wild Bikini* (AIP, 1965) with (*left to right*) Marianne Gaba, Salli Sachse, Patti Chandler, Mary Hughes, unidentified actress, Sue Hamilton, unidentified actress, and Linda Opie.

her fantastic figure, Jo was pushed to the background in her next beach film *How to Stuff a Wild Bikini* (1965) though she makes the first comment about bikini girl Beverly Adams, the new competition on the sand, and joins the beach girls singing "What About Us" to try to get ad man Mickey Rooney to select one of them for his new advertising campaign. Later, she and the other beach girls reluctantly try to teach Adams how to walk seductively. In the lame service comedy *Sergeant Dead Head* (1965), the beach gang once again puts on clothes as Collins played one of Deborah Walley's military friends. Her most outstanding screen appearance was in the satire *Lord Love a Duck* (1966), directed by George Axelrod. The former Playmate looked fantastic and gave a surprisingly droll performance as a shapely, bored starlet seen lounging on a yacht. The star of *Cold War Bikini* and plaything of producer Martin Gabel, Collins finds him to be "a drag" when he announces she is too over-exposed and will now be playing the older sister to new discovery Tuesday Weld in his upcoming beach movie extravaganza, *Bikini Countdown*. Jo Collin's last feature film was *Fireball 500* (1966) wherein the beach party gang abandons the shores of Malibu for the dragstrip. Collins was part of a gaggle of groupies who coo over handsome racer Fabian, rival to Frankie Avalon on and off the track. After she stopped acting, Collins continued visiting Vietnam while working as a Playboy Bunny in clubs.

**The Beginning:** She was born Janet Canoy of Norwegian and Spanish descent on August 5, 1945, in Lebanon, Oregon. Blossoming into a beautiful young woman with dark hair, cream-colored skin, blue-gray eyes, and a figure measuring 36-24-36, it is no surprise that she caught the attention of a *Playboy* talent scout while she was working as a page on the TV program *Queen for a Day*.

**The '70s & Beyond:** In 1970 Jo married former baseball player Bo Belinsky. That marriage ended in divorce in 1975 and Collins dropped out of the limelight, working at Playboy, Inc., as a Bunny Mother. In the January 2000 issue of *Playboy*, Collins was named one of the 100 Centerfolds of the Century, placing seventeenth. She appeared as herself in the DVD release *Playboy: 50 Year of Playmates* (2004) and in "Hugh Hefner: Girlfriends, Wives and Centerfolds" on *E! True Hollywood Story* (2006).

# Yvonne Craig

A vibrant, gorgeous, green-eyed brunette, she was one of the Sixties' busiest decorative actresses as she had the talent and looks to convincingly play ingénues, trollops, Elvis girls, snow bunnies, spy chicks, space aliens, and a superhero in numerous films and TV shows throughout the decade.

**You May Remember Her Most From:** TV's *Batman* as the motorcycle-riding, high-kicking crimefighter, Batgirl, a.k.a. Barbara Gordon.

**Her Groovy '60s Credits:** In 1960, television viewers were treated to Yvonne Craig playing the sweet ingénue on episodes of *The Barbara Stanwyck Show*, *Channing*, *The Dick Powell Show*, *Dr. Kildare*, *Follow the Sun*, *Hennessy*, and many others. On the big screen she played a brainy college coed in the 1960 Bing Crosby comedy *High Time* (where she met her first husband Jimmy Boyd; they divorced two years later) and a young nurse held captive by the Japanese in the World War II adventure *Seven Women from Hell* (1961). Craig then surprised her fans when cast as the town tramp who vamped rich playboy George Hamilton in *By Love Possessed* (1961). Sitting in his car, the amorous Craig seductively purrs, "If, ah, I get drunk and pass out... it's no fun for me. If you get drunk and pass out... it's no fun for me." After their roll in the hay, he gives her the brush-off. Furious, the gold-digging tart accuses him of rape. Craig's big-screen persona softened during the mid–Sixties after signing a contract with MGM and co-starring twice with Elvis Presley. In *It Happened at the World's Fair* (1963) she was a small town girl in a tight dress, caught making out on the family sofa with playboy pilot Elvis by her gun-toting father who runs the poor boy out of his house. In *Kissin' Cousins* (1964) she vied with her hillbilly sister Pamela Austin for the charms of distant cousin GI Presley. In a surprising twist, brunette Craig lands the King while blonde Austin has to settle for another.

Craig was next wasted in a small part as a saloon girl in the comedy western *Advance to the Rear* (1964) starring Glenn Ford and Stella Stevens, and then played the spoiled fiancée of meek news reporter Robert Morse who almost loses him to half–Maori girl Anjanette Comer while on assignment in Antarctica in the lightweight romantic comedy, *Quick, Before It Melts* (1964). In *Ski Party* (1965), a beach party in the snow starring Frankie

Avalon and Deborah Walley, Yvonne played the love interest of Dwayne Hickman. When she and Walley go gaga over ladies man Aron Kincaid, the guys, determined to discover what women look for in a man, dress in drag and pretend to be British lasses. Craig gives a perky performance and looks fetching in her ski outfits but unfortunately she is nowhere to be found when the bikini girls gyrate poolside to a warbling Avalon. At this time Yvonne started landing better and more memorable roles especially in the spy genre on TV beginning with an appearance on *The Man from U.N.C.L.E.* ("The Brain Killer Affair") as the young innocent who joins Robert Vaughn's Napoleon Solo as he searches for U.N.C.L.E. chief Mr. Waverly, who is being held prisoner by THRUSH agent Elsa Lanchester, the creator of a mind-altering machine whose rays render the captive ineffectual. On *The Wild Wild West* Craig gave a passionate performance as the amusingly named Ecstasy La Joie, a seductive assassin whose every attempt to kill a Middle Eastern despot is foiled by Robert Conrad's agent James West in "The Night of the Grand Emir." For marquee name value only, Craig appeared in added scenes in two theatrically released *Man from U.N.C.L.E.* features. In *One Spy Too Many* (1966) she played Leo G. Carroll's niece who is attracted to Robert Vaughn's virile agent. But the role was just created for gratuitous titillation as topless Craig is seen lying on her stomach in a bikini, tanning under a sun lamp while working in the communication room at UNCLE headquarters. *One of Our Spies Is Missing* (1966) featured Craig as agent Wanda, who unfortunately keeps her uniform on but has no interaction with any of the other actors in her brief scenes in the control room. She next played a sexy mini-skirted scientist who recites a lot of scientific mumbo jumbo in the sci-fi cheapie *Mars Needs Women* (1966) opposite Tommy Kirk as a Martian sent to bring nubile Earth lasses back to the Red Planet, whose female population has plummeted. Despite the film's tag line "They were looking for chicks… to go all the way!" it is not as fun as it sounds and both leads give very stiff performances, draining any life out of it. After putting her ballet skills to good use in the more high profile role of a Russian ballerina-enemy agent in *In Like Flint* (1967), Yvonne landed the role that will make her live on in infamy—Batgirl on TV's *Batman*. With the ratings falling during the second season, the producers wanted to spice up the series with a female crimefighter. The network was skeptical but after watching Craig (who, measuring 37-23-35, was a knockout in her skintight purple suit during a short promo film), *Batman* was renewed for a third season in 1967. Her meek librarian Barbara Gordon by day morphed into Batgirl by night, aiding the Dynamic Duo in keeping Gotham City safe from felonious felons. Her best episode was perhaps the one that introduced her to the series (Barbara Gordon is kidnapped by Burgess Meredith's Penguin, who aims to marry her, making him the son-in-law of the city's police commissioner). Though Craig brought more excitement to the show, it did not translate into bigger ratings so the series was cancelled in 1968. She finished up the decade playing various roles on *The Mod Squad* as a singer with meningitis on the lam from the mob ("Find Tara Chapman!"), *Star Trek* as a demented green-skinned alien denizen of a space asylum ("Whom Gods Destroy") and *Land of the Giants* as a time-traveling researcher ("Wild Journey").

**The Beginning:** Yvonne Joyce Craig was born on May 16, 1937, in Taylorville, Illinois. When her family relocated to Dallas, Craig began ballet training with Edith James. A superlative dancer, Yvonne wowed guest teacher Alexandra Danilova, who chose her to be her protégé. It was through Danilova that Craig won a scholarship to the School of American Ballet in New York, which led her to become the youngest member of the

**Yvonne Craig strikes a provocative pose to help promote** *One of Our Spies Is Missing* (MGM, 1966).

Ballet Russe de Monte Carlo where she progressed to soloist. While on tour in Hollywood, she passed on film offers but when she returned in 1957 (after abandoning a career in ballet possibly because she was a bit too voluptuous to be a dancer), she accepted the female lead in the handsomely produced western *The Young Land* (1959) starring Patrick Wayne as a lawman torn between the Anglos and Mexicans in the newly formed state of California. Craig with cleavage amply on display played his senorita girlfriend. When filming was delayed, she accepted a supporting role in the teenage exploitation film *Eighteen and Anxious* (1958). More movie roles followed: the disapproving high school friend of Sandra Dee's surfing sweetie in *Gidget* (1959) and a pony-tailed teenage vixen who puts the moves on shy drummer Sal Mineo in *The Gene Krupa Story* (1959). Craig also began appearing on the small screen with guest roles on *Schlitz Playhouse of Stars*, *Perry Mason*, *Bronco*, *Philip Marlowe*, and a few appearances on *The Many Loves of Dobie Gillis*.

**The '70s & Beyond:** Yvonne Craig returned to the big screen wearing a auburn wig in the comedy *How to Frame a Figg* (1971), playing a duplicitous secretary aiding crooked politicians to set up bookkeeper Don Knotts to take the fall for their looting of the town's coffers. She is quite seductive in her fur coats and mini-dresses as she tries to romance Knotts to keep him from catching on to the politicians' scam, and she disappears from the movie far too soon. The remainder of the decade saw her mired in forgettable TV roles that were a waste of her charms. Proving she had comedic talent from her past performances, she made four appearances on *Love, American Style* and two on the forgettable Don Adams sitcom, *The Partners*. The rest of her credits include small dramatic roles in the made-for TV movie *Jarrett* (1973) and on *O'Hara, U.S. Treasury*; *Mannix*; *The Magician*; *Kojak*; *The Six Million Dollar Man*; and *Starsky and Hutch*. Tired of being typed in sexy roles, Craig instructed her agents not to accept them any more. Hence, her career came to a screeching halt as she wasn't able to progress to mother-type roles. Needing to support herself, she obtained a real estate license while accepting an occasional acting role such as in "Remember... When?" on *Fantasy Island* in 1983. Yvonne received a resurgence of popularity when Tim Burton's *Batman* movie was released in 1989, which led to many talk show appearances and a small role in the direct-to-video comedy *Diggin' Up Business* (1990). At this time, she began doing autograph conventions where she was a fan favorite. Her popularity inspired her to write her memoirs entitled *From Ballet to the Batcave and Beyond*, which was released in 2000 by Kudu Press. After appearing as herself, reminiscing about her dancing days in the documentary *Ballet Russes* (2005), she announced her retirement from making personal appearances in 2006 to spend more time with her husband Kenneth Aldrich, whom she wed in 1988.

# Pamela Curran

Coming across as a flaxen-haired, hazel-eyed Julie Newmar, this sophisticated Amazon was mired in bit roles on the big screen though she landed larger-than-life parts in B-movies and on fantasy television shows due to her glacial persona, highlighted by long, lithe limbs and wide, mysterious eyes.

**You May Remember Her Most From:** TV's *The Man from U.N.C.L.E.* for her two appearances as THRUSH bad girls who try unsuccessfully to eliminate Robert Vaughn's slick agent, Napoleon Solo.

**Her Groovy '60s Credits:** As the decade started, Pamela Curran turned up on TV's

*Thriller* playing a turn-of-the-century streetwalker terrorized by a maniacal psychopath in the memorable episode, "Yours Truly, Jack the Ripper" and a beauty queen murdered by a sniper in "Lady Killer" on the syndicated series *Tallahassee 7000*. Minor roles quickly followed in the early Sixties on *Surfside 6* as a murdered former classmate of Lee Patterson in "The Old School Tie," *Alfred Hitchcock Presents*, *The Roaring 20's*, and *Perry Mason*, among many others. On the big screen Curran had an amusing bit as the Happy Girl, spokesmodel for Happy Soap, spoofing Jayne Mansfield in *The Thrill of It All* (1963). The camera opens on the luscious Curran taking a bubble bath. Rising from her sunken tub clad in nothing but a towel, she shares the joys of being a movie star with the audience and then says that you need to learn "what clothes to wear and what hair style—oh, and how to act." She goes on to pitch the soap, promising "you'll smell like a movie star." Displeased with her performance ("couldn't sell me a cake of that soap"), the owner of the company replaces her with housewife Doris Day. The comedy *Under the Yum Yum Tree* (1963) featured Curran in another bit as one of lecherous landlord Jack Lemmon's nubile tenants who likes to exercise scantily clad. In the Elvis Presley musical *Girl Happy* (1965) Curran didn't have much more to do than look good in a bikini playing the annoyed, vague date of band member Gary Crosby, who keeps deserting her to help Elvis chaperone coed Shelley Fabares on Spring Break in Fort Lauderdale. Pamela journeyed from the beaches of Florida to a cemetery in Los Angeles for her small part as a Whispering Glades hostess who assists Jonathan Winters' Rev. Glenworthy in the funny satire on the funeral arts, *The Loved One* (1965).

Curran finally landed a lead role in the low-budget Grade Z movie *Mutiny in Outer Space* (1965). She was cast as an astronaut who with her crew is trapped in a space station where a deadly parasitic fungus in this pre–*Alien* adventure. Smitten with the captain who has turned a blind eye to the situation; she follows his orders and doesn't send a mayday to Earth, putting the entire crew in danger. The remainder of the decade, Curran concentrated on television. She made two appearances on *The Man from U.N.C.L.E.* playing the Amazonian bad girl to good effect. In "The Sort of Do-It-Yourself Dreadful Affair" she was a love-starved, buttoned-up THRUSH agent in charge of financing for the production of indestructible humanoid assassins who falls for U.N.C.L.E. agent Robert Vaughn; "The Deadly Smorgasbord Affair" featured her as a Swedish THRUSH agent (masquerading as a college professor's assistant) who makes several attempts to kill Vaughn to no avail. Curran, so good playing the bad girl, continued her evil ways playing a nasty, dark-haired Persian princess who enslaves Larry Hagman's Major Nelson in "My Hero" on *I Dream of Jeannie*; the aptly named Vanessa Vane, a duplicitous health spa worker in "Beautiful Dreamer" on *The Green Hornet*; and a sexy alien in "Counterattack" on *The Invaders*. Her last movie appearance was in *The Chase* (1966) starring Marlon Brando as a small town sheriff and Robert Redford as an escaped con heading back to town. Clad in a tight white sequined evening gown a la Marilyn Monroe, Curran played the small role of a blonde bimbo and trophy wife of an older businessman who makes a drunken fool of herself at a birthday party for the town's richest man E.G. Marshall. Divorced from her second husband in 1964, the remainder of the decade found Curran fodder for the gossip columnists due to her romances with George Hamilton, producer Sam Spiegel, and actor Lance Fuller.

**The Beginning:** A daughter of privilege, Pamela Helene Dudley Curran was born June 2, 1930, and grew up a debutante in New York City. Her parents, William Greathead and

**Pamela Curran (1963).**

Helen Curran, divorced when she was young and her mother married Frank M. Gould, a wealthy Detroit advertising executive. She spent time both in New York City and at Beechwood, her mother's estate in Old Westbury, Long Island, where the teenager became an expert horsewoman and a crack shot with a rifle. Pamela was featured on the cover of *Life* magazine on November 24, 1947, where she was dubbed a "Top New York Subdeb" and she graced the April 11, 1950, cover of *Look* along with five other debutantes clad in strapless gowns. A short-lived marriage (1951–1954) to commodities broker Joseph Austin

Wade, Jr., produced two sons and ended in a scandal as private detectives hired by Wade found Curran nude in the hotel room of millionaire banker and amateur golfer Robert Sweeny, whom she eventually wed in 1957. The socialite took an interest in acting and began studying with Lee Strasberg, which helped her land a small part in Norman Krasna's *Who Was That Lady I Saw You With?* on Broadway. A few live television appearances, particularly on *Kraft Mystery Theater*, brought her a lot of press, which led her to Hollywood. Her kissing scene with Spencer Tracy in *Desk Set* (1957) was left on the cutting room floor but her brief make-out scene in *The Blob* (1958) was retained.

**The '70s & Beyond:** In the early Seventies, Curran guest starred on *The FBI* as a hair stylist in "Summer Terror," *Hogan's Heroes* as a German girl infatuated with Werner Klemperer's Colonel Klink in "Klink's Escape," and *Adam-12* as a bank hostage in "Log 26: LEMRAS." Her last acting credit was "Love and the Note," a 1971 *Love, American Style* with James Brolin, before she returned to New York due to her engagement to multimillionaire Bruce Norris. As of 1977, she was still living in Manhattan. Her whereabouts today are unknown.

# Danica d'Hondt

A talented, statuesque blonde who never got the opportunity to prove she was more than just another beautiful Glamazon in Hollywood, she was hired mainly to decorate B-movies and major studio productions though television offered her more of a chance to demonstrate her acting talent.

**You May Remember Her Most From:** TV's *The Man from U.N.C.L.E.* as the villainous vixen Lucretia Nazarone who beats up Robert Vaughn's Napoleon Solo twice and ranks as one of the series' most memorable Amazonian bad girls.

**Her Swinging '60s Credits:** Danica d'Hondt made her film debut in the low-budget Chicago-lensed exploitation melodrama *Living Venus* (1960), directed by Herschell Gordon Lewis. She was a vision of loveliness in this swipe at Hugh Hefner and *Playboy* playing a waitress who goes from slinging hash to international cover girl. A disastrous marriage to the gruff publisher who treats her cruelly and practically pimps her out to prospective advertising clients leads her to drink. During a drunken binge the souse takes an accidental header into a swimming pool and drowns. In Hollywood after doing some television work, d'Hondt landed a contract at Universal and was cast in the frivolous farce *Wild and Wonderful* (1964) as a sexy French girl named Monique; she and the rest of the cast, including Tony Curtis, were upstaged by a scene-stealing French poodle. Danica next co-starred as one of a number of beauties whom con man Marlon Brando tries to charm in one of his rare excursions into comedy, *Bedtime Story* (1964). Stardom slipped by her when she turned down the role of Ginger on *Gilligan's Island* to play a harlot in the low-budget *A House Is Not a Home* (1964), the movie bio of New York madam Polly Adler (played by Shelley Winters). A change-of-pace role came her way when the fresh-faced twenty-three-year-old was cast as a late-thirty-something judge, complete with her temples dyed grey, in the romantic comedy *A Very Special Favor* (1965) starring Rock Hudson as a rich oil man who romances business rival Charles Boyer's spinster daughter Leslie Caron.

As with Julie Newmar and Francine York, movie producers just didn't know what to do with d'Hondt and her height lost her parts due to insecure leading men. Television offered d'Hondt some powerful roles, most notably in "Escape from Venice" on *Voyage to the Bottom of the Sea* as the government liaison between the *Seaview* submarine and the naval institute, and "The Girls of Nazarone Affair" on *The Man from U.N.C.L.E.* as a luscious THRUSH operative and racecar driver (a role reminiscent of Pussy Galore in *Goldfinger*) who allows herself to be riddled with bullets to test the powers of a rejuvenation potion that instantly heals injuries. Her assignment is to stop Robert Vaughn's Napoleon Solo from retrieving the formula. Immune to his suave sex appeal and bursting with renewed energy, d'Hondt thrashes Solo in her hospital room after telling him, "I don't like your face." She gets another shot at doing him in (this time by strangling him) before she succumbs to the potion's deadly side effect—advanced aging. Danica looks simply smashing and made a worthy adversary for the U.N.C.L.E. agents. Danica's last big-screen role was in the outrageous bedroom farce *Mother Goose a-Go-Go* (1966) playing the Amazonian Dr. Marilyn Richards, a curvaceous sex therapist counseling Tommy Kirk, a newlywed who blacks out before having sex with his nubile bride because of his obsession with Mother Goose rhymes. The unorthodox Dr. Richards takes notes with a feathered pen, dons a skimpy purple bikini and pretends to be a guest where Kirk is honeymooning, and administers a psychedelic drug to the boy before sending him to a discothèque to get his libido groovin'. Back on the small screen, d'Hondt had meaty roles in "The Night of the Deadly Bed" on *The Wild Wild West* playing the wicked accomplice of a deranged general who is building an underground steel plant in Mexico to use for his takeover of the country. In "A Life for a Life" on *Tarzan*, she was a photographer whose blood type could save a young boy. Soon after, Danica d'Hondt left Hollywood to live in San Francisco where she worked as a theatre director, magazine writer, producer of educational films, and acting teacher at her own school, The Actor's Lab.

**The Beginning:** The 5-foot-9 beauty had quite a pedigree before going Hollywood. Born in London of Irish and Belgian descent, her parents ran a hotel. Danica made her film debut at age nine singing the French national anthem with her classmates in a film shot at Shepperton Studios in England before relocating with her family to Canada. While attending high school in Montreal, the young d'Hondt worked in radio, TV, and on stage. Unbelievably the stunning beauty even found time to enter and win the Miss Canada pageant in 1958. While attending the University of British Columbia, she earned tuition money by working on CBC Radio and then returned to London, working in the theatre and on the BBC Radio.

**The '70s & Beyond:** Danica d'Hondt, with a new husband in tow, returned to Hollywood from San Francisco in 1971. She did a little acting including an appearance in the TV-movie *A Step Out of Line* (1971) starring Peter Falk and then began working behind the scenes as a writer and associate producer. On camera she was chosen to be a consumer and financial reporter for the syndicated daytime TV show *Breakaway*. When the show ended, Danica, at age forty-six, gave birth to her sixth child and completely retired from show business. Residing in Northern California, d'Hondt works with her husband tending their vineyard and running their restaurant called Sequoia. She also found the time

Danica d'Hondt as bad girl Lucretia Nazarone threatens U.N.C.L.E. agent David McCallum in *The Man from U.N.C.L.E.* (MGM Television, 1965) abetted by Sharon Tate and Kathy Kersh.

to author two works of nonfiction, the latest being *The Da Vinci Code: The Final Analysis*, relating to society's reaction to Dan Brown's *The Da Vinci Code*. She tours the country teaching seminars and participating in debates on this and other esoteric subjects.

## *Danica d'Hondt speaks out on…*

*Living Venus*: This was horrendous. I had been in touch with an agent in Chicago named George Liberace who was Liberace's brother. George contacted my agent in Toronto who had never really handled actors. Most of his clients were variety acts. George booked me in this movie and said everything was going to be on the up-and-up. But when I got there they told me that they wanted to do a European version with nude scenes. I was not twenty-one yet so I think I used that as my way out of doing it. But later they spliced in someone else's body. There are nude scenes in this but it is not me but only my very closest friends would know!

**Herschell Gordon Lewis**: Herschell Gordon Lewis reminded me of a used car salesman. I thought he was the kind of man who would exploit anyone just to make a name for himself in the movie business. He thought this film was a way to make money. I never got any artistic vibes from him. But we had Harvey Korman in the movie and he was great because he was a real actor from the Second City in Chicago. We became really good friends and we would work out things in our scenes together. We did the best we could with what we were stuck with.

In those days, especially with filmmakers like Lewis, there was no concern for people's safety on the set. I was almost electrocuted in the swimming pool during my drowning scene by a lamp that was blown over by the wind. One of the crew members grabbed it in time and luckily saved my life.

*Wild and Wonderful*: I was told if I fit the costume I got the role. I ran down to the studio that day to try it on but it didn't fit. The wardrobe people were so nice and told me, "You're going to fit this costume by tomorrow morning so don't worry." The next day it fit perfectly. I'm five foot, nine inches and towered over Tony Curtis. In the middle of the scene I was supposed to kiss him. He was so far below me that I literally picked him up because I was not about to bend over in my skimpy costume. He was supposed to be so bedazzled by my kiss that he was to fall backwards into a closet. But picking him up was even funnier. The director just loved it but I incurred the wrath of Tony Curtis. He hated me from then on.

*Bedtime Story*: I thought Marlon Brando was very immature. I was not impressed even though I had idolized him since I saw him in *On the Waterfront*. He looked really silly in this because he wore prosthetic rabbit teeth thinking it would make him look funny. He was constantly playing with the teeth and goofing around. He was also rude and so insulting to the director. Marlon and I would talk about how we would do the scene. When the director said, "Let me show you how we are going to do it," Marlon responded, "No, let us show you how we're going to do it." He was a bit much and unprofessional. I felt very awkward working with an actor like that.

**Passing on playing Ginger in** *Gilligan's Island*: I was on hold for this part for the longest time. I auditioned and thought it was the dumbest show I had ever come across. I thought, "No way am I going to do this." I wasn't worried about it being a flop, I was worried that it would be a success! But my agents insisted and said it was going to be big money. I had a chance to be in the movie *A House Is Not a Home* with Shelley Winters. I wanted to work with Shelley so I asked my agents to pull me out of [*Gilligan's Island*] and they did. Tina Louise played the part and the rest is history.

*A House Is Not a Home*: This was a nice ensemble cast. It was Raquel Welch's first movie. She was a sincere, wonderful person and I really liked her. I was impressed with her dedication and professionalism. Raquel worked very hard but when it came to her actually speaking in the movie she became very nervous and would throw up in the bathroom. The director gave me her lines so I don't think she ended up saying anything in the movie.

I got along well with Shelley Winters too. We became really good pals and years later when I went into production we worked together in a TV show I wrote and co-produced called *Marilyn, Remembered*. The only one on the set who was aloof was Robert Taylor. He was not very warm but everybody else was great.

**Typecasting**: In those days, if you were tall, it was the kiss of death. You were considered a body and nothing else. I would be sent for roles requiring a Julie Newmar type. It was very frustrating being typecast because I thought I had more to offer. *Playboy* kept asking me to pose in the magazine and I turned them down a number of times. I was represented by the William Morris Agency. There is something to be said for being with a big agency because you get good opportunities but it is hard to get small parts with a big agency unless they're packaging a film and they include you. I auditioned for big parts quite often but I was always taller than the leading man.

One film I lost out on was *Seven Days in May*. I read for director John Frankenheimer who really wanted me for the lead role [Burt Lancaster's former lover]. But then Kirk Douglas came along and said, "I have to approve her." Basically, he had a reputation for being very "friendly" with the females he worked with. I gave him every indication that I wasn't interested. It was the old casting couch, which was prevalent back then—not so much today. A lot of girls, some featured in this book, went that way and they didn't wind up with bigger roles than I did. Kirk turned me down and I think it was because of my height. He also had a problem with my name. It is my real name and I insisted on keeping it. The movie had all men in it and they wanted audiences to know for sure that there was a woman in it. John Frankenheimer sold out his interest in the film to Seven Arts Productions. Ava Gardner owed them one more movie so she got the part.

*The Man from U.N.C.L.E.*: David McCallum was a nice guy and very professional. I wasn't so impressed with Robert Vaughn who acted "the star." Sharon Tate was so sweet and we socialized a bit after this shoot. When I heard about her murder, it was extremely disturbing to me. She was such a lovely girl.

**Stunt work**: I had to learn how to drive a finely tuned sports car called a Cobra on *The Man from U.N.C.L.E.* They had one that was the show's car and another that was this guy's prize possession that they were going to use for the speed scenes. Well, the TV car's back axle locked so we could only use the really fancy one. The guy who owned it did *not* want me driving it. The stuntman had parked the car with the wheels turned and I didn't notice that. They gave me strict instructions not to baby the car but to put my foot on the gas and go. I got in the car with this actor [Ben Wright], I said my lines, I put my foot on the gas and since the wheels were turned, I was headed for about fifty crew members. I swung the car around and careened down the road. I think it was being in character that saved me, otherwise I would have been too scared to do that. They got it all on film and everyone was thrilled to death except the poor guy in the car with me who I think had to go and change his underwear.

*Mother Goose a-Go-Go:* I had a manager at the time whose name was Cal Ross, who convinced me to do the movie because it was a nice-sized part. I wasn't thrilled with the role or the movie. Jack Harris [the producer, director, and screenwriter] was cut from the same cloth as Herschell Gordon Lewis but maybe a step above. I was so naïve back then so I didn't know Tommy Kirk's strange behavior was from drugs. It makes sense to me now. He was quite a space cadet. In his drug-induced stupor I think he had a crush on me and would follow me around, which was silly because he was quite a bit younger than me. Anne Helm had a lot of emotional problems going on and I spent a lot of time with her, helping her.

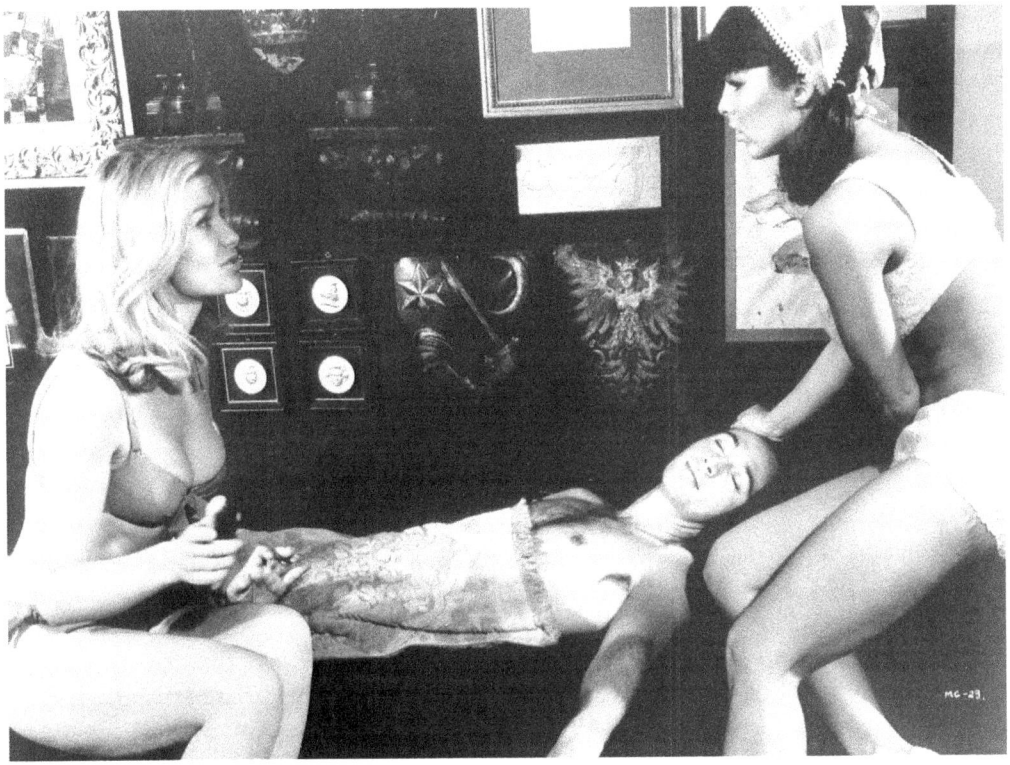

Danica d'Hondt and Anne Helm try to revive newlywed Tommy Kirk in *Mother Goose a-Go-Go* (U.S. Films, 1966).

In the scene where I dive into the pool to rescue Tommy Kirk they used a double. I am not a very good swimmer and am terrified to dive. That is why they had to do it in fast motion and had me don a swim cap before I jumped in. It was funny—the poor guy is drowning and my character is worried about getting her hair wet!

**A missed opportunity**: I had a husband and child to support so I took whatever roles were offered. When I did a TV episode of *Tarzan*, that was sad because I had been auditioning for a part in the stage musical *Oh, What a Lovely War!* I really wanted to be in that and kept getting call backs. I was waiting and waiting and waiting but we didn't hear a thing. I accepted the offer to do *Tarzan*, which was shot in Brazil, and after I arrived in Rio my manager called to tell me that I got *Oh, What a Lovely War!* If I was able to do the musical, I think I would have had a different career.

**Directing**: I always wanted to become a director. It was extremely difficult in those days to [become a director] because women were never given the chance. The only one I knew of was Ida Lupino. I knew a few more actresses who wanted to direct. Most of us just worked in the industry and we did whatever we could. We took every job we could get so we could keep accumulating experience so when our opportunity came we'd at least know as much as we could. On every set that I was on, I always made friends with the crew such as the cameraman and the lighting director. I would always converse with them and ask them how they did their job. They were always great guys—hard-working, patient, and supportive. The producers and directors treated you like cattle at times but the crew never did.

**Her life today**: I live with my husband in the Sierra Foothills of California where we own a vineyard and restaurant called Sequoia. I have six children and many grandchildren. My new book entitled *The Da Vinci Code: The Final Analysis* was released in early 2007 and it is my versions of "the wrap-up" of the Da Vinci Code controversy. I have been traveling around the country teaching seminars and participating in debates on the subject. My current activities can be found on the Internet at www.whisperedhistory.com.

---

# Phyllis Davis

A striking, dark-haired stunner with curves galore, she was similar in appearance to Edy Williams and was usually hired only to fill a bikini though she found fleeting fame in the Seventies in exploitation movies and on television.

**You May Remember Her Most From:** TV's *Love, American Style* as the shapely brunette usually wearing a bikini or mini-dress, lusted after during the blackout segments; or from the detective series *Vega$* as Robert Urich's glamourous blonde assistant.

**Her Groovy '60s Credits:** Due to Phyllis Davis' sultry looks and knockout body highlighted by a gleaming smile, the 5-foot-6 beauty began playing minor, scantily clad roles in such films as *Lord Love a Duck* (1966), *The Swinger* (1966), and *The Last of the Secret Agents?* (1966) where she turned up in bikini and sunglasses and holding a small dog in a series of blackouts on a train. Her bit television roles included a saloon girl in "The Night of the Steel Assassin" on *The Wild Wild West*, a "Kitty Kat" in "Jethro's Pad" and "Brewster's Baby" on *The Beverly Hillbillies*, and a showgirl in "The Windfall" on *Petticoat Junction*. She appeared in a number of Elvis movies including *Spinout* (1966) and *Live a Little, Love a Little* (1968) and continued popping up on television, usually (un)dressed for swimming. Despite these minor parts, Davis got noticed by studio insiders and was voted a Hollywood Deb Star in 1966. She was offered a role in *The Arrangement* by esteemed director Elia Kazan but passed on it because she didn't want to bare her breasts on the big screen. Instead, she accepted another bikini role in *The Big Bounce* (1969), playing a bimbo with nothing more to do than splash around a pool with an older rich guy. But the brunette beauty filled a wild swimsuit so lusciously that she was hired for the blackout skits of the new series *Love, American Style* beginning in 1969. For the next four years Phyllis was seen either in the skimpiest of bikinis or shortest of mini-dresses for the brief sketches where she was usually the object of desire for bungling nebbish Stuart Margolin. In 1969, she snagged a role in what she thought would make her a star—the character played by Barbara Parkins in *Valley of the Dolls* in the unofficial sequel *Beyond the Valley of the Dolls* (1970), directed by Russ Meyer. Davis' character, a fashion designer and aunt to aspiring rock star Dolly Reade, comes to LA with her friends seeking fame and fortune. With her long black mane parted in the middle and hair sprayed stiff, a pale-looking Davis comes across like Vampira in this loose take-off on Hollywood excess, giving one of the film's most wooden performances playing a character supposedly oblivious to the weird goings-on surrounding her. Though the movie was a hit and became a cult classic, Davis washed her hands of the picture due to her unpleasant experiences with Meyer, including his springing a topless scene on her. (It was seen at the beginning of the movie as part of a montage while Reade and friends drive across country to LA.)

**The Beginning:** Phyllis Davis was born on July 17, 1947, in Port Arthur, Texas. Growing up in Nederland, Texas, she lived above a funeral parlor owned by her parents. A lonely child, she began making herself up to look like her favorite actress Elizabeth Taylor. Her first foray to Hollywood landed her extra work only, though she did screen test at Warner Bros. Returning to Texas, she spent a year at Lamar College and acted in a few plays. She then regrouped and headed back to Hollywood where, using the stage name Phyllis Elizabeth Davis, she studied acting at the Pasadena Playhouse. She was content working as a movie extra but this knockout wouldn't remain anonymous for long.

Phyllis Davis (ca. 1968).

**The '70s & Beyond:** While continuing on TV's *Love, American Style*, Phyllis lost out on being a Bond Girl to Lana Wood in *Diamonds Are Forever* (1971) but snagged the lead in *Sweet Sugar* (1972), an outrageous exploitation women-in-prison film, after Celeste Yarnall turned it down. She played a prostitute working in Latin America, set up on a bogus drug charge by a crooked politician and sent to a chain gang to work on a sugar plantation. As with most of her contemporaries who wanted to keep working in film, Davis (looking fantastic clad in a mid-riff and short shorts) got over her shyness, doffing her blouse in many a scene to the delight of her male admirers. She again went topless in *Terminal Island* (1973) playing another sexpot. Exiled for life to a penal colony on an island off the coast of California for murder, Davis (with her hair cut short and dyed blonde) was cast as bimbo killer Joy who loves to sexually tease her male compatriots. When she and three other tough chicks escape from the bad guys (led by Sean Kenney) and team up with Don Marshall's renegades, her experience with a bow and arrow, not to mention her seduction technique, proves useful. Despite the hardships of deserted island living, the glamourous Davis always looks like she just stepped out of a beauty parlor. A much smaller role came next for Phyllis in Mike Nichols' disappointing *The Day of the Dolphin* (1973): a bubble-headed blonde receptionist more interested in her personal phone call than helping George C. Scott, who is waiting to see her boss. She then channeled Scarlett O'Hara in the extended dream sequence in *Train Ride to Hollywood* (1975), directed by Charles Rondeau who helmed many episodes of *Love, American Style*. Davis got noticed playing a dominatrix in the otherwise dismal *The Choirboys* (1977) and then was cast as private investigator Robert Urich's brainy assistant in the popular light-hearted series *Vega$*, a part she played from 1978 to 1981. Though this brought Davis back into the limelight, the show didn't give her much to do other than to look sexy aiding Urich in his investigations. Her career in the Eighties was undistinguished with guest star roles on *Hotel*, *Fantasy Island*, and *The Love Boat*, among others, but the fact that she outlasted many of her contemporaries was an accomplishment in itself. She also made tabloid headlines for her romance with Dean Martin and for suing *High Society* magazine for printing nude photos of her. In 1986, she began a recurring role on *Magnum, P.I.* as Cleo Mitchell, a love interest for Larry Manetti's playboy character. Her final screen role was the small part of a hostage in the Steven Seagal action flick *Under Siege 2: Dark Territory* (1995). Soon after, Davis retired from show business.

# Susan Denberg

A popular, shapely Playboy Playmate, this blonde German with the faraway look in her eyes was handed a lead role in a Hammer horror movie after playing a few bit roles but never capitalized on the notoriety it brought her.

**You May Remember Her Most From:** *Frankenstein Created Woman* (1967) as a deformed barmaid, brought back to life by the infamous doctor as a beautiful vixen with revenge on her mind.

**Her Groovy '60s Credits:** After studying at the Desilu Studio Workshop, Susan Denberg made her film debut in the lurid over-the-top melodrama *An American Dream* (1966) starring Stuart Whitman as a TV talk show host who may or may not have killed his wife and is being pursued by the police and the mob. Prior to the film's opening, Warner Bros. sponsored a contest to rename the Teutonic beauty. She rejected the winning moniker and came up with Susan Denberg herself. Small TV roles followed, playing a German girl on an episode of *Twelve O'Clock High* and a gorgeous alien humanoid in "Mudd's Women" on *Star Trek*; Denberg looked stunning in her blue off-the-shoulder tasseled mini-dress as one of the three loveliest women in the universe. The gals are "cargo" on the *Enterprise*, being transported by Roger C. Carmel, who acts an intergalactic pimp providing brides

Susan Denberg, *Playboy*'s Miss August 1966.

to lonely men. It turns out that they have a hypnotic effect on males that comes from a Venus drug that transforms them from hags to glamour girls. Standing 5-foot-7 and measuring 34-25-34, Denberg had the same effect on Hugh Hefner, who chose her to be *Playboy*'s Miss August 1966. She lists "Harold Robbins" as her favorite author and her turnoffs as "impoliteness, bad dressers, and self-admiration." Susan's pictorial was quite popular and she was one of the finalists for Playmate of the Year in 1967. She lost but kept busy doing photo shoots and dating many eligible Hollywood bachelors. Gossip columnists had a field day reporting on her romances with such actors as Stuart Whitman, Sammy Davis, Jr., and Nicholas Pryor. She made headlines doing a poolside striptease at a party thrown by Frank Sinatra, who reportedly was not amused with her antics.

Denberg's notoriety was noticed by Hammer Films in London who selected her for the female lead in *Frankenstein Created Woman* (1967) opposite Peter Cushing. Wearing a long auburn wig, she played an innkeeper's timid, disfigured and crippled daughter infatuated with the assistant to Cushing's Baron Frankenstein (Robert Morris). When Morris is set up for the murder of her father and beheaded before her eyes, the despondent lass jumps off a bridge and drowns. Frankenstein retrieves both bodies and melds Morris' soul with the remodeled Denberg, now a ravishing pigtailed blonde beauty. However, things go terribly wrong when Frankenstein's creation tarts herself up and goes on a murder spree, killing those who framed Hans. After getting her revenge, she meets a tragic end. The movie was a hit for Hammer in part due to the misleading title and promo photos that led audiences to believe that Frankenstein creates the scantily clad Denberg (her suggestive poses in a makeshift bra and panties were not part of the actual movie). Though Denberg's voice was purportedly dubbed by British actress Jane Hands because her German accent was too thick, she still had the beauty and on-screen poise to become a Hammer Girl like Veronica Carlson and Ingrid Pitt. But Susan got caught up in the excesses of the Swinging Sixties. She turned down many film offers and was content to live off her savings, blowing all her dough on clothes and jewelry by day, and partying by night.

**The Beginning:** Born Dietlinde Zechner in Bad Polzin, Germany, on August 2, 1944, Susan grew up in Klagenfurt, Austria. At age eighteen, the green-eyed blonde traveled to London where after working as an au pair she became a Bluebell dancer in 1963. About a year later she accompanied the famous dance troupe to perform at Las Vegas' Stardust Hotel where she met and married singer Tony Scotti, future star of *Valley of the Dolls*. The marriage lasted only six months but the beautiful showgirl was bitten by the acting bug and relocated to Hollywood.

**The '70s & Beyond:** Susan Denberg worked as a topless showgirl and was in and out of mental clinics. In 1972, while toiling as a bar hostess, she had a son. In 1974, she returned to performing, getting a job as a topless dancer on the Vienna nightclub scene. While there she attempted suicide. A year later she was admitted into a mental institution and bore a second child. Contrary to the abounding rumors of her demise, Denberg was still alive as of 2007 and living in Austria.

# Lyn Edgington

A pretty brunette with all–American girl-next-door appeal, she specialized in playing fun-loving coeds on the big screen and intelligent ingénues on TV.

Lyn Edgington (ca. 1967). *Courtesy of Dr. James Platler.*

**You May Remember Her Most From:** the Elvis Presley musical *Girl Happy* (1965) as one of Shelley Fabares' college roommates who accompanies her on Spring Break in Fort Lauderdale.

**Her Groovy '60s Credits:** Lyn Edgington made her film debut playing a proud college coed who leads Sandra Dee and other students in a sit-in ("Bottoms always on the floor!") protesting book censorship in the comedy *Take Her, She's Mine* (1963) starring James Stewart. She then transferred universities when cast as one of Carol Lynley's envious sorority sisters who revel in the coed's plan to live platonically with her boyfriend Dean Jones to see if they are marriage-compatible in the comedy *Under the Yum Yum Tree* (1963), also starring Jack Lemmon as an amorous playboy landlord determined to deflower Lynley. On television, Edgington had a bit in "Tour of Duty" on *The Lieutenant* and then nabbed the lead guest role as a nurse pursued by factory worker Phil Silvers and his pal in "Cyrano DeGrafton" on *The New Phil Silvers Show*. Back on the big screen, she played a perky coed who challenges poet James Stewart's diatribe against science in the comedy *Dear Brigitte* (1965).

*Girl Happy* (1965) gave her more to do as she and Chris Noel convince roommate Shelley Fabares to defy her father Harold J. Stone and join them on a Spring Break jaunt to Fort Lauderdale. However, the coeds aren't as clever as they think as Stone hires Elvis Presley and his combo to secretly chaperone the trio while performing at a local nightclub. As the girls drive south they sing the snappy tune "Spring Fever" along with Elvis and the guys in a scene that cuts back and forth between them. As the naïve friend who thinks boys prefer the brainy types, Lyn has a few amusing moments at the hotel when the manager threatens to evict the three girls for having a boy in the room even though they were only playing cards. Later, on the beach, Edgington feels uncomfortable and suggests to her friends that she feels like they are being stared at (Gary Crosby is spying on them from a nearby sand dune). The gals later get drunk and wind up in the slammer when a melee breaks out at a club where Fabares decides to do a sloppy impromptu strip tease.

In *The Loved One* (1965) Lyn is lost amongst the myriad of starlets playing funeral parlor hostesses, cosmetologists, and scantily clad good-time girls. During the next couple of years Edgington was relegated to the small screen beginning with the Clint Eastwood western *Rawhide* where she was a militant suffragette in the 1965 episode "Clash at Broken Bluff." In 1966, she was fought over by two men in "Prime of Life" on *Gunsmoke* and was part of a family trying to claim an inheritance in "Four Sisters from Boston" on *Bonanza*. The producers of *The FBI* were supportive and cast her three times. She played a helpful nurse in "Line of Fire" in 1967 and closed out the decade caught up in an espionage ring in "Wind Up and It Betrays You" in 1968. Around this time Lyn's husband of five years Ken Kendrick, whose family owned a petroleum company, died of a brain tumor. Devastated by her loss, she took a respite from acting.

**The Beginning:** Lyn Edgington was born on July 27, a native of Los Angeles. Her father Ralph Edgington was a cowboy from Montana who earned a law degree before going into the oil business and her mother Ethel Loretta Jones was a socialite from a very prominent Long Island family. When Lyn was sixteen years old, the esteemed ballet dancer: choreographer George Balanchine spotted her strolling along Rodeo Drive with her mother and approached the pair and asked to train Lyn, who he felt had that special gift of movement to become a prima ballerina. He was turned down flat by Mrs. Edgington but she later relented. Lyn danced with Balanchine and was supposed to perform with the troupe in Las Vegas but her parents put an abrupt halt to it when they viewed a performance where Lyn acted the snake slithering around a male dancer's body and thought it obscene. Edgington enrolled at the University of Wisconsin where she developed an interest in acting. She won favorable reviews for playing the lead in *Our Town* and also proved to be an excellent student, receiving a Junior Phi Beta Kappa pin for her academic prowess.

**The '70s & Beyond:** In 1970, Lyn Edgington returned to acting and was cast for the third time on *The FBI* in "The Stalking Horse" as the wife of a spy. Next, she co-starred in the very popular *Dirty Harry* (1971) where she reunited with Clint Eastwood, who played a hard-boiled San Francisco detective who throws away the rule book in tracking a perverted psycho nicknamed the Scorpio Killer. As the wife of Eastwood's injured partner Reni Santoni, Lyn has a poignant scene where she confesses to Eastwood her insecurities about being married to a cop. Edgington also turned up in an unbilled small part in the Brian DePalma–directed comedy *Get to Know Your Rabbit* (1972), her last movie appearance. She continued acting in minor parts on television until the late Seventies. Her second marriage to Andras Maros produced two daughters, Guilyn and Bryonie Lyn. After getting a divorce, she met Dr. James Platler and they wed in 1985. They remained married until her death in 2005. Remembering his wife, Dr. Platler remarked, "What Lyn did after retiring was to enrich the lives of her two girls, my two sons, and me. She filled us with excitement, enthusiasm, and wholesome fun every day. One of her girlhood friends wrote a note after Lyn died. It read, 'With Lyn every day was a treat-day—in every way.' It was a perfect statement. The world lost much the day she passed."

# Dolores Faith

A luminous, dark-haired beauty who eerily resembled Elizabeth Taylor with the classiness of Grace Kelly, she projected a sweet persona and was usually cast as fragile ingénues or vixenish vamps but never rose out of Grade Z movies.

**You May Remember Her Most From:** *The Phantom Planet* (1961) as the mute space girl who falls in love with an astronaut from Earth.

**Her Groovy '60s Credits:** A natural blonde who bucked the trend in the halcyon days of Sandra Dee and the flaxen-haired Barbie Doll by dying her hair black to match her olive skin, Dolores Faith began the decade with bit parts as a young bride in *All in a Night's Work* (1961) and a pie-throwing coed in *Love in a Goldfish Bowl* (1961). The fledgling starlet next grabbed a lead role in the low-budget exploitation movie *V.D.* (1961), which was also released under the title *Damaged Goods*. She played a dark and temperamental teenage trollop who seduces her friend's beau and pays for it by getting the Clap. Unbelievably heavy-handed and preachy, the movie plays as if it was one of those high school short films warning of the dangers of having premarital sex (and in fact has the hero forced by his doctor to view one). Faith's next role was her most memorable but unfortunately that is not saying much. In the cult sci-fi movie *The Phantom Planet* (1961) she is a mute inhabitant of the planet Rehton who falls in love with stranded astronaut Dean Fredericks. At first he is treated as a hostile until he rescues the beautiful Faith from the icky creatures the Solarites. In the process, she regains her voice. Faith received a lot of press for this (she was billed as "The Girl from Outer Space" on the film's posters) and from a purported romance with dashing Sean Flynn, son of Errol Flynn. More notoriety came her way when she was selected to be a Hollywood Deb Star in 1962; however it did not lead to any significant movie roles for her and she was back in exploitation land, re-teaming with Dean Fredericks in the totally obscure drama *Wild Harvest* (1962). He was a brutish manager of

**Dolores Faith as a sexy space babe is comforted by Earth astronaut Dean Fredericks in *The Phantom Planet* (AIP, 1961).**

a vineyard who mistreats the migrant workers and she played his mistress who at first enjoys his chicanery. But when she finally realizes how horrendous he is to the workers, she aids them in getting their revenge. On television she turned up as the daughter of a former Communist colonel marked for death due to his tell-all book in "The Last Chapter" on *Ripcord* and a Nepalese princess on the lam in "Caravan" on *Have Gun, Will Travel* in 1963. That same year *Life* magazine did a feature story on her but all it led to was a cameo appearance as a towel-clad American woman in Italy who gently convinces a jealous sergeant to help his rival and girlfriend escape from the Germans in the World War II adventure *Shell Shock* (1964). It was a respite before Dolores returned to far-out roles in two Grade Z sci-fi productions from the directing-writing team of Hugo Grimaldi and Arthur C. Pierce. In *Mutiny in Outer Space* (1965) she joined Glamazons Pamela Curran and Francine York as astronauts on a space station being terrorized by a creeping alien fungus. As the crew's bio-chemist, Faith is the one who first discovers the creature. *The Human Duplicators* (1965) had space visitors trying to take over the world by replacing some Earth inhabitants with lookalike androids. Dolores played the sexy blind niece of a scientist whose space lab has been taken over by the aliens, one of whom has fallen in love with Faith.

Her career sliding into the muck, Faith's next movie was a step down from even the previous two but that is not surprising since schlock horror filmmaker Jerry Warren was brought in to try to save it. *House of the Black Death* (1965) featured Dolores as the innocent girl caught between two battling warlocks, John Carradine and Lon Chaney, Jr., out to control the Desard family to which Faith belongs. Faith next turned up in a small role as a fashion model who decides to aid U.N.C.L.E. agent Robert Vaughn locate her missing scientist father but she is strangled with a telephone cord by a THRUSH agent before she can meet with him in "The Bridge of Lions Affair" on *The Man from U.N.C.L.E.* This two-part episode was edited into the feature film *One of Our Spies Is Missing* (1966) and released overseas. Dolores Faith's last big screen appearance was in the low-budget hillbilly musical *That Tennessee Beat* (1966) playing a sweet local girl romanced by rebellious country western singer Earl "Snake" Richards. His awful warbling not only scared audiences away, it sent Dolores Faith fleeing from pictures. Though not seen on the big and small screens any longer, she was still a fixture around Hollywood, turning up at the hottest night spots on the arm of millionaire Bob Neal, heir to the Maxwell House fortune.

**The Beginning:** Dolores Faith was born Dolores Faith Hedges in 1942 of Hungarian and Italian descent. As a child she was stricken with temporary deafness when her eardrums inexplicably burst. After slowly regaining her hearing, she developed a lisp but was able to return to public school. She spent her early years in Cleveland, Ohio, before her parents divorced and her mother relocated with Dolores, age twelve, and her sister Gigi to a house on Beachwood Canyon in the Hollywood Hills. She spent some time in an orphanage because her mother lacked the means to care for her children but the family reunited when Faith became a successful model. Work as a dance instructor for Arthur Murray led to acting with an early role playing a witness on a TV court show.

**The '70s & Beyond:** After several years of courtship, Dolores Faith married Bob Neal in November of 1972 in Las Vegas. She is reportedly retired and living in Florida as of 2006.

# Linda Foster

A pretty blonde in the mode of Pamela Austin, she was more ingénue than sexpot and was usually cast as the wholesome girl-next-door though she gave her roles a jolt of sex appeal.

Linda Foster and Robert Vaughn in a publicity photo for *The Man from U.N.C.L.E.* (MGM Television, 1966).

**You May Remember Her Most From:** the Matt Helm spy spoof *The Ambushers* (1967) as a Slaygirl with a loaded bra.

**Her Groovy '60s Credits:** After graduating from high school in Van Nuys, California, Linda Foster was studying to become a secretary when she was discovered by a talent agent while shopping at the Hughes Supermarket. He began representing her and she immediately landed a lead guest role as a popular high school student who Don Grady's Robbie Douglas vies for in "The Ever-Popular Robbie Douglas" on TV's *My Three Sons* in 1963. She got noticed playing an aspiring starlet, basically herself, in "Sirens, Symbols, and Glamour Girls" on *Hollywood and the Stars* in 1963. This led to roles on *Burke's Law*,

*Gunsmoke*, and a second appearance on *My Three Sons*. Foster also began being cast in minor roles on the big screen. She played a college student in *Roustabout* (1964) starring Elvis Presley, a newlywed in the farcical comedy *Honeymoon Hotel* (1964), and then joined a gaggle of starlets including Ann Morell, Eve Bruce, Jane Wald, Barbara Bouchet, Irene Tsu, and Teri Garr as harem girls in the mega-disaster *John Goldfarb, Please Come Home* (1965). She signed a contract with Universal and the studio kept her busy with roles in two episodes of *Bob Hope Chrysler Theatre* (in one, "Think Pretty," she played Fred Astaire's daughter); *The Virginian*; *Tom, Dick and Mary*; and four episodes of *McHale's Navy*. Not happy with the parts offered to her, Foster got released from her contract and went freelance. She landed a small role as one of playboy Dean Martin's sexy secretaries in *Marriage on the Rocks* (1965) and played the ingénue in the low-budget A.C. Lyles western *Young Fury* (1965) starring Rory Calhoun as a retired gunslinger forced out of retirement to save the town from a gang of young hellions led by his estranged son Preston Pierce. Warner Bros. took a shine to her and offered her a regular role on their new sitcom *Hank* in 1965. Dick Kallman was Hank, a student who, unwilling to see his sister sent to an orphanage, masquerades as various characters to make the authorities believe that they are being cared for by adults. He also "dropped in" on college courses that he could not afford to take and romanced Doris (Foster), the daughter of the university's registrar. Doris was well aware of Hank's schemes and at times joined in on them. After *Hank* was cancelled after only one season, Linda returned to playing guest lead roles. She popped up on *F Troop* as the refined daughter of town drunk Frank McHugh in "Will the Real Captain Try to Stand Up," *Rango*, *Bonanza*, and her third *My Three Sons*.

The spy genre offered her two memorable roles. On TV's *The Man from U.N.C.L.E.* she played an innocent schoolteacher whose dental work picks up THRUSH radio messages of a plot to assassinate a Gandhi-like leader in "The Thor Affair." On the big screen she was a sexy Slaygirl named Linda in *The Ambushers* (1967). Envied by the other Slaygirls, she is chosen to demonstrate to Dean Martin's Matt Helm one of the new weapons developed by ICE at their rehabilitation center. While necking on a couch, Helm is shot by a blank from Linda's halter top with a retractable gun barrel that fires on contact. After the smoke clears, Helm quips, "How do you like that? I didn't even get to squeeze the trigger. When you say you are a 38, you ain't just kidding." After their lesson, the amorous Slaygirl tries to entice Helm back to the couch but not trusting her—"those things come in pairs"—he exits. As did Linda Foster, who marched down the aisle with actor Vince Edwards and took a respite from acting to raise a family.

**The Beginning:** Linda Foster was born on June 12, 1944, in Lancaster, England. She was the only child of Nicholas and Hilda Foster. Her father was a nautical engineer and her mother owned a dance school where a six-year-old Linda took ballet and modern dance. In 1957, the family relocated to Toronto, Canada, and two years later they settled in Los Angeles.

**The '70s & Beyond:** It should come as no surprise that when Linda Foster resumed her acting career, *My Three Sons* would be the show she would return to. After progressing from high school senior to novice student teacher to a hippie college coed previously on the show, her last appearance featured her as a parent of a second grader. More TV roles followed on *Ironside*, *The Rookies*, and *Project U.F.O.* She played a military captain opposite her husband Vince Edwards in the made-for-TV movie *The Courage and the Passion* (1978) about the trials and tribulations of a group of Air Force test pilots. Soon after she divorced Edwards and married character actor Edward Winter. Foster's final credit was a small role as a reporter in "Tender Comrades" on *Dynasty* in 1983. She remained married to Winter until his death in 1991.

# Marianne Gaba

A pretty, curvaceous blonde indistinguishable from others with similar looks, this former beauty queen and Playboy Playmate was more famous for her romance with teen idol Ricky Nelson than for any of her acting roles. During her short stay in Hollywood she mixed decorative minor roles in big studio productions with major supporting roles in B-movies.

**You May Remember Her Most From:** *How to Stuff a Wild Bikini* (1965) as surfer chick Animal, who helps teach awkward beach babe Beverly Adams how to groove.

**Her Groovy '60s Credits:** A former Playboy Playmate, Miss September 1959 began the Sixties with small parts in the comedy *Please Don't Eat the Daisies* (1960) as one of David Niven's drama students and the children's movie *Raymie* (1960) starring David Ladd. In *G. I. Blues* (1960) Gaba had another minor role as a bargirl with a perpetual smile working at the nightclub where G.I. Elvis Presley and his combo get their first break performing live on stage. Alas Gaba does not receive screen credit, has no lines, and has no interaction with the King. She was next seen in a co-starring role in the youth gone wild JD flick *The Choppers* (1961). Clad in a tight sweater one size too small, the former Playmate looks fantastic but is only around for decorative purposes as the whiny, nagging girlfriend of an insurance investigator out to nab punk Arch Hall, Jr., and his gang The Choppers, who strip cars for parts. After two more bit roles in *Island of Love* (1963) and the Jerry Lewis comedy *The Patsy* (1964) as a scantily clad nightclub waitress, Gaba donned a bikini for her role as man-hungry beach girl Animal in *How to Stuff a Wild Bikini* (1965). She followed in

Marianne Gaba (ca. 1962).

the footsteps of Valora Noland, Meredith MacRae, and fellow Playmate Donna Michelle, all of whom played the part in previous beach party movies. Gaba gets lots of screen time, even leading the shapely beach girls in the song "How About Us?" to try to convince Mickey Rooney to select one of them for his ad campaign by extolling their charm, looks, and brains. In the course of the movie, Gaba reluctantly agrees to teach Rooney's choice Beverly Adams some poise and has to break the news to Annette that Frankie, away in the naval reserve, has been cheating on her with an island cutie. On television Gaba had a memorable role as a beatnik named "Squirrel" who digs that big lunkhead Jethro for his personality not his money as most other gals did in "Big Daddy, Jed" and "Cool School Is Out" on *The Beverly Hillbillies* in 1965. Gaba's final film role was as one of the anonymous gold lamé bikini–clad robots in *Dr. Goldfoot and the Bikini Machine* (1965) starring Vincent Price and Frankie Avalon. Considering how well she performed as Animal, here she is absolutely wasted as she has no lines and is lost amongst all the other curvaceous cuties hired solely for their ability to fill bikinis. Perhaps seeing the writing on the wall, Gaba dropped out of show business.

**The Beginning:** Marianne Gaba was born on November 13, 1939, in Chicago, Illinois. Working as a model led her to entering and winning the Miss Illinois contest in 1957. This propelled her to the Miss USA pageant where she was a finalist for the crown but did not win. Relocating to Southern California she enrolled in USC and then made her film debut in *Missile to the Moon* (1958), a semi-remake of *Cat-Women of the Moon*, cast with other "International Beauty Contest Winners" as sexy Moon Maidens clad in high heels and showgirl-type costumes. She then appeared in the pages of *Playboy* as Playmate of the Month for September 1959. Measuring 34-24-34, she was not one of the bustier models to pose and bared only a portion of her derriere while clad in a striped shirt and high heels. Still, this was a surprising move considering her beauty queen titles and the fact that she was receiving loads of press due to her romance with teen idol Ricky Nelson, whom she mentioned in her *Playboy* profile as one of her turn-ons along with "beaches and sunsets." She became such fodder for the movie rags of the time that *TV and Movie Screen* hired her to write a monthly gossip column.

**The '70s & Beyond:** Marianne Gaba, still looking terrific, popped up as herself in "Hugh Hefner: Girlfriends, Wives and Centerfolds" on *E! True Hollywood Story* in 2006. She revealed that her mailman father was so proud of her *Playboy* centerfold that he would show all the folks on his route while her mother was terrified that their parish priest would find out about it.

# Sue Hamilton

Cute as a button, she was a petite blonde who at 4-foot-11 was one of the shortest Playmates to grace the pages of *Playboy* and frolic on the shores of Malibu as a beach girl in a number of AIP beach party movies.

Sue Hamilton, *Playboy*'s Miss April 1965.

**You May Remember Her Most From:** *How to Stuff a Wild Bikini* (1965) as a beach bunny nicknamed Peanuts who beguiles Mickey Rooney.

    **Her Groovy '60s Credits:** Sue Hamilton came to *Playboy* via modeling. Her measurements of 34-20-34 certainly suited her diminutive frame. As Miss April 1965 she used the name Sue Williams. Her turn-on was "eating popcorn in a Paul Newman movie" and one of her hobbies was "motorcycle riding." The blonde beauty was signed to a movie contract by American International Pictures when a talent scout spotted her photograph in a magazine ad. She was rushed into *How to Stuff a Wild Bikini* (1965) playing beach girl

Peanuts, who interacts with Mickey Rooney as an advertising executive. Along with Marianne Gaba and the other beach girls, they belt out the song "How About Us?" praising their charm, looks and brains to Rooney, who is searching for a spokeswoman for a new line of motorcycles. In her next movie, *Sergeant Dead Head* (1965), she morphed into Sue Hamilton to play a WAC and then was just one of the many beauties hired to play bikini-clad robots created by mad doctor Vincent Price in the spy spoof *Dr. Goldfoot and the Bikini Machine* (1965). As No. 7, Sue is assigned to marry and eliminate a rich Dutch oil man. As usual, Hamilton stands out from all the other girls due to her size, or lack thereof, and was selected along with Mary Hughes, Patti Chandler, and Salli Sachse to dance during the film's end credits as well as in the promotional TV special, *The Wild Weird World of Dr. Goldfoot*.

On television, Hamilton did background work on a number of *Gidget* episodes and was handed a line as one of the surfer's classmates in the episode where Gidget tangles with her overbearing English teacher. In *The Ghost in the Invisible Bikini* (1966) starring Tommy Kirk and Deborah Walley, Hamilton was pushed to the background without much screen time though she could be seen dancing poolside and lolling around Nancy Sinatra's bedroom during Piccola Pupa's musical number. A bigger role followed as a sexy farm nymph in *Fireball 500* (1966) starring Frankie Avalon and Annette Funicello. Clad in short shorts and a red plaid top, Hamilton is caught by her hillbilly daddy while she is making out with race car driver Frankie in the family barn. Chased by the irate pitchfork-wielding farmer, Avalon kisses the protesting beauty goodbye before hopping into his car and speeding off, leaving Sue and her film career in the dust. After being dropped by AIP, Hamilton returned to modeling and was the cover girl for Sheer Magic beginning in May of 1966. Sadly, Hamilton committed suicide on September 9, 1969, and is interred in Forest Lawn Memorial Park in Los Angeles.

**The Beginning:** She was born Karen Susan Hamilton on May 13, 1945, in Glendale, California. After graduating high school she passed up a chance to enroll at USC and instead began modeling despite her petite size. Her sister is responsible for Sue being chosen a Playboy Playmate as she submitted photographs of Sue taken by her company Figge Photography.

# Joy Harmon

A busty blonde with big blue, expressive eyes and a perpetual tan, she was a favorite pinup in all the popular girlie magazines of the time except *Playboy*. She had the looks, body, and comedic talent to become a star but this flaxen-haired beauty was more comfortable in minor roles and bit parts and had no interest in stardom.

**You May Remember Her Most From:** *Cool Hand Luke* (1967) as the sexy farm nymph who teases members of a chain gang by tantalizingly washing her car.

**Her Groovy '60s Credits:** After gaining notoriety on Broadway and television due to her voluptuous figure, Joy Harmon relocated to Hollywood in 1962 to become a regular on the short-lived *Tell It to Groucho* series (where she was billed as Patty Harmon) and began getting small movie roles after switching back to Joy. She was a gun moll in *Mad Dog Coll* (1962) and later in *Young Dillinger* (1965), and the gal pal of coed Carol Lynley who is living platonically with her boyfriend Dean Jones to see if they are compatible for marriage in *Under the Yum Yum Tree* (1963). In *The Loved One* (1965) Harmon had only one line but stood out as a top-heavy starlet in a form-fitting white polka-dot dress. Due to her giggly voice, infectious laugh, and naïve, blank stare, Harmon could always be counted on to get a snicker from the audience and she became a fixture on TV, especially in sitcoms. Usually seen in a bikini or low-cut mini-dress, Harmon brightened up a number of series with her effervescent personality including *Bewitched* as a Miami vacationer who befriends the "fun side" of Darrin in "Divided He Falls" and *That Girl* as a kooky actress auditioning for a play in "Pass the Potatoes, Ethel Merman." On *Gidget* Joy played one of the surfer girl's overly developed friends in "In God, and Nobody Else, We Trust" and then showed up doing the Frug as surfer Richard Sinatra's bikini-clad girlfriend in "A Hearse, a Hearse, My Kingdom for a Hearse." *Batman* cast her as bug-eyed beauty contest winner Miss Galaxy in "A Riddle a Day Keeps the Riddler Away."

Returning to the big screen, Joy graduated to playing the lead bad girl in *Village of the Giants* (1965), a fantasy about teenage delinquents (including Beau Bridges, Tisha Sterling, and Gail Gilmore) who grow to enormous size and terrorize a town. Harmon was amusing as the bubble-headed blonde who instigates most of the teen's dirty deeds but the film was more noteworthy for its poster art featuring Johnny Crawford hanging onto the bikini top of her giant-sized bosom. In the little-seen *One Way Wahine* (1965) bikini-wearing Joy played the title character of a newcomer to Hawaii working as a waitress who gets involved with beach bums in a plot to steal stolen money from the crooks who snatched it. Despite receiving good notices for her comedic abilities ("she is a joy to behold" quipped one critic), it was back to bit roles for Joy as a mini-skirted party gal fawning over cheating husband Robert Morse at a restaurant bar in *A Guide for the Married Man* (1967). Her most infamous role came next in *Cool Hand Luke* (1967) where a sexy Joy, in a tatty housedress with her cleavage clearly on display, teases members of a chain gang including Paul Newman and George Kennedy as she soaps up her jalopy (and herself in the process) in a scene that is truly one of Sixties cinema's most provocative moments. Joy holds the nozzle of the hose suggestively, squeezes the soap from the sponge and drenches her dress, and presses her bounteous bosom on the passenger-side window as she washes the roof, putting on quite a tantalizing show for the frustrated prisoners who have nicknamed her Lucille. She then hoses down the car, driving the men on and off the screen into a frenzied state. Without uttering a line, Harmon is amazing as she plays it innocently with a twinkle in her eye that reveals that her every move is to purposely titillate the prisoners.

Offers poured in for Joy, including a contract with AIP starting with a lead in *Born Wild*, but she accepted a marriage proposal instead. She continued acting but was happy with small parts and bit roles. On TV's *The Monkees* she appeared in "The Picture Frame" as a doe-eyed teller working for the bank that The Monkees are duped into robbing, thinking they are playing roles in a movie. In "Monkees on the Wheel" she is a casino hanger-on in a silver-lame mini-dress, Zelda, who attaches herself to Mickey Dolenz after he innocently wins big at a rigged roulette wheel. She was also a recurring player on the TV variety series *That's Life* (1968–69) starring Robert Morse. In the big screen comedy *Angel*

Luscious Joy Harmon turns the simple task of washing a car into a sex act in the classic *Cool Hand Luke* (Warner Bros., 1967).

*in My Pocket* (1969) she is very amusing as the wide-eyed, bubbly Miss Holland, a burlesque dancer who assures Reverend Andy Griffith that she keeps "her anatomy within the code" and then asks him to check the wiring on her costume. Thinking it is for her hearing aid, he obliges and then is shocked to see the windmills on her bosom begin to rotate. "Good Lord," he exclaims, "twin engines!" It was an apropos sendoff for Joy Harmon to end the decade.

**The Beginning:** Patti Joy Harmon was born on May 1, 1940, in Flushing, New York, but spent most of her childhood growing up in Wilton, Connecticut. As a teenager she was an extra in the movie *The Man Who Came to Dinner* (1956) and later was crowned Miss Connecticut. Her amble bosom (41-22-36) was her ticket to Broadway in the comedy *Make Me Laugh* (1958) starring Sam Levene. On television she became a favorite of talk show hosts Steve Allen and Garry Moore who would make double-entendres at Joy's expense; she would just glide across the stage and the comparisons to platinum-blonde sex goddess Jayne Mansfield were unavoidable. In between variety show appearances, she found time to make her film debut as a tough chain-smoking broad in the juvenile rock 'n' roll flick *Let's Rock* (1958). She also became a popular pinup as her voluptuous body was on view in all the top men's girlie magazines (*Rex, Nugget, Show*, etc.). But unlike June Wilkinson and others, she always kept her top on and rebuffed Hugh Hefner's many offers to pose semi-nude for *Playboy*.

**The '70s & Beyond:** Joy continued working on television in such series as *Love, American Style* as a ditzy blonde who sets up her friend, an ex-nun, on a date in "Love and the Secret Habit," *The Odd Couple* as a waitress in "Don't Believe in Roomers," and a Follies Girl in "Twentieth Century Follies" on *The ABC Comedy Hour* before calling it quits to devote time to her son and two daughters. Her final credit was a bit role on the forgotten sitcom *Thicker Than Water* in 1973. But Joy stayed connected to show business through her husband, TV producer Jeff Gourson, and did some voiceover work for his hit Eighties series, *Quantum Leap*. Today, Joy Harmon is a very successful businesswoman as the owner of Aunt Joy's Cakes, the leading supplier of desserts to movie and television studios across Southern California.

# Ena Hartman

A stunning model-turned-actress with a long slim nose, penetrating dark eyes, and petulant lips, she was one of the very few African-Americans to play decorative roles during the Sixties and became a frequent cover girl for the prevalent black publications of the decade, *Ebony* and *Jet*. Though she never found stardom, she, along with Sixties actresses Judy Pace and Mimi Dillard, paved the way for the blaxploitation stars of the Seventies such as Pam Grier and Tamara Dobson.

**You May Remember Her Most From:** *Terminal Island* (1973) in the role of the tough, ass-kicking black convict who finds herself banished to a tropical jungle to serve a life sentence for murder.

**Her Groovy '60s Credits:** Ena Hartman was the first African-American actress signed to a contract with NBC-TV. The network gave her small roles on *Bonanza* and *Profiles in Courage*. She made her film debut as a nurse in *The New Interns* (1964) before being cast as a military assistant to Lee J. Cobb's head of Ice in the hit spy spoof *Our Man Flint* (1966). The role was a minor one (all she did was field his phone calls a la Lt. Uhura on *Star Trek*), but Hartman brought a touch of glamour to it even clad in a drab military uniform. Leaving NBC, Hartman signed a contract with Universal after playing a sophisticated New

Ena Hartman (*right*) with Patty Poulsen as air hostesses working an ill-fated flight from Chicago to Rome in *Airport* (Universal, 1970).

Yorker in the TV-movie *Fame Is the Name of the Game* (1966). This was followed by a number of television roles including an unbilled bit as an *Enterprise* crew member in "The Corbomite Maneuver," the first official episode of *Star Trek*; three appearances as Laneen, a tribeswoman, on *Tarzan*; and an actress' ex-maid in "A World of Jackals" on *Ironside*, one of three appearances she made on the popular detective show.

Back on the big screen, Hartman played a party guest in the psychological thriller *Games* (1967) starring James Caan and Simone Signoret. In 1968, Ena made news when she was "elected" the first African-American mayor of Universal City Studios. The position was just ceremonial but she received lots of press coverage. She came close to co-starring with Elvis in *Change of Habit* but lost the role to Barbara McNair. She ended the decade playing a nurse in the TV-movie *Prescription: Murder* (1968) starring Peter Falk in his debut as Detective Columbo and made guest appearances on the debut episode "Log 1: The Impossible Mission" on *Adam-12* and "I Can't Hear You Scream" on *The Outsider* as a woman who enlists the aid of private eye Darren McGavin to save a hoodlum wrongly sentenced to death for murder.

**The Beginning:** The daughter of sharecroppers, Ena Hartman was born in Moscow, Arkansas, where she spent her first thirteen years being raised by her grandparents in a shack before relocating to Buffalo to live with her mother. She left high school before graduation and opened her own restaurant where she served as cook, cashier, and waitress in hopes of making enough money to go to New York. Blossoming into an exquisite beauty, she was discovered by a photographer sitting in the lobby of a modeling agency that had just rejected her and became one of the most successful black fashion models of the decade. She studied drama with Josh Shelley and Lloyd Richards, which led to a television career when she was brought to the attention of the vice-president of NBC Talent Relations.

**The '70s & Beyond:** Ena Hartman began the decade in the box office smash *Airport* (1970) as a flight attendant working in the tourist section on Global Airline's ill-fated flight to Rome; passengers included little old lady stowaway Helen Hayes and mad bomber Van Heflin. Unfortunately, the role gave her nothing more to do than serve coffee and then comfort passengers after Heflin detonates his bomb blowing a hole in the plane's cabin. Tired of the subservient roles, Ena with much fanfare walked out on her contract with Universal Studios. She became a regular on the action-packed Quinn Martin series *Dan August* (1970–71) starring Burt Reynolds as a detective working in the Southern California community where he grew up. Hartman played a secretary in the police department. When the series ended after only one season, Hartman abandoned her good girl image, grew her hair into an Afro, and played Carmen Simms, a tough chick sentenced to life imprisonment on *Terminal Island* (1973) where condemned killers are sent to permanent exile. The low-budget exploitation movie full of tits and violence was directed by Stephanie Rothman. Hartman's initiation to the island is to get beaten up by burly Roger Mosley as ordered by sadistic leader Sean Kenny and informed that women are merely sex slaves to pleasure the male population at their whim. But this sista takes no guff and she quickly leads the other three women on the island against the abusive male prisoners as they join up with a renegade group headed by Don Marshall. A brutal war breaks out between the two factions and the good bad guys win due to their guerilla warfare tactics and set up a tranquil hippie-type commune to spend the remainder of their days. Though she looks terrific with her seventies do and short shorts, the soft-spoken Hartman never quite projects the toughness of a Pam Grier and it is probably why she never became a staple of blaxpoitation cinema. Long retired from acting, she resides in Southern California.

# Alexandra Hay

A long-haired, wispy blonde with waif-like, delicate features, she played a number of cool chick roles in the late Sixties before turning to exploitation films and television during the Seventies.

**Alexandra Hay (ca. 1969).**

**You May Remember Her Most From:** *Skidoo* (1969) as gangster Jackie Gleason's nubile hippie daughter, who lusts after hoodlum Frankie Avalon.

**Her Groovy '60s Credits:** Alexandra Hay made her film debut in *Guess Who's Coming to Dinner* (1967) playing a gum-chewing teenage carhop at Mel's Drive-in who, with a deadpan delivery, rattles off the burger joint's list of ice cream flavors for Spencer Tracy, who is craving a flavor he can't remember. Later, as Tracy pays the check, Hay looks on quizzically as the happy customer goes on and on about the Oregon Boysenberry ice cream. She had a smaller though memorable decorative role in the Matt Helm spy adventure *The Ambushers* (1967) as Kurt Kasznar's secretary, attired in a mod multi-colored zigzag-striped mini-dress, who jumps up and gushes when agent-fashion photographer Dean Martin enters. When he asks if she'd be willing to pose for him, the excited blonde coolly turns him down and calmly returns to her desk. Alexandra began 1968 as "Miss Golden Globe" at the Hollywood Foreign Press' Awards Ceremony where each year a promising starlet is chosen to hand out the trophies to the winners. In the trying-to-be-with-it comedy *How Sweet It Is!* (1968) Hay played one of Donald Losby's hippie friends he accompanies on a tour of Europe with his bickering parents in tow.

The pretty blonde's bid for stardom rested with her next two movies but both were failures at the box office. Otto Preminger's debacle *Skidoo* (1968), a nonsensical comedy that tried to merge hippies with gangsters to attract a mixed audience, cast Alexandra (receiving "and introducing" in the credits sung at the end of the movie) as ex-mobster Jackie Gleason's vapid teenage daughter who falls in with hippie John Philip Law and his friends. When Gleason goes missing when pressured by head mobster Groucho Marx as God to rub out Mickey Rooney in prison, both Hay and Carol Channing try to seduce baby-faced gangster Frankie Avalon to learn Gleason's whereabouts. Hay's bikini-clad body adorned with painted flowers and the words "love" and "kiss" as seen in the movie was used in the film's posters and trade ads. Better received was *The Model Shop* (1969), director Jacques Demy's homage to Los Angeles, about one day in the life of alienated, unemployed architect Gary Lockwood, who trapped in a loveless relationship has just learned he has been drafted and takes a photography class where he falls in love with married French woman Anouk Aimée. The sweet-looking Hay was cast against type as Lockwood's live-in girlfriend, a pushy, grasping starlet who aches for marriage. Demy lovingly captured the City of Angels by giving the movie a sun-drenched desert hue but what transpired in front of the scenery did not live up to expectations. During the Sixties, Hay was known for her outspokenness in interviews and would routinely slam the studios, her agents, and anybody else she felt was holding her back. Finally free from Columbia, she pinned her hopes for super-stardom on director Robert Aldrich, who chose her to play a teenage nymphet forced into stripping by her nasty stage mother in *The Greatest Mother of 'Em All*, a thinly disguised story of Errol Flynn's underage wife Beverly Aadland and her mother Florence. The film was never made.

**The Beginning:** Born in Los Angeles on July 24, 1944, Alexandra Hay began modeling at age twelve. Her mother died when Alexandra was just sixteen and soon after she married her legal guardian, retired British naval officer Cedric Kehoe, so she could spend time in Europe. She continued modeling and made international headlines when she rescued Prince Francesco Borghese, who was knocked unconscious in a boat racing accident. She held him above water until help arrived. Returning to California, she had her marriage amicably annulled and concentrated on acting. She performed on stage in *The Beard* in San Francisco and Los Angeles, where she was arrested fourteen times for obscene language and doing stage nudity. She then landed a long-term contract with Columbia Pictures.

**The '70s & Beyond:** Alexandra Hay's last major movie was *The Love Machine* (1971) as one of the many lovelies who jump into the sack with handsome but egotistical newscaster John Philip Law. She then followed other Sixties glamour girls into the world of Seventies drive-in exploitation movies with *1000 Convicts and a Woman!* (1971). She received top billing as the poisonous nymphet daughter of a British prison governor who is an equal opportunity seducer, bedding guards and inmates alike. Despite its lurid plot, Hay remains clothed throughout most of the movie except for one brief semi-nude scene. The box office failure of this and her other movies drove Hay to television, where she appeared on *Mission: Impossible* as an IMF agent taken hostage on a hijacked plane in "The Code," *Love, American Style* as a woman who likes her men big and mean in "Love and Mr. Nice Guy," and in the suspenseful TV-movie *The Screaming Woman* (1972) starring Olivia de Havilland as a rich matron just released from a mental institution who fears a woman is buried alive on her property; none of her greedy family members (including Hay) believe her. She was unnervingly vulnerable on the British TV series *Thriller* (renamed *Wide World of Mystery* in the US) in "A Place to Die" as a doctor's young, refined wife newly arrived in a small village after a skiing accident injured her leg. The devil-worshipping inhabitants agree she has the requirements as prophesied to become the bride of Satan. Realizing they've made a mistake, they plot to sacrifice her instead. Alexandra next appeared in two theatrical movies, *How to Seduce a Woman* (1974), a stiff sexploitation comedy starring Angus Duncan as a lothario who beds five women including Hay as an art gallery owner tricked into thinking Duncan is the creator of eleven paintings she covets, and the unreleased *That Girl from Boston* (1975) starring Mamie Van Doren. To give her career a needed boost, Hay posed nude for the February 1974 *Playboy* in a pictorial entitled "Alexandra the Great." It was a beautifully photographed salute to the glamourous Golden Age of Hollywood as Hay posed semi-nude as if she was the new Jean Harlow. But the best that came of it was the road movie *How Come Nobody's on Our Side?* (1975) starring Adam Roarke and Larry Bishop as popular biker movie actors so bored with their films that they steal a pair of motorcycles and become drug runners with Hay as the obligatory love interest. On TV, she could be seen in "The Man Who Thought He Was Dillinger" on *The Manhunter* as the moll of a deranged David Hedison, who thinks he is the infamous gangster, plus episodes of *Kojak*, *The Streets of San Francisco*, and *Police Story*. Her last acting credit was a small role in the *Dirty Harry* rip-off *The One Man Jury* (1978) starring Jack Palance as a vigilante-type cop. Alexandra Hay retired from show business in the early Eighties. She passed away on October 11, 1993, at the age of forty-nine.

# Marianna Hill

A flaxen-haired beauty who was a natural with dialects and made a career playing various ethnic types as a blonde, brunette or redhead, she was one of the busiest and most versatile actresses to rise from minor roles to second leads. However, her chameleon-like appearances prevented her from developing a screen persona, which hampered her from garnering lead movie roles while less talented actresses such as Diane Baker and Stefanie Powers prospered. The Seventies saw her starring in a number of low-budget horror movies between supporting roles in A-productions.

**You May Remember Her Most From:** *Paradise, Hawaiian Style* (1966) as a slinky chanteuse who seductively warbles "Scratch My Back" to Elvis Presley.

**Her Groovy '60s Credits:** With a fair amount of stage experience behind her despite her young age, nineteen-year-old Marianna Hill began working in television in 1960, landing minor roles on *77 Sunset Strip*, *The Man and the Challenge*, *Tate*, *The Westerner*, and *Michael Shayne*, among others. In 1961, she was cast in a recurring role on the western series *The Tall Man* as the girlfriend of Clu Gulager's Billy the Kid, who is trying to stay a law-abiding citizen. Her film debut was in the teenage exploitation movie *Married Too Young* (1962), playing a bad girl involved with a hot-car ring. This was followed by the low-budget fright flick *Black Zoo* (1963), the first of many horror movies appearances for her. More film roles followed but she was wasted playing minor bit parts in *Wives and Lovers* (1963), *The New Interns* (1964), and *Roustabout* (1964) starring Elvis Presley. Television gave Hill a chance to show her range in a variety of roles such as a Mexican senorita pursued by all three Cartwright brothers in "Ponderosa Matador" on *Bonanza*, a sexy psychologist romanced by Gene Barry in "Who Killed Molly?" on *Burke's Law*, and a carnival performer with marital problems in "The Last of the Strongmen" on *The Greatest Show on Earth*. The latter brought her to the attention of director Howard Hawks who cast her as a French sexpot in his soap opera-ish racecar drama *Red Line 7000* (1965). The exciting Hill plays a groupie passed on to racecar driver James Caan by his rival James Ward.

Marianna Hill (ca. 1972).

She steals the movie with her energetic dance numbers at a nightclub and in front of a hotel's Pepsi machine where she is watched by Caan. In *Paradise, Hawaiian Style* (1966) Hill has the second female lead as one of the many Hawaiian beauties romanced by helicopter pilot Elvis Presley to send tourists his way to drum up business. Hill is simply charming and, exhibiting a sexy, throaty voice, she duets quite impressively with the King on "Scratch My Back." Later the duo gets stranded on an island along with nine-year-old Donna Butterworth when his helicopter malfunctions. Despite being saddled with an unflattering long black wig thanks to jealous co-star Suzanna Leigh, who admitted in her autobiography that she demanded to be the only blonde in the movie, the stunning Marianna still looked gorgeous.

Curiously, Hill was off the big screen for the next three years and instead concentrated on television, turning up on many popular series of the time beginning with *Batman* as King Tut's aptly named moll Cleo Patrick in "The Spell of Tut" and "Tut's Case Is Shut." She followed that with guest roles on *Star Trek* as a physician and former paramour of Capt. Kirk's, accompanying him to an interplanetary penal colony where the head doctor is experimenting on the inmates in "Dagger of the Mind"; *My Three Sons* as a French exchange student who jilts Don Grady's Robbie for his friend in "The Best Man"; *The Wild Wild West* as a bad girl named Belladonna who aids villainous Michael Dunn in trying to dispose of Robert Conrad's virile James West in "The Night of the Bogus Bandits"; and *Mission: Impossible* as a Spanish vixen who frames her lover for murder in "The Condemned." Hill finally returned to the big screen in director Haskell Wexler's highly praised experimental film *Medium Cool* (1969), starring Robert Forster as a TV news cameraman covering the 1968 Chicago Democratic Convention. The film took on a *cinema-verite* approach as it was actually filmed amid the tumultuous protests outside the convention hall. Hill played a sexy nurse whose relationship with Forster is waning. After he takes her to a roller derby match they have a full-frontal nude love scene at her apartment. Proving what an unconventional and versatile actress she was, Hill ended the decade on the family-oriented *Mayberry R.F.D.* playing a sexy model who unsuccessfully tries to entice series star Ken Berry away from good girl Arlene Golonka.

**The Beginning:** Marianna Hill was born Marianna Schwarzkopf, cousin of General H. Norman Schwarzkopf, on February 9, 1941, in Santa Barbara, California of German and Spanish descent. Her father was a building contractor who lived all over the world. She grew up attending schools in California, Spain, and Canada. When Marianna was a teenager her father bought a restaurant in Southern California and the family settled down. At fourteen, she was bitten by the acting bug and she worked as an apprentice at the Laguna Playhouse where she danced in a production of *Pal Joey* and played a peasant in *Miss Julie*. She eventually moved on to the La Jolla Playhouse for three summers and spent one winter working at the Globe Theatre in San Diego. In between stage productions, Marianna modeled and took acting lessons with Sanford Meisner at the Neighborhood Playhouse in New York.

**The '70s & Beyond:** Throughout the Me Decade, Marianna Hill juggled traditional TV roles with more ambitious parts, usually as the bad girl on the big screen. After appearing on TV's *Love, American Style* and *Daniel Boone*, Hill (now being billed as Mariana Hill) starred in the exciting, violent western *El Condor* (1970) as the often undressed mistress of General Patrick O'Neal, trying to protect the secret of his Mexican fortress from scoundrels Jim Brown, Lee Van Cleef and a tribe of Apaches out to steal the gold supposedly hidden inside. Critics raved but audiences stayed away from Hill's next film *The Traveling Executioner* (1970) where she played a murderess ca. 1918 who keeps getting a stay of execution to the chagrin of paid executioner Stacy Keach, who eventually falls for the beautiful inmate and tries to save her life. In the hippie drama *Thumb Tripping* (1972) she played half of an ill-mannered, battling married couple who gives a lift to hitchhikers Michael Burns and Meg Foster. She then co-starred in two of the strangest horror films of the decade. *The Baby* (1973) featured Hill as a wild-haired member of a wacko family of women who keep their adult brother in diapers and treat him as an infant while trying to outsmart nosy social worker Anjanette Comer, leading to a truly surprising ending. The low-budget, dark *Messiah of Evil* (1973) featured Hill as a young woman who comes to a California coastal village searching for her missing father and encounters townsfolk who have turned into zombies.

More popular was the Clint Eastwood–directed western *High Plains Drifter* (1973) with Hill as a feisty town belle who comes out swinging—insulting and slapping mysterious gunslinger Eastwood, who has just killed a man in self defense. He rapes her with no consequence ("Isn't forceful rape in a broad daylight still a misdemeanor in this town?" she exclaims) and, though she comes after him guns blazing, she pretends to fall for him as he is hired to protect the town from advancing gunfighters. In cahoots with the bad guys, she sets him up for an assassination attempt. *The Godfather: Part II* (1974) should have brought Marianna lots of attention as the grasping, complaining wife of John Cazale's weak-willed Fredo Corleone but her best scenes were cut from the final print though they resurfaced on the deluxe DVD release years later. During this period, Marianna also made the requisite episodic TV appearances on such shows as *The Name of the Game*, *Harry O*, *Kung Fu*, *The Magician*, *S.W.A.T.*, and *Quincy, M.E.* She deserved better than that and the roles offered to her in Grade Z horror movies such as *Schizoid* (1980) as a newspaper advice columnist who is in communication with a serial killer and *Blood Beach* (1981) as a woman investigating the mysterious death of her mother who was devoured by an underground creature while strolling on the sands of Santa Monica Beach. The best thing about the movie was its tag line lampooning *Jaws*: "Just when you thought it safe to go back into the water, you can't get across the beach." Though she gave it her all in these parts, it was at this point that Marianna Hill's career trailed off, most likely from the actress' frustration in not obtaining roles that were worthy of her talent. Hill then began working as an acting coach and in the Nineties moved to London to teach Method Acting at the Lee Strasberg Studio. In 2005, she made a surprising return to film in the little-seen *Coma Girl: The State of Grace*.

# Susan Holloway

Another cute, long-legged baby doll blonde who couldn't make a name for herself in Hollywood, she went from playing a kooky co-ed in a teenybopper musical to lusting after some bikers in a violent motorcycle flick during her short career.

Leggy Susan Holloway (1967).

**You May Remember Her Most From:** *Point Blank* (1967) as a mini-skirted, ditzy blonde looking to buy a used car.

**Her Groovy '60s Credits:** Susan Holloway made her film debut in the totally lame teenage musical *When the Boys Meet the Girls* (1965), a remake of *Girl Crazy* featuring Herman's Hermits and Liberace. Sporting a cute, pixyish hair style, she played a coed who catches the eye of frat boy Joby Baker who is aiding his friend Harve Presnell in saving local gal Connie Francis and her deadbeat daddy from losing their home. She next was selected to be a Slaymate in *The Silencers* (1966) but was just one of the many scantily clad beauties hired to decorate the background of agent Dean Martin's bedroom in a promo added to the film to announce the sequel, *Murderers' Row*, which she did not appear in though she was chosen to tour the country to promote the original.

The movie that brought her fleeting notoriety was the violent noir *Point Blank* (1967), directed by John Boorman. In it she was cast as a sexy customer whom two salesmen fawn over before vengeful criminal Lee Marvin takes the owner on a test drive from Hell to find out where the mobster who double-crossed him is hiding. Holloway adds nothing more to the plot than being a decorative diversion. In the biker flick *Angels from Hell* (1968) Holloway played the bimbo mini-skirted girlfriend of successful biker-turned-actor Steve Rogers whose former gang descends on his Hollywood home. While the gang tries to convince Rogers to return to the fold, his agent thinks a biker flick with his former members would be a great moneymaker. While this is going on, Holloway is lasciviously eyeing the virile, leather-clad biker studs. But their jealous babes make sure she keeps her hands off. This was Holloway's last screen appearance during the Sixties.

**The Beginning:** Not much is known about Susan Holloway's early life except that she was a very successful model who appeared in dozens of TV commercials before becoming an actress.

**The '70s & Beyond:** After an eleven-year absence from the big screen, Holloway surprisingly turned up in the B-movie *Delta Fox* (1979) as the kittenish girlfriend of crooked tax lawyer Stuart Whitman. Her whereabouts today are unknown.

# Teri Hope

A former Playboy Playmate, she was a cross between a buxom bombshell and an underage tease. Never quite fitting into either type, it is not surprising that this Joy Harmon lookalike had a very brief career.

**You May Remember Her Most From:** *Fun in Acapulco* (1963) as a teenage hellion who gets deckhand Elvis Presley fired at the start of the movie.

**Her Groovy '60s Credits:** Teri Hope, *Playboy*'s Miss September 1958, guest starred on *The Ed Sullivan Show* in 1960 playing a sexy nurse in a skit with comedians Wayne and Shuster. This brought her to the attention of former classmate Tony Anthony, who was producing an independent movie. Hope snagged the female lead in the juvenile delinquent drama *Force of Impulse* (1961) playing a rich sex kitten named Bunny. Despite objections from her father, Hope falls in love with Anthony, a boy from the wrong side of the tracks. Trying to impress her, the stupid kid robs his father's grocery store before their date, leading to an all-night chase which culminates on the beach. Shooting on location in Miami, Hope spends most of the film in nothing more than a bikini, which was apropos for a former Playboy Playmate. In conjunction with the movie, noted pinup photog-

Teri Hope flees from her lover in the low-budget programmer *Force of Impulse* (Sutton Pictures, 1961).

rapher Bunny Yeager shot photos of Hope frolicking on the beach (with her luscious figure measuring 39-19-33 clearly on display) for *Pageant* magazine.

Back in Hollywood, Teri landed a recurring role as a coed named Susan on the 1961–62 TV sitcom, *Mrs. G Goes to College* starring Gertrude Berg as an elderly widow who becomes a college freshman. In between she played a nurse in "The Best Man" on *Hennessy* and one of Cynthia Pepper's classmates in "Madame President" on the 1920s-set sitcom *Margie*. She lost out on *Lolita* but landed a bit role in the musical *Gypsy* (1962) starring Natalie Wood. In the Elvis Presley musical *Fun in Acapulco* (1963) Hope played the spoiled, underage brat who gives Elvis nothing but trouble at the beginning of the film. Hope's Jenny is the sexy daughter of a rich businessman who owns the yacht where Elvis works as a deck hand. Attired in skimpy shorts, the shapely teen comes on to him but he rejects her advances, infuriating the little witch. Later she and her friends follow him to a smoky gin mill. When her father storms in and catches her drinking whiskey, she blames Elvis. "It is Coke, isn't it, Daddy?" she asks innocently. The father believes his little girl and fires Elvis, bellowing, "You're lucky I don't have you arrested for contributing to the delinquency of a minor." An infuriated Elvis retorts, "She was a delinquent long before anyone contributed anything" and storms out. Unfortunately, it is the last we see of Hope's interesting vixen. Hope would work again with Elvis in *Roustabout* (1964), albeit in a much smaller role. The petite blonde turns up very early in the movie along with Raquel Welch as smart-mouthed college students who give Joan Staley's waitress a hard time at a club where motorcycle-riding Elvis Presley sings and plays guitar. When the gals flirt with Elvis (who sings "Poison Ivy League," mocking their frat boy beaus), a melee ensues, landing the King in jail. Hope's last movie appearance was in AIP's *Pajama Party* (1964) starring Annette Funicello and Tommy Kirk. Hope had a minor role as one of the fashion models who work in Dorothy Lamour's dress shop. Wearing a sort of red jumpsuit dress with red- and white-striped blouse and matching headband, she announces to another gal that that they will be modeling a topless bathing suit when a cute three-year-old girl emerges wearing it. Later she is in the changing room clad in her slip when Buster Keaton's bumbling Indian chief bursts in looking for "Swedish blonde bombshell." Soon after, Teri Hope gave Hollywood the slip and disappeared from show business.

**The Beginning:** The pretty blonde was born Natalie Hope Reisberg on February 19, 1941, in Kittaning, Pennsylvania (population 8,000). She began taking dancing lessons at the age of three and after performing in front of a live audience she decided a career in show business was for her. To reach that goal she enrolled at Carnegie Tech after graduating high school. An operative soprano, while studying acting a friend snapped a picture of her at a frat party and submitted it to *Playboy* magazine, which led Hope to become a Playmate. As Miss September 1958, she was one of the magazine's smallest models (5-foot-2) and posed topless holding a frilly party dress. The pictorial didn't stop the determined coed from acting and after two years at the university she moved to New York, where she appeared in the live drama series *The Oldsmobile Show*, *The Reynolds Aluminum Hour*, and *Playhouse 90*.

**The '70s & Beyond:** Her whereabouts after she quit show business are unknown.

# Mary Hughes

A sexy, statuesque blonde in the tradition of Brigitte Bardot, she was the perpetual Sixties beach bunny and stood out from all the other girls on the sand due to her eye-popping proportions—standing 5-foot-9 and measuring 36-22-36. None of the other bikini girls could turn as many heads as she.

Beach babe Mary Hughes (*right*) looks on as Susan Hart serves up a winner in *Pajama Party* (AIP, 1964).

**You May Remember Her Most From:** any one of the Frankie and Annette beach movies (beginning with *Muscle Beach Party*, 1964) where she could be ogled gliding her tan, bikini-clad body across the sand or shaking it at the local dance club.

**Her Groovy '60s Credits:** To populate the background of *Muscle Beach Party* (1964), the sequel to the previous year's *Beach Party*, Mary Hughes was literally whisked off the sands of Malibu and brought to the attention of AIP. Though she had nothing more to do in the movie than to look good in a bikini, nobody did it as sexily as Mary. She quickly followed this with appearances in *Bikini Beach* (1964) and *Pajama Party* (1964). The latter featured a beach volleyball game and, though one of the players was the sexy Susan Hart, male viewers couldn't take their eyes off of the stunning Hughes just standing on the right watching the antics. AIP signed the lissome sexpot to a contract, sending her on public relation tours around the country to promote the beach films. Despite the fact that she rarely uttered a line of dialogue, she became one of AIP's most popular starlets. In

*Beach Blanket Bingo* (1965) she has an amusing bit during the film's opening song as she smashes an ice cream cone into the face of surfer boy Mike Nader ("Right blanket, wrong miss," sing Frankie and Annette) before she fades into the background. *Ski Party* (1965) gave Hughes billing on its poster ads but she does not appear in any of the ski scenes filmed in Sun Valley. *How to Stuff a Wild Bikini* (1965) features an entertaining segment with Hughes (actually speaking a line), Patti Chandler, Marianne Gaba, and the other beach girls who through song try to persuade ad man Mickey Rooney that they had what it takes to be "the girl next door" in his motorcycle ad campaign. When they cavort and sing the song "What About Us?" extolling their looks, smarts, and curvy bodies, you could not help but agree. In *Dr. Goldfoot and the Bikini Machine* (1965), Hughes played Robot No. 6 programmed by Vincent Price as the evil Dr. Goldfoot to marry then kill a wealthy surgeon in Denmark. AIP's *The Ghost in the Invisible Bikini* (1966) features Hughes wearing an unflattering thick red headband throughout the movie but her curvy body is prominently on display as she dances and shakes poolside. Hughes next put on some clothes for her final two movies at AIP. In *Fireball 500* (1966), she was one of the many fawning fans of racecar driver Fabian. The gals trail him wherever he goes and wear his name on the butts of their shorts. In another AIP racecar movie, *Thunder Alley* (1967) starring Fabian and Annette Funicello, Hughes pops up dancing at the local club where the drivers hang out and unwind. In between, she was cast as one of the Slaymates in the Matt Helm spy spoof, *Murderers' Row* (1966). Though draped in widow's weeds, Hughes is easily recognizable from the other girls due to her golden flaxen hair. Later she is seen scantily clad as Miss September as she and the other Slaymates surround Martin's enormous bathtub.

Hughes' final film was the swinging London-set musical *Double Trouble* (1967) starring Elvis Presley, where she was hired as a Watusi dancer. Remaining in England, Hughes became part of that hip late Sixties music scene and had romances with Jeff Beck, Eric Clapton, and Roger Daltrey. While a member of The Yardbirds, Beck composed the song "Psycho Daisies" to prove his devotion to Hughes. Returning to Hollywood, Hughes' last professional show business gig was as one of the four "Operation Entertainment Girls" along with Sivi Aberg, Thordis Brandt, and Eileen O'Neill on the 1968 TV variety series *Operation: Entertainment*. She performed each week with guest stars, entertaining the troops around the U.S. and the world.

**The Beginning:** Mary Hughes was born on February 25, 1944, in Hollywood and attended University High School. A true California beach girl, the tanned beauty with the long white-blonde hair would drive the surfers of Malibu crazy every time she set foot on the sand. It was there where she was discovered by director William Asher.

**The '70s & Beyond:** Mary returned to the U.S. from London after marrying musician-singer Lee Michaels and resided in Northern California for eighteen years. After her divorce, she returned to Southern California where she wed a very wealthy man and had two sons. After years of living in relative obscurity, Mary Hughes was featured in an August 2006 *Vanity Fair* article on Malibu surfers of the '60s. Still a gorgeous blonde, she has been a personal trainer for thirty years, owns a boogie board, and still can turn heads while traipsing across the sands of Malibu, where she currently resides.

# Melodie Johnson

A willowy blonde sex kitten with a bewitching quality along the lines of Sharon Tate, she had a chameleon-like quality to play varied roles which may have hindered her career as she was usually cast in period films.

**You May Remember Her Most From:** *Coogan's Bluff* (1968) as the adulterous housewife who bathes and then makes love with sheriff Clint Eastwood in her bathtub during the film's opening scenes.

**Her Groovy '60s Credits:** With much fanfare, Melodie Johnson made her TV debut playing a murderous mantrap in "Kicks" on *The Bob Hope Chrysler Theatre* opposite Mickey Rooney. Johnson was a hit as she injected her desperate, selfish character (indebted to her bookie) with a softness that made the audience empathize with her despite her dirty deeds. Universal's publicity machine went into overdrive touting the newcomer as a combination Jean Harlow, Marilyn Monroe, and Deborah Kerr. Johnson had a good dramatic scene clad in a slinky slip as the girlfriend of a murder victim in one of the very first made-for-TV movies, *Fame Is the Name of the Game* (1966) starring Tony Franciosa and Jill St. John. Her big screen debut was in the quickie western *Ride to Hangman's Tree* (1967). Playing a sexy chanteuse, she is torn between outlaws Jack Lord and James Farentino, who join together to rob the Wells Fargo train line which they were hired to protect. Before her next movie, Universal kept the blonde busy guest starring on TV, particularly in westerns. Among her varied roles were a comely circus tiger tamer-bank robber in "Any Way the Wind Blows" on *Laredo*, a saloon girl in "The Claim" on *The Virginian*, a photographer trying to protect ocean wildlife in "The Time of the Sharks" on *Run for Your Life*, and a fiery efficiency expert in "Efficiency Is for the Experts" on *The Rounders*. Back on the big screen, she was next clad in a ratty loose housedress with her cleavage clearly on display in the hit detective drama *Coogan's Bluff* (1968) playing an adulterous wife who, after some cajoling from deputy sheriff Clint Eastwood, agrees to a romp in the hay but only after he agrees to a bath first. Her screen time was minimal but memorable.

Unhappy with being typed as the sexpot, she and Universal parted ways. Now freelance, Melodie got a chance to strut her stuff in three big-budget films but none made it at the box office. She copped a supporting role as the beautiful, duplicitous niece and ward of George Kennedy's crooked politician in the lavish turn-of-the-century comedy *Gaily, Gaily* (1969) starring Beau Bridges as "Bible-toting country boy" Ben Harvey, who comes to Chicago in quest of fame and fortune. Based on the life of writer Ben Hecht, the film was directed by Norman Jewison and co-produced by Hal Ashby. With this much talent behind the scenes, *Gaily, Gaily* was predicted to be a hit. Unfortunately, movie audiences didn't find it very gaily and it flopped.

**The Beginning:** Melodie Johnson was born on December 23, 1943, in Los Angeles, California. At the age of fifteen she was discovered by a modeling agent, William Adrian, while she was lunching at the Huntington Hotel in Pasadena. She blossomed into a voluptuous young beauty standing 5-foot-7 with a tantalizing figure measuring 35-23-35 and quickly graduated from print ads to TV commercials. At age twenty-one Johnson, who was attending USC majoring in English, landed a husband (record producer Bones

**Melodie Johnson as a western chanteuse in *Ride to Hangman's Tree* (Universal, 1966).**

Howe, complete with three small children), an agent, and a contract with Universal Studios.

**The '70s & Beyond:** *Rabbit, Run* (1970) featured Johnson as a staid minister's trashy wife who lusts after former high school football star James Caan, who is busy juggling drunken spouse Carrie Snodgress and hooker Anjanette Comer. *The Moonshine War* (1970) won the pretty blonde some of her best reviews though it was her last big-screen appearance. A lively and violent film in the tradition of *Bonnie and Clyde*, it starred a young Alan Alda as the owner of 150 gallons of illegal (Prohibition) whiskey being fought over by various mountain folk. Johnson is simply charming as a hotel clerk who loves Alda. Unfortunately, both movies failed to find an audience and did nothing to further Johnson's career, which may explain her retreat to the small screen. She turned up on episodes of *Bewitched* as a staid girl transformed by Endora into a sex kitten attracted to Darrin in "The Generation Zap" and *Mannix* as a suspect in the murder of a golfer at a country club in "Babe in the Woods." Having that perfect early Seventies hip look, Johnson turned up three times on *Love, American Style* playing a worldly waitress enamored by a nerdy teenager in "Love and the High School Flop-Out," a sex kitten in "Love and the Lovesick Sailor," and a wife seeking spiritual fulfillment in "Love and the Guru." As the decade progressed, Johnson co-starred in the TV-movie *Powderkeg* (1971) with Rod Taylor and in episodes of *Baretta*, *Barnaby Jones*, and *Project UFO* between TV commercials but her real passion was writing. In 1980 she wrote a play called *The Lady of the House*, which was produced by the Los Angeles Theatre Center. She quit acting and never looked back as she authored two acclaimed mystery novels, the Edgar-nominated *The Mother Shadow* (1990) and *Beauty Dies* (1996) featuring California private detective Clair Conrad and her assistant Maggie Hill. Her entertaining books draw from her own experiences—good and bad—in Hollywood. And her Diana Poole short stories, published in *Ellery Queen*, feature a middle-aged actress as her protagonist. Still married to record executive Bones Howe, Melodie Johnson continues to write successfully and her recent Diane Poole short story "Facing Up" was nominated for a Barry Award.

## *Melodie Johnson speaks out on...*

**Playing a murderous blonde mantrap in "Kicks" on** *The Bob Hope Chrysler Theatre*: This was my very first acting role though I played a dead body being carried into an ambulance in a previous *Bob Hope Chrysler Theatre* episode. Dick Berg was the producer and he was a lovely man. He believed in me and gave me a shot at this. I played the lead and killed Mickey Rooney. It was a shock because working with Mickey Rooney, it is *all* about Mickey Rooney. It was like acting with a standup comic. He was always on and acting for the crew. His ego was relentless but to me he was very nice and helped me. I was so young when I did this and scared. I barely knew how to hit my marks.

*Ride to Hangman's Tree*: The part called for someone who could sing and dance. I could do neither but Universal still wanted me for it—*welcome to being a contract player*. I learned to dance. It's amazing when you have that quality in you. I could not dance now if you asked me to. I have no sense of rhythm and even finished dancing before the music ended in the movie. But I didn't fall down. Luckily they let me lip-synch so I didn't have to sing. We filmed this in seven days and it was padded with outtakes from the 1948 movie *Black Bart* starring Dan Duryea and Yvonne DeCarlo despite the fact that James Farentino and I had opposite hair colors of the former stars.

Jack Lord was a pain in the ass. I remember him sitting in front of the mirror putting on his own mascara and that sort of stuck with me because it just sort of fits him. We had a scene in a stagecoach and I think he had to knock a gun out of my hand or something. But it was like he wouldn't reach for it. He was just a really weird, difficult guy and not likable. James Farentino, however, was a wonderful, lovely guy. We were both under contract and he is a very good actor before he became a stalker—*who knew?* [Farentino pleaded no contest for stalking his ex-girlfriend Tina Sinatra in 1993.]

*Coogan's Bluff*: That was all me—no implants—but the wardrobe people had ways to push your breasts up and out. The dress stayed on as it always did back then. I remember after doing that scene with Clint Eastwood, I went home and said to my husband, "God, he's a lovely man but he can't act. I don't think he is going to make it." The tension that he projects on the screen wasn't always evident while working with him. Don Siegel was a gruff, wonderful man and he loved Clint Eastwood. They were perfect for one another. Don was great with me because it was one of my first real roles. He gave you space and was very creative to work with. He wasn't strict like a lot of the directors were back then.

**Posing for cheesecake photos**: I refused to straddle an oversized rocket in a Universal Studio publicity shoot. Edy Williams and I were posing in Fourth of July outfits. I told the photographer that it was a phallic symbol and he replied, "So?" I still wouldn't do it. He looks at Edy and, God love her, she leaps up on it and wraps her legs around the sides straddling away. I watched Edy and thought, "You know you're just not going to make it in the movies, Melodie."

Adulterous lovers Clint Eastwood and Melodie Johnson get it on in the bathtub in *Coogan's Bluff* (Universal, 1968).

**Stardom:** You have to understand that I never really wanted to be an actress. I wanted to be a writer so I was always of two minds about this. It was that I just looked like a movie star. Universal also wasn't pleased that I had married a man with three children. They went nuts when they found out. It wasn't easy and I lived a sort of dual life—very strange and very uncomfortable.

You needed the drive to become a star like Raquel Welch had. She had the cojones and that's what it takes. Universal wanted me to play a belly dancer in one movie and I wouldn't even come out in my costume. They painted my skin this dark color and I looked like I had leprosy. The makeup was beginning to crack and I refused to do it. They kept begging me and I just said no.

*Gaily, Gaily*: Director Norman Jewison was a wonderful man and a lot of fun to work for. He loves actors—just adores them. I had a long, involved lovemaking scene with Beau

Bridges, who was a sweetheart. That was a lot of undressing and as it was a period piece we had all these clothes on. On the third take I sensed that it was going on for too long a time and our lips were getting raw from kissing. Finally, we looked up and there was no one. Norm and the crew tip-toed away and left us there rolling around this bed. Then we heard the howls of laughter from everyone off in the corner.

I was in a funeral scene with Melina Mercouri and watched her try to upstage Brian Keith. I will never forget that as long as I live. She was wearing this black veil and take after take she'd let it drift in front of his face. They were supposed to kiss and her face was in perfect camera position but he was swathed in all this black. Finally, Brian took her, pressed the veil against her face and gave her a big smack [kiss] on the mouth. She was just stunned.

**James Caan in *Rabbit Run*:** Jimmy Caan was what I call a busy actor. In our scenes he would always find something to fiddle with when I was talking.

*The Moonshine War*: Alan Alda was a bit of a limp rag to work with, in all honesty. Richard Widmark was a wonderful pro but Patrick McGoohan could scare you to death. On the set he was very aloof but that helped acting in scenes with him. I loved this part because I was not playing a sex object.

**Why she think the roles dried up:** People just didn't know how to cast me so I kept working however I could. Depending how you photograph me, my face could change. I think by appearing in movies set in the present and then in period pieces, it threw people off and I never developed a persona. If that were happening today I do not think people would be thrown by it. Back then it was the time women were running around in polka-dot bikinis with funny white go-go boots.

**Why she stopped acting**: I always wanted to be a writer and kept taking writing courses all the time I was acting. In 1980 I wrote a play called *The Lady of the House*, which was produced by the Los Angeles Theatre Center. I was still working steadily in TV commercials pitching everything from deodorant to Kool Aid. At an audition for a dog food commercial I was sitting in a room with other aging blondes and realized what I really wanted to do was write. I walked out. I've never looked back and I'm still happily married to Bones.

# Alena Johnston

A gorgeous blonde blue-eyed Glamazon who resembled Catherine Deneuve, she progressed from bit roles in the Sixties to an exploitation film lead in the Seventies before fading away.

**You May Remember Her Most From:** the T&A exploitation cult classic *War Goddess* (1973) as the topless, mud wrestling, javelin-throwing, man-hating Queen of the Amazons.

**Her Groovy '60s Credits:** Alena Johnston made her film debut playing a Slaygirl in the third Dean Martin Matt Helm spy caper, *The Ambushers* (1967). Surprisingly, the six

**Alena Johnston as the scintillating Springtime Bride in** *Funny Girl* **(Columbia, 1968).** *Billy Rose Theatre Division, The New York Public Library for the Performing Arts, Astor, Lenox and Tilden Foundations*

foot Amazon did not receive screen credit even though she had more lines than most of the other Slaygirls and was featured on the cover of *Pageant* magazine with Martin to promote the movie. After appearing with the other scantily clad girls throughout the opening montage in pursuit of would-be paramours as the title tune is sung over the credits, Johnston is one of the Slaygirls at ICE's rehabilitation center getting a refresher course on the agency's latest weaponry. She later turns up giving Martin's Helm a rubdown. When he comes on to her, the staid young woman responds, "I'm just a masseuse," much to the amorous Helm's disappointment. The part garnered the 39-25-38 beauty enough attention for her to be cast in *Funny Girl* (1968) as one of the most astounding of Ziegfeld Girls. She was chosen (along with Inga Neilsen) to open the lavish production number "His Love Makes You Beautiful" playing a bride combing her hair as she prepares for her wedding day. A bit later, she and the other showgirls descend a long staircase. As a Springtime Bride she recites only one line—"The Springtime Bride is starry-eyed"—before the other brides take over but her beauty is so exquisite you can't take your eyes off of her. Her topless torso was on display in *Playboy*'s pictorial salute to the girls of *Funny Girl* but Johnston disappeared from the public eye after wedding a much older man.

**The Beginning:** Alena was purportedly born in 1949 and was discovered by comedian Bill Dana.

**The '70s & Beyond:** After divorcing her husband, Alena Johnston returned to the big screen, albeit dubbed with a grating voice, as the star of the 1973 Italian adventure epic *Le Guerriere dal seno nudo* (*The Warriors with Naked Breasts*), better known internationally as *The Amazons* or *War Goddess*. A semi-serious take-off on the European peplums combined with a women's lib twist, it was directed by Terence Young and written by Robert Graves (*I, Claudius*). Set in ancient Greece, the movie opens with a busty, beautifully made-up Johnston complete with heavy eyeliner beheading a man before returning to her tribe of six-foot-plus Amazons for a series of challenges a la *Survivor* to crown a new queen. She emerges victorious after defeating her large-breasted half-sister Sabine Sun in a topless oil-wrestling match. As queen, the amazing beauty leads her Sisters of Sappho in their annual dreaded mating ritual with a tribe of Greeks and, horror of horrors, develops feelings for handsome Angelo Infanti as the king of Greece, masquerading as a warrior! Johnston subsequently gives birth to the king's son who is left for dead in the desert, has an oiled-up rematch against her rival that ends in a draw, becomes a willing hostage of her lover just to be with him, and watches helplessly as her Amazons are defeated by the Greek army. The film ends as the two lovers quarrel over a woman's place in Greek society. This was Alena Johnston's swan song as she was never seen on the silver screen again. The movie, picked up by AIP for distribution in America, tanked at the box office but has since become a cult favorite. Johnston's current whereabouts are unknown.

# Joi Lansing

Technically a Fifties glamour girl, this stunning platinum blonde in the tradition of Marilyn Monroe was still only appearing in minor decorative roles by the start of the Sixties. She finally received critical recognition due to her amusing performance as Dean Martin's secretary in *Marriage on the Rocks* in 1965. This led to a few lead movie roles albeit in awful Grade Z drive-in movies. She deserved much better.

Joi Lansing (1965).

**You May Remember Her Most From:** *The Beverly Hillbillies* as country singer Lester Flatt's elegant, citified wife Gladys, who was able to hold her own with the hillbilly ways foisted on her by the Clampetts.

**Her Groovy '60s Credits:** Perennial minor player Joi Lansing began the decade with a small part in the convoluted comedy *Who Was That Lady?* (1960). She and Barbara Nichols played the bubble-headed Coogle sisters who, after being rejected by *The Ted Mack Amateur Hour*, go on a double date with Tony Curtis and Dean Martin and are mistaken for double agents by Martin's wife Janet Leigh. While Nichols was completely at home as the dumb blonde, Lansing was too refined to be believable. On the small screen, she played saloon girl Goldie from 1960–1961 on the western series *Klondike* starring Ralph Taeger and a young James Coburn as cowboys searching for gold in snowy Alaska. After the series' cancellation in 1961 after only eighteen episodes, Lansing continued working in television on *The Joey Bishop Show* and *Rawhide*. In 1963, she made the first of her five popular appearances on *The Beverly Hillbillies* in "Jed Throws a Wingding." When country musicians Lester Flatt and Earl Scruggs write Jed and tell him they are coming to Beverly Hills for an engagement, the hillbilly thinks one of them is going to propose to Cousin Pearl, but the duo show up with their new city gal brides. Lansing played the glamourous Gladys Flatt who is at first jealous when she mistakes Elly May for Pearl. She returned to the show the following year in "A Bride for Jed" as the country duo scheme to land their rich friend a wife while Gladys tries to transform tomboy Elly May into a lady. The comedy series was a huge hit and brought Joi lots of exposure and new fans.

While fellow platinum blondes Jayne Mansfield and Mamie Van Doren were doffing their tops for *Playboy* and other nudie magazines as the roles began drying up for Fifties brassy bombshells, Lansing remained clothed and started a singing career. She landed a recording contract and cut her first album with songs composed by Jimmie Haskell. Soon after, she began appearing in nightclubs across the country and became one of Scopitones' most popular female vocalists as she performed such songs as "The Silencer," "Web of Love," and "The One I Love Belongs to Someone Else" in their video jukeboxes. An eye-popping Joi Lansing returned to the big screen in the Frank Sinatra-Dean Martin comedy *Marriage on the Rocks* (1965). Always on the busty side, Joi's breasts never looked bigger than in her role as playboy Martin's secretary and there was much speculation that she had her breasts enlarged to help her get roles since she was now in her mid-thirties. Boob job or not, Lansing is extremely amusing as she takes dictation in a polka-dot bikini with a ruffle bottom, massages the boss's neck, and works around the office clad in the low-cut dress fit so snuggly that audiences held their breath waiting for her bosom to pop out. Her performance was so well-received that the annual publication *Screen World* named her one of the year's Most Promising Personalities, which was a real head-scratcher since she was no newcomer. Had they really not seen any of her prior work? Bikini-clad photos of Joi from *Marriage on the Rocks* were hot sellers and she became one of the most requested pinups by GIs in Vietnam. After her success in the movie, Joi reprised the role of Gladys Flatt three more times on *The Beverly Hillbillies*, most memorably in "Delovely and Scruggs" where Gladys gets a screen test and Lester pays Jethro to direct it hoping he'll screw it up. He doesn't but, in love with her husband, Gladys opts for the hills of Tennessee. The popular pinup finally landed a lead (after Mamie Van Doren turned it down) in the Grade-Z musical *Hillbillys in a Haunted House* (1967), a sequel to the previous year's *Las Vegas Hillbillys*. She played singer Boots Malone who with two other country singers, Ferlin Husky and Don Bowman, takes refuge in a haunted mansion on the way to a gig in Nashville and discovers the house is being used by international spies after a rocket fuel formula. In between the unfunny shenanigans, the cast belts out fourteen songs! Lansing rode out the Sixties on the small screen playing the sexy wife of a businessman in "Steve, the Apple Polisher" on *Petticoat Junction* in 1968 and Richard Deacon's new, distracting secretary in "Take Her, He's Mine" on *The Mothers-in-Law* in 1969. During this period she also concentrated on stage work, appearing in *Gentlemen Prefer Blondes* in Memphis and *Follies Burlesque '69* in New York.

**The Beginning:** Though it has been reported differently, Joi Lansing was most likely born Joy Rae Brown in Salt Lake City, Utah, on April 6, 1928, to strict Mormons Jack Glen Brown and Virginia Shupe Brown. When she was about twelve years old, the family relocated to Los Angeles. She blossomed into a stunning young lady standing 5-foot-6 with curvaceous measurements of 39-23-35 and began modeling. Discovered by MGM, she was signed to a contract, which led to bit roles in *Easter Parade* (1948), *Take Me Out to the Ball Game* (1949) and *Neptune's Daughter* (1949) using the name Joy Lansing. She was on the cover of *Life* magazine in March 1949.

After being dropped by MGM she went freelance. From 1950 to 1956 she was usually cast due to her stunning blonde looks rather than any acting talent in bit parts as a model, showgirl, hatcheck girl, bathing beauty or cocktail waitress in a string of colorful musicals and comedies, the most memorable being *Singin' in the Rain* (1952) where she played a gushing admirer of movie star Gene Kelly. During this period she came close to playing the role of the ambitious sexpot in *All About Eve* (1950) and Louis Calhern's mistress in *The Asphalt Jungle* (1950) but lost both roles to another stunning blonde, Marilyn Monroe. Lansing did snag the role of Mrs. Lance Fuller but the marriage was short-lived. Changing the spelling of her first name to Joi, she finally broke out of bit roles for a short period when she proved that she had a flair for light comedy: She was more than just a pretty face when cast in the recurring role of sexy model Shirley Swanson who, clad in tight sweaters two sizes too small or swimsuits, is constantly hit on by playboy photographer Bob Cummings in *The Bob Cummings Show* from 1956–1959. She was able to parlay her notoriety from the series to a few supporting parts albeit in the low-budget programmers *Hot Cars* (1956) as a mink-draped man-trap who involves an honest married car salesman into a stolen car ring and *Hot Shots* (1956), a Bowery Boys comedy. She played small roles in more prestigious fare such as the Academy Award–winning *The Brave One* (1956), Orson Welles' *Touch of Evil* (1958) as the blonde stripper seen tooling around in a convertible at the beginning of the movie, and *A Hole in the Head* (1959) as the bimbo girlfriend of wealthy Keenan Wynn. But by the late '50s Joi was unjustly relegated once again to bit parts in *Queen of Outer Space* as the girlfriend who bids adieu to her spaceman, *It Started with a Kiss* as a hatcheck girl, and *The Atomic Submarine* again as the girlfriend who stays behind as her beau goes off on his adventure. On television she made memorable guest appearances as an undercover detective in "Superman's Wife" on *Adventures of Superman* in 1958 and as "Miss Low Neck" on *The Lucy-Desi Comedy Hour* in "Lucy Wants a Career" in 1959.

**The '70s & Beyond:** The start of 1970 found Joi Lansing headlining at the Thunderbird Hotel in Las Vegas in a production of *Come Blow Your Horn*. That summer she underwent an operation to remove a cancerous tumor. She then copped the female lead in her last movie *Bigfoot* (1970), another ridiculous low-budget drive-in clunker. Joi played a beautiful pilot who, after removing her jumpsuit, is clad in a low-cut mini-dress more suitable for a cocktail party than the cockpit. She parachutes into the woods and is almost immediately chased by a hairy beast. It captures the poor girl and brings her back to its lair where two female creatures tend house and keep an eye on her and a biker chick (tied to trees) while Bigfoot lurks in the forest. A motorcycle gang comes to her rescue. Lansing looks terrific in the movie, especially while bouncing through the forest, and audiences would never guess that she recently turned forty! Lansing's final TV credit was *The Governor and J.J.* in 1970 where she played a woman who claims to have had a secret love affair with Governor Dan Dailey in "P.S. I Love You." In July of 1972, the stunning blonde once again underwent surgery. Joi Lansing died on August 7, 1972, in Santa Monica, reportedly from breast cancer. She was survived by her husband Stanley Todd, her parents, and a brother. In 2006, *thirtysomething* creator Joseph Doughterty authored a book entitled *Comfort and Joi* about his exploits researching the career of the exquisite blonde whom he aptly described as a "beautiful beacon in a Sargasso of bad filmmaking."

# Anna Lavelle

Not just another shapely blonde beach babe who could fill a bikini, she possessed comedic talent but disappeared into the foam before realizing her potential.

**You May Remember Her Most From:** *Beach Ball* (1965) as the bikini-clad groupie who is smitten with surfer dude Edd Byrnes; *he* only has eyes for new beach babe Chris Noel.

**Her Groovy '60s Credits:** Starting off in bit roles, pretty blonde Anna Lavelle appeared briefly in the comedy *Goodbye, Charlie* (1964) as a boisterous smock-clad beauty spa patron dissatisfied with the dye job on her hair and then in *John Goldfarb, Please Come Home* (1965) as one of many harem girls hidden under lots of flowing chiffon (though she was one of the girls who belly dances). Lavelle could also be briefly glimpsed as one of handsome daredevil Tony Curtis' many fawning admirers in the adventure comedy *The Great Race* (1965). Audiences finally got to see a lot of Anna when she donned the skimpiest bikinis ever worn in a teenage surf party in *Beach Ball* (1965). Edd Byrnes, looking more like a professor than student, played a college dropout and manager of a band (The Wigglers) consisting of his roommates Aron Kincaid, Don Edmonds, and Robert Logan. Lavelle has some amusing moments as the addled-brained groupie Polly (dig her leopard print bikini) who hangs around the guys' beach house running errands for them when not mooning over Byrnes. But poor Lavelle is used by Byrnes to distract the old codger to whom they owe money as they concentrate on the new hip chicks on the beach (including Chris Noel, Brenda Benet, and Gail Gilmore), unaware that they are the nerdy coeds in disguise who tore up their student loan check (those bad boys were going to use it to pay off their instruments and not for tuition) and who are determined to get these dropouts to return to school. When the gals show up on the sand *sans* swimsuits, Anna and her friends outfit them in some teeny bikinis. Once the guys see these gals in the flesh, poor Lavelle is dropped liked yesterday's newspaper. Anna is scantily clad again as one of the specialty dancers in *The Silencers* (1966). Unfortunately, most of her routine in the film's nightclub scene was cut from the final print though she popped up standing around Dean Martin's rotating bed in the film's tacked-on promo for *Murderers' Row*. Her last screen role was in *Wild Wild Winter* (1966) playing a pretty bus passenger who falls for the charms of lothario beach boy Gary Clarke, who has abandoned his surfboard and the sands of Malibu for skis and snowy Alpine College. Reaching his destination, he disembarks trailed by the amorous, wildhaired Lavelle, whom he promises never to forget as he puts her back onto the bus. It goes off to parts unknown, as did Anna Lavelle. Though that same year she received lots of press as "Miss Thrifty Drug Store," she never appeared on the big screen again.

Anna Lavelle as a surfer chick in *Beach Ball* (Paramount, 1965).

**The Beginning:** Not much can be found on Anna Lavelle's early days. She was born in 1944 and trained as a classical ballet dancer, becoming one of the few non-Russians to dance with the Bolshoi Ballet. To help pay the rent, Anna worked as a model before she turned actress and by 1965 she had already been married and divorced.

**The '70s & Beyond:** Her whereabouts after she quit show business are unknown.

# China Lee

An Asian beauty noted for her long jet-black hair, this Playboy Centerfold never rose out of minor roles and was almost always bikini-clad in her movies, to the delight of her many male admirers.

**You May Remember Her Most From:** Woody Allen's spy spoof *What's Up, Tiger Lily?* (1966) as the curvaceous siren who strips during the film's closing moments.

**Her Groovy '60s Credits:** China Lee became *Playboy*'s first Asian-American Playmate of the Month when she disrobed as Miss August 1964. She listed "vanity" as her pet peeve and "corn beef" as her favorite food. She was one of 1964's most popular centerfolds and came close to being named Playmate of the Year but lost out to Jo Collins. With an alluring smile and a 35-22-35 figure, it is no wonder movies beckoned for this captivating beauty though throughout her career she was considered a sort of poor man's Irene Tsu who was sort of the poor man's Nancy Kwan. Lee made her film debut playing a hooker in the obscure comedy *The Troublemaker* (1964). She then joined a gaggle of starlets as anonymous gold lamé bikini-clad robots in *Dr. Goldfoot and the Bikini Machine* (1965), a takeoff on James Bond's *Goldfinger*. She has a fair amount of screen time in the film's beginning when the shapely robots are first introduced as they are ordered by Vincent Price to observe a surveillance screen where Susan Hart as No. 11 is trying to seduce rich playboy Dwayne Hickman. The following year Lee kept busy in a string of minor roles beginning with *Harper* (1966) where she is seen briefly clad in a yellow halter top dancing at a discothèque where private eye Paul Newman is trying to pry information out of blowsy Shelley Winters. In *The Swinger* (1966) she played a model for *Girl Lure* magazine. When writer Ann-Margret, trying to peddle her stories, is mistaken for a model and refuses to pose on a swing, Lee takes her place. Later, still wearing the same bikini, she is introduced as one of the international models at the *Girl Lure* press conference. In *Paradise, Hawaiian Style* (1966) she, along with Edy Williams and Ann Morell, is one of the curvaceous candidates vying to be Elvis' secretary.

The film that brought China the most notoriety was Woody Allen's spy spoof, *What's Up, Tiger Lily?* (1966). Allen took a serious Japanese spy adventure, threw out the original dialogue and plot, and re-dubbed it, turning the movie into a comedy about an agent trying to stop an evil organization from getting their hands on the world's best egg salad recipe. China Lee doesn't appear until the very end in a new scene added with Allen. As he lounges on a sofa munching on an apple, the curvy lass dressed in a tight black dress begins stripping for him as the end credits roll. Just as she is about to remove her black panties, Allen stops her and says directly to the audience, "I promised I'd put her in the film... somewhere" as the screen freezes and then fades to black. Lee's curvaceous, bikini-clad figure was prominently displayed on the movie's poster art. Though the movie brought Lee to the masses (a still of her in her swimsuit was used to promote the movie worldwide), it didn't bring her any significant film roles. She was back playing bits in the Sonny and Cher musical *Good Times* (1967) as one of movie mogul George Sanders' secretaries and in the satire *Don't Make Waves* (1967) as a topless bikini girl swimming in the pool that skydivers Tony Curtis and Sharon Tate land in. Lee's last film role was a bit as a rowdy roller derby patron sitting next to Robert Forster and Marianna Hill in Haskell Wexler's groundbreaking *Medium Cool* (1969).

**Woody Allen flips as China Lee strips in the spy spoof** *What's Up, Tiger Lily?* **(AIP, 1966).** *Billy Rose Theatre Division, The New York Public Library for the Performing Arts, Astor, Lenox and Tilden Foundations*

**The Beginning:** China Lee was born Margaret Lee in New Orleans on September 2, 1942. Her parents had emigrated to the U.S. from Shanghai, China. Along with her three brothers and four sisters, she was raised with traditional Chinese customs. She worked as a waitress and model before becoming a Bunny at the Playboy Clubs in Chicago and New York. Her experience led her to become a "training Bunny" traveling to Playboy Clubs around the country to teach and guide new employees in the ways of a being a Bunny.

**The '70s & Beyond:** China Lee, who married political comedian Mort Sahl in October 1970 after a long courtship, retired from show business in the early Seventies. Lee had a son, Mort Sahl, Jr., late in life but the nine-year-old died in 1996. She had divorced his father prior to that. In the January 2000 issue of *Playboy*, Lee was named one of the 100 Centerfolds of the Century coming in at 49.

---

# Lara Lindsay

A sultry sexpot who resembled actress Jean Simmons, this blue-eyed, auburn haired beauty arrived in Hollywood at a time when the hippie-type chick was in vogue. Had she come along earlier, more opportunities playing decorative roles in the fantasy/sci-fi realm of TV may have come her way but alas by 1968 that genre was a dying breed.

**You May Remember Her Most From:** the surf movie *The Sweet Ride* (1968) as a Malibu party girl and paramour of tennis bum Tony Franciosa.

**Her Groovy '60s Credits:** Lara Lindsay was signed to a contract by 20th Century–Fox in the mid–Sixties and entered their talent school where her classmates included Tom Selleck and Corinna Tsopei. The school's coordinator, the esteemed Pamela Danova, predicted big things for sexy Lara but she never fulfilled her promise. After playing bit parts on TV's *Peyton Place* and in *In Like Flint* (1967) as a spa denizen, Lara landed her first noteworthy role in *The Sweet Ride* (1968), one of the last Hollywood surf movies of the Sixties, which took a serious and melodramatic look at aimless youths and thirtysomethings who refused to grow up while enjoying the carefree life in Southern California. Lindsay was cast as dim-witted beachcomber Martha, one of lothario tennis hustler Tony Franciosa's many playthings. The first shot of Lara, whose hair was dyed bright red to distinguish her from brunette leading ladies Jacqueline Bisset and Michele Carey, is as the sexy, disheveled girl wakes up nude in Franciosa's beach house, unaware where she is. She is soon rudely told to hit the road by Franciosa when he receives a phone call with news that his surfer roommate Michael Sarrazin's girlfriend Bisset has wound up in the hospital after being left for dead by the side of a road. In flashbacks, Lara is seen accompanying the guys to hear third roommate jazz musician Bob Denver perform at a seedy bar that is invaded by a motorcycle gang. After some bikers make rude comments about Lindsay, Franciosa's quick wit enables him and his friends to exit without getting hurt. Lara is last glimpsed dancing at a discothèque before Franciosa replaces her in his bed with tennis player Corinna Tsopei. Lindsay was impressive as Martha and deserved better than what came next—a small part in the failed TV pilot *Braddock*, about a private eye of the future. She then landed a supporting role in the fact-based *The Boston Strangler* (1968) starring Tony Curtis as the notorious killer. As victim number eight, clad in an orange coat, Lindsay steps into her apartment after kissing her date goodnight; hearing the door buzzer, she opens it thinking it is her beau, only to be greeted with a sharp knife held to her throat by the Strangler. Though Lara doesn't have many lines, her image was used in

Lara Lindsay (ca. 1968).

a number of promotional materials. After playing an unbilled minor role in *Hello Dolly* (1969) and making two guest appearances on the TV detective series *Felony Squad* ("A Fashion for Dying" as a model and "Matched for Murder" as yet another murder victim, this time of a psychotic killer with whom she was matched by a computer dating service), Lara Lindsay abandoned her acting career to try her luck behind the camera.

**The Beginning:** Lara Lindsay was born Gladys Irene Jacobs on January 1, 1942, in Chicago. As with Carol and Nina Wayne, she was an expert ice skater as a child, which led to a stint with the Ice Capades when she got older. A short-lived early–Sixties marriage produced a son in 1963. While living in Tucson, Arizona, she began appearing in TV commercials and then was hired to be Charlene Holt's stand-in in the movie *El Dorado* which was filming in the area. Bitten by the acting bug, she then went to Hollywood where she changed her name (taking Lara from *Dr. Zhivago* and Lindsay from her brother who had that name).

**The '70s & Beyond:** Lara Lindsay abandoned her contract with Fox in 1970 to pursue a career in motion picture production. She made a rare return to acting in *Logan's Run* (1976) where she also worked as the assistant to the producer. Lara played an anonymous Woman Runner, fleeing from the Sandmen after reaching her thirtieth birthday, and she also provided the voice for the computer at Sandman headquarters. Her whereabouts today are unknown.

# Vicki London

A raven-haired beauty, this talented actress-singer only amassed a handful of movie credits as she preferred working on stage to film and passed on a few opportunities in Hollywood.

**You May Remember Her Most From:** *Village of the Giants* (1965) as one of the delinquent teenagers who grows to gigantic heights and terrorizes a town.

**Her Groovy '60s Credits:** Arriving in Hollywood from Memphis, Southern gal Vicki London's first professional job was to tour the U.S. as a red-headed Yum Yum Girl to help promote the comedy *Under the Yum Yum Tree* (1963) starring Jack Lemmon and Carol Lynley. The ten-city jaunt kept London busy as she appeared on twelve TV shows, seventeen radio shows, and gave twenty-five print interviews. Her first acting role was as a nurse in "Season for Vengeance" on the legal drama *Sam Benedict* in 1963. Preferring singing and dancing over acting, she turned down a part as a call girl in *A House Is Not a Home* in 1964 so she could appear in the Las Vegas musical revue *Blackhawk Gunfighters*, which eventually wound up at the New York World's Fair. During the show's run Vicki made headlines not because of her performance but because she was the last person to speak with singer Frank Sinatra, Jr., before he was kidnapped. She found her fifteen minutes of fame distasteful, which soured her on Hollywood. On television she played a bit part on *Dr. Kildare* and then the guest lead as Rick Nelson's coworker who arouses jealousy in his wife Kris in "Rick and the Girl Across the Hall" on *The Adventures of Ozzie and Harriet* in 1964.

London's film debut was in the cult classic teenage sci-fi movie *Village of the Giants* (1965), directed by Bert I. Gordon and loosely based on H.G. Wells' *Food of the Gods*. London joined Beau Bridges, Joy Harmon, Tisha Sterling, Gail Gilmore, Bob Random, and Mickey Rooney, Jr., as troublemaking teenagers who stumble upon a small town where ten-year-old "Genius" (Ronny Howard) has created goop that can make animals and people increase in size tenfold. When Bridges is hesitant to ingest the goop, London's

Georgette takes the plunge. The teens grow to gigantic proportions, literally bursting from their clothes, and bully the town. Law enforcement is helpless to stop them so it is up to good teens Tommy Kirk, Johnny Crawford, and Charla Doherty to knock them down to size, which they do due to Genius who produces an antidote. London's next and last movie appearance was in a biting satire on teenage popular culture, *Lord Love a Duck* (1966). She along with Lynn Carey played high school friends of grasping teenager Tuesday Weld, whose dreams of popularity and movie stardom are spurred by the Svengali-like actions of classmate Roddy McDowall. That same year Vicki London retired from show business after marrying a man from Chicago. They had two children and moved to Tarzana in the San Fernando Valley.

**The Beginning:** Vicki London was born Victoria Blumenfeld in Memphis, Tennessee. She began doing children's theatre at age ten. She could sing and dance and at sixteen years old she began performing locally in cabarets and revues. She even cut a single called "Summer's Here" for Mercury Records. Though she trained as a jazz singer, the record company forced her to sing in the style of Connie Stevens and Annette Funicello, who were popular at the time, so the record never charted. In 1962, Vicki was cast in a movie called *The Promoter* to be shot in Memphis but it was never made. Relocating to Hollywood, she began attending acting classes with her friend Linda Evans. Their coach was the esteemed Vincent Chase, who was the drama director for Stella Adler.

**The '70s & Beyond:** After a stint as a stay-at-home mom and wife, Vicki London became an entrepreneur, opening her own business called Vicki's Fantasies, which provided specialized gift wrapping within the entertainment industry. After her divorce, she moved to Malibu and started the first higher consciousness children's program for kindergarten through third grade, Creative Expressions. In 1996, she authored the children's book *This Is Not Goodbye... It's Halo: Awakening the Angelsoul Within*. Today, a thriving real estate agent, she lives in Carmel, California.

## *Vicki London speaks out on...*

**Why she passed on *Petticoat Junction*:** I was hired to play the middle sister [Bobbi Jo]. I turned it down because my agent at the time didn't want me to be typecast as a hillbilly. He was afraid, since I was from Memphis, all that would be offered to me would be hillbilly roles. Of course we know what happened with *Petticoat Junction*.

**Her involvement in the Frank Sinatra, Jr., kidnapping:** This was not a good time for me and actually I think it was the end for me in terms of show business. I just did not want to do anything after that. I knew Frank Sinatra, Jr., and we had talked on the phone the night of the kidnapping. There was a knock on his door and he put the phone down to answer it. The next thing I knew, the phone was hung up. I thought he did it and didn't know what happened until the next morning when the FBI showed up at my door. I was eighteen years old and living with my grandparents at the time. A few hours later our house was descended upon by photographers and reporters. I had my fifteen minutes of fame with the paparazzi and it was absolutely horrible. I don't know how celebrities handle it, I really don't. I was on tour with *Blackhawk Gunfighters* and I was actually subpoenaed to go to trial right in the middle of dress rehearsal. Nobody ever told me I would have to appear in court, which I did wearing my cowgirl costume. It was just about the worst situation of my life.

Vicki London (*far right*) grows to gigantic proportions and terrorizes a town with pals (*left to right*) Beau Bridges, Joy Harmon, Tisha Sterling, and Gail Gilmore in *Village of the Giants* (Embassy, 1965).

**Frank Sinatra:** After it was reported that I was the last person to speak with him, Frank Sinatra, Sr., called me, just frantic, wanting to know what happened to his son, naturally. I told him what I knew, which of course was nothing. He later called George Axelrod and he got me an acting job in *Lord Love a Duck*.

*The Adventures of Ozzie and Harriet*: This was the weirdest shoot of my career. After it was over I ended up talking like the Nelsons. You have no idea how they all had this cadence when they spoke. It was almost robotic and it wasn't real. That was a very strange

**Vicki London (1966).**

family. I'm sure they were nice people underneath it but it almost felt like being on a set with robots. They were polite but nothing seemed genuine to me.

**Her audition for *Village of the Giants*:** I had to audition for this but it was an easy interview and I was told I got one of the lead roles. During the wardrobe fittings, they wanted us [Vicki, Joy Harmon, Tisha Sterling, Gail Gilmore] to remove our blouses because they wanted the girl with the biggest breasts to play the part Joy Harmon wound up with. I refused and Tisha did too. They still gave Tisha a very nice part. It was downhill after this for me, though. But now that I am older and think back on it, I understand that Bert [Gordon] just wanted to see who would fit that part since her chest was used in the ad posters with Johnny Crawford hanging off her bra straps. But at the time it just didn't feel right to me. They made an issue out of me being unwilling to show my breasts so they threatened that if I didn't do it they were going to cut me out of everything and they did. They filmed me talking behind a screen where you only see my silhouette in one scene and when we become giants I am not even shown. I think they didn't do this to Tisha because her parents were famous.

***Village of the Giants*' infamous mud scene:** The mud scene didn't bother me as much as it did the other girls. It was messy and hard to move around. I found it to be kind of stupid but the movie was stupid—yet it is so popular. It is on DVD, there is a website devoted to it, and I still get contacted to talk about it. It is unbelievable.

**The cast:** Tisha Sterling was fabulous. She should have become a major star because she was absolutely gorgeous. I don't even know today who we could liken her to in the movies—maybe Scarlett Johansson. Joy Harmon was not a pretty girl. She had a bubbly personality and was very sweet but she didn't have that movie star look. Gail Gilmore was nice also. Beau Bridges was wonderful. I also met his brother Jeff and his father Lloyd and they were all so down-to-earth. That is a really nice family and really great people. Beau I think was the nicest of them all. Tommy Kirk was kind of standoffish, from what I remember. Bob Random and Mickey Rooney, Jr., were nice guys. I think I was paired with Bob in the movie.

**Why she turned down working with Elvis Presley in** *Girl Happy*: I was cast in a small part—I don't remember what—but I then got offered the role of Gloria in a production of *Damn Yankees* in Memphis. I wanted that more so I dropped out of the movie. Whenever a singing and dancing part on stage was offered to me, I always took it. I enjoyed it more and much preferred to be on stage. I found Hollywood back then to be so disrespectful to actresses. Girls today demand more and they get more. In the Sixties it was a hard time to be an actress.

*Lord Love a Duck*: George Axelrod was a wonderful man and a fabulous director—much, much, much higher caliber than Bert Gordon. I had a number of scenes with Tuesday Weld and Roddy McDowall but if you reach your hand down into your popcorn container you're going to miss me. I don't know if my scenes were cut out or they used close-ups of the stars. Tuesday was great to work with though. She had her own trailer and she'd invite us all in. Roddy McDowall was fabulous and I loved him. He was incredible. We were both working since we were children so I think we connected.

**Why she stopped acting:** It was because of the Frank Sinatra, Jr., kidnapping. I did not want to deal with that [fame] and it was too much for me. Also, Hollywood just did not get me. They did not understand where I came from and what I was all about.

# Darlene Lucht

A fetching sandy-haired brunette who graced the backgrounds of a number of comedies and beach movies during the Sixties, she ratcheted up the cheesecake factor. Wanting to be taken seriously as an actress, she changed her name to Tara Ashton but still could not make it to the top.

**You May Remember Her Most From:** *The Haunted Palace* (1963) as a sweet young thing terrorized by evil Vincent Price.

**Her Groovy '60s Credits:** Arriving in Tinsel Town in the summer of 1961, Darlene Lucht toiled as product presenter on the daytime TV show *Queen for a Day* and rotated in and out as one of the "Billboard Girls" on *The Steve Allen Show*. She landed very minor bit roles in two Jerry Lewis films, *The Bellboy* (1960) and *The Errand Boy* (1961), before coming to the attention of American International Pictures. She was cast as a near-victim of warlock Vincent Price, who performs rituals to interbreed mortals with demigods,

Darlene Lucht (ca. 1964). *Billy Rose Theatre Division, The New York Public Library for the Performing Arts, Astor, Lenox and Tilden Foundations*

in *The Haunted Palace* (1963), loosely based on a short story by H. P. Lovecraft. AIP then promoted Lucht as one of their most promising starlets. She posed for many pinup cheesecake shots and the film company sent her out frequently on publicity tours. Lucht joined the ranks of their anonymous beach girls with roles in 1964's *Muscle Beach Party* (she can be seen twisting away, clad in a red and white striped blouse opposite Jody McCrea, while Dick Dale and Donna Loren belt out the song "Muscle Bustle" on the porch of a Malibu beach house) and in *Bikini Beach* (she is a decorative background player). In between beach movies, she was able to squeeze in one more Jerry Lewis comedy, *The Patsy* (1964), in a bit nonspeaking role as a checkroom girl, and a few TV shows. She was cast in minor roles as an Alaskan model in "Many a Slip" on *Surfside 6*, a carnival princess in "A Funny Thing Happened on the Way to the Game" on *Checkmate*, and a waitress in "Who Killed the Strangler?" on *Burke's Law*. Back at AIP it was no secret that director William Asher overtly favored Mary Hughes, Patti Chandler, Salli Sachse, and Linda Opie, whom he discovered on the beaches of Southern California, so by the time *Beach Blanket Bingo* (1965) was filmed, Lucht's screen time was skimpier than her bikinis. After leaving AIP, Darlene's new agent Henry Willson, who represented Tab Hunter and Rock Hudson during the Fifties, convinced her to start anew with a name change to boost her career. As Tara Ashton, she snagged the role of Bunny in the sex comedy *Marriage on the Rocks* (1965) as one of the many beautiful women surrounding playboy ad man Dean Martin (who accidentally winds up married to his partner Frank Sinatra's ex-wife Deborah Kerr). When Martin's secretary Joi Lansing has to leave to tend to her sick mother, she sends Lucht in as her temporary replacement, hoping her married status will deter Martin from flirting. When Lucht tells Dino that she can take shorthand at 200 words per minute, he quips, "I can't say 200 words per minute!" Mishaps ensue as Sinatra takes over Martin's swinging lifestyle and inherits his girls, including Lucht. Next, Ashton was able to land the female lead in director Al Adamson's sadistically violent western *Five Bloody Graves*, which was filmed in 1967 but not released until 1970. Lucht played a stalwart dance hall girl stranded in hostile Indian territory along with Robert Dix as a loner gunfighter and others who are picked off one by one by the rampaging tribe. The movie offered the pretty brunette her most screen time as she bares her back while changing clothes, has a catfight with saloon girl Julie Edwards and, in a surprise ending, takes a bullet meant for Dix whom she had wed in January 1967 before filming began. She quit show business shortly after to raise their son Robert, who was born in 1969.

**The Beginning:** Darlene Lucht was born in Milwaukee, Wisconsin. After graduating high school, she worked as a secretary, then embarked on a modeling career. Bitten by the acting bug, she performed at a local regional theatre before being crowned Miss Milwaukee in 1959 and placing first runner-up in the Miss Wisconsin contest. This led to her being chosen to represent the state in the first Miss Sun Fun U.S.A. contest in Myrtle Beach, South Carolina. She walked away with the tiara and a new car, which she drove cross-country to find fame in Hollywood. Though she found the city, stardom eluded her.

**The '70s & Beyond:** Darlene Lucht and Robert Dix split in the early 2000s. She purportedly resides in Wisconsin.

# Deanna Lund

A sexy strawberry blonde beauty, usually bikini-clad, she had a special vitality not found in most glamour girls of her ilk and decorated a number of lightweight Elvis musicals, beach movies, and spy spoofs before going dramatic as a lesbian in the hardboiled detective film *Tony Rome*.

**You May Remember Her Most From:** TV's *Land of the Giants* (1968–70) as mini-skirted spoiled-rich-girl Valerie Scott, one of the seven people on a suborbital flight from New York to London who end up on a planet identical to Earth except that everything is twelve times larger.

**Her Groovy '60s Credits:** Deanna Lund made her film debut as a waitress disguised as a boy in the obscure comedy *Once Upon a Coffeehouse* (1965) and then appeared in two more Florida-lensed movies, *Run for Your Wife* (1965) as a blonde bimbo who goes for a joy ride with Ugo Tognazzi and *Johnny Tiger* (1966) as James Brolin's promiscuous girlfriend. Arriving in Hollywood, she quickly went the glamour route with minor bikini roles in *Dr. Goldfoot and the Bikini Machine* (1965) as a robot, *The Oscar* (1966) as a bathing beauty, and *The Swinger* (1966) as a pinup model. More bit parts followed in the Elvis movies *Spinout* (1966) as a redheaded beauty (Elvis sings to her from the stage during the film's opening and closing scenes) and *Paradise, Hawaiian Style* (1966) as a nurse who briefly flirts with Elvis while caring for his hospitalized friend, James Shigeta. In the low-budget spy movie *Dimension 5* (1966) Lund was "Miss Sweet," a sort of sexy younger version of Miss Moneypenny from the James Bond films. Her most amusing role came next as an enemy assassin in the beach/spy spoof *Out of Sight* (1966). Appropriately named Tuff Bod, Lund traded in the bikini for a black leotard under a see-through dress and was ordered to eliminate secret agent Jonathan Daly. Her plan fails when she can't resist shimmying to a groovy beat, allowing Daly to escape. Television offered her small guest roles on *Amos Burke, Secret Agent*, *The Road West*, *Laredo*, *T.H.E. Cat* and most memorably *Batman* where she played a feisty bad girl named Anna Gram; teamed with John Astin's hyperkinetic Riddler, she goes on a crime spree in Gotham City in "Batman's Anniversary" and "A Riddling Controversy." Not wanting to get trapped in "bikini roles," she passed on *In Like Flint* and then turned up in a bra and panties in *Tony Rome* (1967) as a trailer trash stripper with a jealous, blowsy lesbian lover played by Joan Shawlee. As private eye Frank Sinatra questions her, the uncooperative Lund undresses and argues with Shawlee, who hauls off and wallops her. The sobbing lovers then fall into each other's arms as a bemused Sinatra exits.

Deanna was so embarrassed about her role that she had her name removed from the credits but her performance impressed producer Irwin Allen, who hired her to play intergalactic castaway Valerie Scott on his new TV series *Land of the Giants* in 1968. Three crew members and four passengers are on a suborbital flight from New York to London in 1983 when they pass through an electrical storm and crashland on a planet identical to Earth except that everything is many times larger. Now aliens in a strange world, they are dubbed "the Little People" by the inhabitants and a bounty is placed on their heads. Lund's character began the show as a spoiled rich girl who constantly schemes with the equally conniving Kurt Kasznar. But as the series progressed and Lund's skirts got shorter, she mellowed and morphed more into a likable heroine. Photos of a bikini-clad Lund posing with a miniature *Spindrift* spaceship became a favorite pinup shot of boys across America until the series' cancellation in 1970, the same year she married co-star Don Matheson. They eventually had a daughter named Michelle who also became an actress.

**The Beginning:** Deanna Lund was born on May 30, 1937, in Oak Park, Illinois, but was raised in Daytona Beach, Florida. An introvert, she spent most of her childhood with her horse, competing in rodeos. While she was in college, her father suggested she enroll in a drama course and the lithe beauty caught the acting bug. On stage she appeared in productions of *Bus Stop* and *The Crucible*, among others. She turned down a contract offer from Columbia Pictures due to parental objections and instead married a cowboy she met on the rodeo circuit. Four years later she was divorced with two small children. Relocating to Miami, Lund began working as a model and local weathergirl to support her family. Her television exposure led to her movie career.

**The '70s & Beyond:** Deanna Lund rode the wave of her popularity from *Land of the*

**Deanna Lund poses with a replica of the *Spindrift* to promote her hit TV show *Land of the Giants* (20th Century–Fox Television, ca. 1968).**

*Giants* and kept busy on TV, making guest appearances on *Love, American Style* playing a cavegirl who discovers smooching in "Love and the First Kiss," *The Waltons*, and *The Incredible Hulk*. With her bikini girl days behind her, she had a small role in *Hustle* (1975) with Burt Reynolds and then played the radiant love interest of Jerry Lewis as an unemployed circus clown who cannot hold a job in the comedy *Hardly Working* (1981). In between, she had a recurring role as bad girl Peggy Lowell on *General Hospital* in 1976 and played supporting roles in the TV movies *Revenge for a Rape* (1976) and *Hanging by a Thread* (1979), which reunited her with producer Irwin Allen. In the early Eighties, Lund resided in New York where she co-hosted *Good Morning, New York* for two years and toiled on the soap opera *One Life to Live* as Virginia Keyser from 1980 to 1981. With much fanfare, Deanna returned to making movies in the hardboiled detective drama *Stick* (1985), based on the novel by Elmore Leonard and starring Burt Reynolds; unfortunately her role was cut to shreds in the final print. Lund then found herself relegated to low-budget, straight-to-video thrillers such as *Elves* (1989) as a mother from hell, *Transylvania Twist* (1990) in a cameo as a schoolteacher, and *Roots of Evil* (1992) as a rich bitch. After co-starring with Sixties contemporary Jane Wald in *Girl Talk* (1993), Deanna made her final movie appearance to date in the teen comedy *The Girl I Want* (1993). A few years later, Lund was in all the gossip columns when she became engaged to oft-married talk show host Larry King. The couple broke off the relationship before they made it to the altar. Since then Deanna Lund has written a novel entitled *Valerie in Giantland* regarding her character's new adventures and appears at fan conventions throughout the world with her *Land of the Giants* co-stars. More important to her is helping others less fortunate than herself through charity work. In 2005, she and Connie Stevens volunteered as certified Red Cross relief workers and journeyed to Southern Mississippi after Hurricane Katrina tore through.

# Linda Marshall

A pretty strawberry blonde, this busy TV actress, similar in looks to Pamela Austin and Linda Foster, at first essayed the sweet ingénue roles but, with a sophisticated icy air about her, she excelled when cast as the prissy snob or rich bitch.

**You May Remember Her Most From:** TV's *Tammy* (1965–66) as pretentious Gloria Tate, who with her malicious mama made life hell for that li'l bayou gal Tammy.

**Her Groovy '60s Credits:** Linda Marshall made her TV debut in 1963 on *My Three Sons* as one of eight nubile classmates of Don Grady's Robbie, hoping to date him in "The System." This began her run as the all-American girl-next-door on a number of series including *77 Sunset Strip*, two episodes of *Perry Mason*, (in "The Case of the Nebulous Nephew," she was cast as a young nun), and *Mr. Novak* as one of frightened substitute teacher Barbara Barrie's high school students in "How Does Your Garden Grow?" On the forgotten sitcom *Grindl* starring Imogene Coca as a domestic worker for a temp agency, Coca allows Linda and new husband Aron Kincaid to pretend a model home she is caring for is theirs to impress her parents in "The Big Deception." *Hazel* featured Marshall in a recurring role as Don Defore's secretary and in the episode "Marriage Trap" Shirley Booth's meddling maid tries to help her reconcile with her boyfriend, Ken Berry. Marshall then landed her first movie, *The Girls on the Beach* (1965), which is notable for the appearance of the Beach Boys. In it she played one of a quartet of coeds who plot to save their sorority beach house after finding out that their good-natured house mother squandered the mortgage money. The gals then hit the beach (of course) and devise various

Surfer boy Steve Rogers makes a play for coed Linda Marshall in *The Girls on the Beach* (Paramount, 1965).

schemes for their sorority sisters to raise some cash. The honeys think their problems are solved when three smitten surfer boys claim to know the Beatles and trick the girls into thinking the group will perform at a benefit concert. When Marshall and friends realize they have been duped, they don cheap wigs and (badly) impersonate the Fab Four, but good enough for their indiscriminate audience to cheer them on. More hairspray than suntan oil is used in the film as Marshall is only distinguishable from her big bouffant-wearing co-stars Noreen Corcoran and Gail Gerber by the towel she drapes herself in no matter where she goes as the prissy one of the group.

Returning to the boob tube, Linda (still sporting her stiff bouffant) played a biker chick, though she looked more like a prom queen, stranded by her boyfriend for smiling at a cop, and trying to convince new motorcycle rider Dick Van Dyke to give her a ride home in "Br-room, Br-room" on *The Dick Van Dyke Show*. She then re-teamed with Ken Berry on his series *F Troop* in "The Girl from Philadelphia." Sporting dark hair and a snooty accent, she was ideally cast as a stuck-up blue blood and former girlfriend of Berry's Captain Parmenter who tangles with his current love interest (Melody Patterson as fiery cowgirl Wrangler Jane) when she tries to persuade him to return East with her and then announces their engagement to his surprise. Linda's success in the role may have led her to a regular role on the sitcom *Tammy* in 1965 playing snobbish Gloria Tate, a mama's-little-rich-girl who is jealous of all the attention the town's young men are giving to cornpone Debbie Watson as Tammy. Gloria and her mother try various schemes to discredit Tammy but the hayseed always comes out on top and Gloria looks the fool. The series lasted only one season and was cancelled in the spring of 1966. Universal, trying to push Watson as a new teen star, edited the first four episodes into a feature film entitled *Tammy and the Millionaire* (1967). However, audiences were not as dumb as the studio may have thought and passed on seeing it. Purportedly, Marshall next starred in a film called *Pasquallia* in 1968 but no information about it can be found. She then began devoting her time to spreading the word of the Bahá'í religion (she had joined in about 1967). This religion, whose most famous member up to then was crooner Vic Damone, began in Persia in the late 1800s, started by a teacher named Baha U'llah "who wrote 100 volumes on how human beings should live to prepare themselves for life after death."

**The Beginning:** Not much is know about Linda Marshall's early years except that she was born in Dallas and raised in Wichita, Kansas. She studied drama and, while at Colorado State College, landed the lead role in a 1960 stage production of *The Diary of Anne Frank*.

**The '70s & Beyond:** After marrying Sahrab Youssefian, Linda Marshall quit show business and gave up her glamourous lifestyle to relocate to Italy to become more involved with the Bahá'í Faith. As an active believer, Linda toured Europe in the summer of 1970 with thirty followers comprising a group calling themselves The Dawnbreakers. They sang and danced while offering inspiring words about the religion. Linda did go on to have children and remained very active within the Bahá'í Faith. A fervent women's activist, she was part of the European Task Force for Women for ten years and in 1995 organized "Women for the Peace" in Italy. Linda Marshall Youssefian is still residing in Italy and is a high-ranking member of the Bahá'í religion. She leads its European Bahá'í Women's Network and travels the continent giving lectures on finding the meaning of life.

# Lee Meredith

A bosomy, flaxen-haired knockout, she was a standout in two of the most coveted dumb blonde roles of the Sixties and Seventies but wasn't able to find superstardom despite her looks and comedic talent.

**You May Remember Her Most From:** *The Producers* (1968) as the inept receptionist Ulla who can't type a lick and barely speaks English but knows how to shake her shapely booty to a groovy beat.

**Her Groovy '60s Credits:** On her first professional audition, Lee Meredith beat out dozens of more experienced actresses for the role of Swedish secretary Ulla in the zany Mel Brooks comedy *The Producers* (1968). Standing 5-foot-7½ with a figure measuring 39-24-36, the blonde bombshell first appears wearing a very short yellow mini-dress, interviewing to be a receptionist for conniving Broadway producer Zero Mostel and his partner Gene Wilder despite her lack of English. Barely able to pronounce the company's name "Bialystock and Bloom," the ditzy airhead's only noticeable skills are cigar-lighting

**Lee Meredith shakes her groove thing as the buxom Ulla in *The Producers* (AVCO Embassy, 1968).**

and go-go dancing—just the right qualifications for the lascivious Mostel. Later, when he tells her to go back to work, the "Swedish tease" drops her raincoat to reveal her shapely figure clad in only a zebra-print bikini as she once again shimmies and shakes to a rockin' beat. Though the role of Ulla is not as big as it is in the musical version, sexy Meredith gives a very skilled performance and gets the laughs. Her next movie gave her nothing more to do than to look glamourous as one of the Ziegfeld Girls in the hit musical *Funny Girl* (1968). In the family comedy *Hello Down There* (1969), Meredith has a small decorative part playing hip record producer Roddy McDowall's busty, brainy assistant who picks hit songs with aid from a computer. When she predicts that teenage Richard Dreyfuss and his group's new tune "Hey, Little Goldfish" will be a huge seller, McDowall books the group on television, unaware that the band is unavailable and ensconced in an experimental underwater home developed by Tony Randall.

**The Beginning:** Lee Meredith was born on October 22, 1947, in Passaic, New Jersey, and is the daughter of two schoolteachers. Though a shy child, at age fifteen she became a member of the Manhattan Rockets, a precision-dancing group a la the Rockettes who performed at state fairs and with the circus. After graduating high school, she did some local modeling and she was named Miss Body Shop. Moving across the river into New York City, she studied acting at the American Academy of Dramatic Arts.

**The '70s & Beyond:** Lee Meredith began the decade in New York making her Broadway debut in the flop comedy *A Teaspoon Every Four Hours* with Jackie Mason. Back on the big screen, she appeared in 1972's *The Stoolie* as a swimsuit-clad beauty whom loser Jackie Mason tries unsuccessfully to pick up on a Florida beach and in 1973's *Hail to the Chief* with Gary Sandy, a failed anti-establishment comedy ahead of its time. After appearing as Miss Rixey in the made-for-TV musical *June Moon* (1974), an adaptation of the George S. Kaufman–Ring Lardner play satirizing Tin Pan Alley, Meredith returned to Broadway scoring big laughs as the Sketch Nurse in Neil Simon's hit comedy, *The Sunshine Boys*. She successfully recreated the role in the 1975 movie version starring Walter Matthau and George Burns as a bickering vaudeville comedy team reunited after years apart to appear in a TV special. They perform their "Doctor's Sketch" with Meredith as a dumb nurse with a Betty Boopish voice, deep cleavage, shapely derriere, and an exaggerated wiggle in her walk. Despite the notoriety *The Sunshine Boys* brought her, Meredith wasn't able to follow it up with a hit. She returned to doing regional theatre, starring in among other plays *The Seven Year Itch* in Atlanta and Tennessee Williams' *Camino Real* with Earl Holliman and Victor Buono in California. Broadway beckoned again and she appeared in *Once in a Lifetime* with an esteemed cast including Treat Williams, John Lithgow, and Jayne Meadows in 1978, and *Musical Chairs* in 1980. Lee was back in the limelight during the Eighties for a series of popular Lite Beer commercials (she had been their spokeswoman since the mid–Seventies) where she appeared with brawny jocks quarreling over whether the brew "tastes great" or was "less filling." In between shooting commercials she headlined a madcap comedy called *The Hollywood Hotel* in New York. The show didn't win any awards but Meredith was named Best Actress Cook on Broadway for her Beef Stroganoff recipe. Her last movie role was as a sexy barkeep in the telepic *Mickey Spillane's Mike Hammer: Murder Me, Murder You* (1983) starring Stacy Keach as the famed gumshoe searching for his long-lost daughter. Soap fans remember Lee as the outrageous ex-stripper Charmaine L'Amour McColl from 1983 to 1984 on *As the World Turns*. She returned to the stage after an eight-year absence to play an aspiring actress-hooker who helps her despondent neighbor in *Life on the Third Rail* and then she turned up in a bit in the 1991 TV special *Benny Hill's World Tour: New York*. Lee's last credit was a 1996 episode of the failed HBO comedy series *The High Life*, a sort of *Honeymooners* for the Nineties. She then appeared as herself in a "making of" featurette on *The Producers* DVD in 2002. Currently, she resides in New Jersey with her husband Bert Stratford. They met during the early Seventies in a bowling league and have two daughters. Lee keeps busy juggling her works as a teacher's aide in a vocational school and as owner of a pet-sitting service.

## Lee Meredith speaks out on...

**Her early years:** Though I was a dancer with the Manhattan Rockets I always wanted to act... and sing. But I'm not a very good singer. I used to write songs and would go around to the neighbors who would listen to me. My friend Cindy and I would sing together and we'd ask our friends, "What name should we record under?" But we were so terrible. One day I got my grandmother to take us to this recording studio and she was actually going to pay to have us cut a record. But she heard us rehearsing in the back seat and at that moment she gracefully backed out of it.

**How she landed an audition for *The Producers*:** I was attending the Academy of Dramatic Arts and graduation was approaching. Our last show was *Carousel*. I didn't have a big part but the producer of *The Fantastiks* came and saw me in it. He called Mel Brooks and I was invited to read for him. I learned my Swedish accent at the library around the block in Riveredge where I was living with my grandfather at the time. It is funny because I had no idea who Mel Brooks was, *or* Zero Mostel. But looking back I'm glad I didn't know more about them because I would have been a lot more nervous.

**Getting the part of Ulla:** Mel Brooks told me that I was very honest. They wanted someone who was innocent but at the same time sexy. Mel was great to audition for. My grandmother had just passed away and I didn't know what to wear. Miniskirts were in but I didn't own one so I wore my grandma's long suit, which was boxy and down past my knees, with a loose flowered blouse and little gloves. I was very proper and looked like a young image of my grandmother. I hadn't seen the script so when I went to read, Mel Brooks said, "Now, take off the jacket and pull in the blouse so we can see what is underneath all that." They put on the record "Sock It to Me Baby" by Mitch Ryder and I danced like crazy. They really liked it. I had to come back to read again and on my last audition I wore a tight Chinese dress with slits up the side. I think he chose me because I was a challenge in a way because it was like making somebody over.

**Her thoughts on playing a dumb sexpot:** At first it was very exciting for me wearing a bikini and mini-dress because it was the beginning of me really getting into those types of parts. I looked at myself and thought, "Ooh, this looks good." I really didn't mind doing this but in those days things were not proper. When they had me on *The Tonight Show* I couldn't show any cleavage whatsoever. You always had to be careful in what you wore—not like nowadays.

**Mel Brooks as director:** He kept everything almost exactly the same as the audition. He had to block it differently because my earrings kept flying off and it took almost the whole day to shoot. Mel knew exactly what he wanted and he didn't change any lines from the original script when we did our first read-through. That it what was so good about his direction as well. There were times when things got a little tense but basically everything went smoothly.

**Zero Mostel:** He scared me. I was naïve and right out of school. At lunch time he would take a nap and the cameraman would make me go into his dressing room to wake him up. I would and Zero would awaken growling like a giant bear. I would be shaking in my boots. Other than that I really didn't get to know him and stayed by myself a lot, being so new to the business. I didn't quite know how to interact with someone like Zero.

**How the success of *The Producers* affected her career:** For years a lot of the work I got was because of this movie. It did typecast me. But I figured it was better than not working.

*The Sunshine Boys* (MGM, 1974) featured Lee Meredith as the beautiful, bountiful sketch nurse.

***Hello, Down There***: I didn't get to know Roddy McDowall that well but he seemed like a very nice person. Tony Randall was a sweet, sweet man. I adored him and ran into him for years afterwards. I became quite friendly with Richard Dreyfuss who played one of the teenagers in this. Actually, I'm only eight days older than him. He was playing quite younger than what he actually was. We went out to dinner a few times and every time I was in California I'd call him. Years later [1983] I was shopping in Giorgio's and I ran into his girlfriend Jeramie Rain and she told me they were going to be married. They invited me to the wedding. I went to the reception, which was a huge affair on one of the studio lots. There was a backdrop of New York City. He also invited me to the private marriage ceremony but I didn't realize it until it was too late and didn't go.

**Her obscure movies:** I never mention *Hello, Down There* to anyone because most people have never heard of it. Another one I leave off my list of credits is *Cauliflower Cupid* [never released] with Jake LaMotta and Rocky Graziano. I was friendly with them because we worked together on my first commercial for United Airlines. I think we made this in 1970 or 1971. Peter Savage produced it. Another one was *The Stoolie* with Jackie Mason. He was very funny and we were friendly. I worked with him first on Broadway [in *A Teaspoon Every Four Hours*]. He could rewrite a whole script in a night—he was amazing. We'd come in the next day and it was totally different. We went through three directors and ninety-seven previews. The play closed on opening night. In *The Stoolie* I had a silly part and am glad this is hard to find. We shot *Welcome to the Club* in Denmark. It was supposed to look like Japan. We filmed *Hail to the Chief* in New York at the Armory. I had a bubble bath scene where I got electrocuted with a TV. I was terribly sunburned—I had just returned from a trip to Florida—and had to spend the entire day under the water. It was the first time I ever had to drown on camera.

**Broadway versus Hollywood:** I didn't prefer one over the other. When you are an actor, you take what you can get. That's the way it turned out for me. There was a movie I was supposed to do with Mel Brooks but a show had come up called *A Weekend with Feathers*. They offered me the female lead opposite Donald O'Connor so I opted for that instead of the film, which was probably stupid because we closed out of town and never made it to Broadway. I liked doing theatre. It was hard commuting to Hollywood but you have to commute no matter what you do.

***The Sunshine Boys*:** I did both the play with Jack Albertson and Sam Levene and the movie with Walter Matthau and George Burns. It is always more fun doing the show because you become like a family and get to know everybody. We went out on tour together as well. Jack Albertson was a doll. He was a hoofer and I remember the first day of rehearsal he was dancing all around the stage. He was just wonderful. Sam Levene was something else! He would play tricks on you but one minute he could be very nice and the next he could be terrible. He was a tough guy and not so easy to work with. One time he did something really mean to me and hurt my feelings. He was really nasty to me but he sent me flowers and apologized. But then he went back to being nasty again.

**Walter Matthau and George Burns:** Walter Matthau was so easy to talk with. He was a really wonderful father and respected his son's opinion. The movie opened at the Radio City Music Hall. We sat around that day together and he told me that when he gets offered a script he would show it to his son to read first. I thought that was really sweet. He was a real good family man. George Burns was always asking me out to dinner. He put me off and I never went because I am very shy. I thought he was asking me out but I am sure now it was to go with a group of people. But then I didn't know how to react to that.

**Playing the Sketch Nurse in *The Sunshine Boys* on stage and in the movie:** The part was not really different but what happens when they adapt a play is that they cut it from so many different angles. They added a lot of exterior shots so my part didn't seem like much in the movie compared to when I did it on Broadway. My scene was a good portion of the show on stage unlike in the movie because of the way it was edited. My costume was exactly the same in each. I was afraid that they wouldn't be able to make it as good as the one I wore on stage so I brought it with me. I still have it and wear it for certain things like a revue I was in called *Hollywood Hotel*. I've used the dress a lot.

*As the World Turns*: I played Charmaine, the wife of Lisa Hughes' rich husband. He was married to two women at the same time. It was very involved and farfetched if you don't follow the soaps. But it was a very funny part. I loved doing it. In one scene I actually did it standing on my head. [The character] was a health food fanatic and would go around putting down foie gras because of the way geese are force-fed. What is really funny is that today I am very into animal rights but then I didn't know much about it. Nowadays you always see on the news the way they mistreat the geese to make this stuff. Back then I thought it was something the writers made up but it wasn't funny—it was true. Charmaine was a lot smarter than I thought she was!

**Lite Beer commercials**: I started doing these in 1973 and the last one was in 1991. We traveled a lot promoting the product. One year I was on the road about 200 days out of the year. We were called Lite All-Stars. I was Mickey Spillane's sidekick. He was a terrific guy. I got a lot of mileage from these commercials being the only female in them. That was quite a lucrative job.

**The Benny Hill special:** I hated this. We filmed in the winter. It was so cold and we were wearing these little bitty outfits. All we did was dash around Central Park. I was running all over the place like an idiot. When it was actually shot I felt like I wasn't contributing anything. I thought, "What a waste of time!" I didn't get to know Benny Hill at all.

**Why she stopped acting:** Frankly, I got too old. Nobody wanted me. I work out to keep in shape and look very good for my age. But I don't have the determination to go looking for work. I am not an assertive person. I think if I had been more aggressive and had more confidence, I may have done a lot more. I never pushed myself and if they didn't come asking for me, I didn't go out looking for work. You have to do that in this business. As I got older I started to get burned out due to all the traveling. I had a family and just couldn't wait to get home to them.

# Donna Michelle

A wild-haired, petulant, strawberry-blonde sex kitten, she was one of the most popular Playmates of the decade and enlivened a number of comedies and spy capers. Unlike her *Playboy* counterparts, she landed roles with a kick to them due to her simmering sensuality, including a man-hungry beach bunny and a karate-chopping enemy agent, but super stardom still eluded her.

**You May Remember Her Most From:** *Beach Blanket Bingo* (1965) as a voracious beach bunny appropriately nicknamed Animal who turns all the surfers' heads and for a split second makes Frankie forget all about Annette.

Donna Michelle, *Playboy*'s 1964 Playmate of the Year, as a man-hungry beach bunny in *Beach Blanket Bingo* (AIP, 1965). *Billy Rose Theatre Division, The New York Public Library for the Performing Arts, Astor, Lenox and Tilden Foundations*

**Her Groovy '60s Credits:** Donna Michelle emerged on the scene as *Playboy*'s Playmate of the Month for December 1963 and then was voted Playmate of the Year for 1964. Michelle was a male fantasy come to life. Not only was she voluptuous (38-22-27) but she definitely was not your typical woman of 1964, listing "swimming, taking care of and riding my horse, and driving my sports car" as how she kept busy and "scuba diving" as one of her hobbies. Michelle was one of the most popular pinups of the decade. She was the first Playmate who commanded more than ten pages on her and the first Playmate of the Year to receive a multitude of gifts (including a Ford Mustang) with the crown. Hollywood quickly took notice, casting the busty Michelle in roles for her physical attributes only, not realizing that she had more talent than many of the other *Playboy* centerfolds who flickered briefly on the big screen. Audiences couldn't help but notice the blonde in her film debut as a gyrating party guest in a tight, low-cut, yellow tasseled dress that accentuated her figure during the opening scene of the comedy *Goodbye, Charlie* (1964). She then took over from Meredith MacRae as amorous bikini-clad Animal in *Beach Blanket Bingo* (1965) as Frankie, Annette and the beach gang give skydiving a try in between shooting the curl. Michelle was paired with surfer Mike Nader as Mike. Whereas Annette wouldn't dream of having sex before marriage, it was always hinted that the guys stood a good chance of scoring with the sexy Animal. Arguably, Michelle was the best of the gals to play Animal because of the sexual ferocity she brought to the part.

On television, Michelle guest starred in a pair of two-part episodes on *The Man from U.N.C.L.E.*, which were both released theatrically as movies. In *The Spy with My Face* (1965) she played THRUSH bad girl Nina, a masseuse who delivers a mighty karate chop to the neck of Robert Vaughn's Napoleon Solo; in *One Spy Too Many* (1966) she was an adulterous princess torn between U.N.C.L.E. agent Solo and villainous Rip Torn as the diabolical Alexander the Great. The scene where she tries to entice Vaughn into her bubble bath was extremely steamy. In between spy adventures, Michelle received lots of press for her role as "The Girl" in the underrated drama *Mickey One* (1965), directed by Arthur Penn. Not uttering a word, Michelle is mesmerizing as an alluring female predator teasing standup comic Warren Beatty, who is on the run from the mob after witnessing a murder, at a gambling joint. Never have poker chips been used so seductively. Though Michelle had lines in her next movie, she was wasted in the staid Miss Moneypenny–type role in the low-budget Bond rip-off *Agent for H.A.R.M.* (1966). She then was enticed to France where the restrictions regarding sex and nudity were looser. No doubt French producers were wise enough to take advantage of this and have Michelle bare almost all as a lesbian stripper being held captive along with her lover by a fugitive wanted for the murder of his wife in *The Night of the Three Lovers* (1968) and as a fashion model who becomes entangled with a bank manager and a robbery attempt gone awry in *Playmates* (1968).

**The Beginning:** Donna Michelle was born Donna Ronne on December 8, 1945, in Los Angeles. As a child she played concert piano and studied Russian ballet for seven years. When she got older she performed briefly with the New York City Ballet. In college, she majored in Theater Arts while working as a model, which led to *Playboy*.

**The '70s & Beyond:** Returning to the U.S. from Europe, Donna Michelle made one final film appearance in a small role in the crime drama *Company of Killers* (1970), which was originally made for television but given a theatrical run instead. She then retired from acting, parlaying her hobby of photography into a full-time career. She shot a celebrated pictorial entitled "Donna Clicks" that ran in the April 1974 issue of *Playboy*. She retired from show business and moved to a 20-acre ranch in Northern California where she started a catering company. At age fifty, she was coaxed to pose for the magazine in a three-page semi-nude spread entitled "Playmate Revisited" (October 1996). Four years later she cracked the Top Ten of the 100 Centerfolds of the Century finishing ninth, which ran in the January 2000 issue. Sadly, shortly after, Donna Michelle died of a heart attack on April 9, 2004. She was 58 years old.

# Ann Morell

A sultry, petite, raven-haired Texan with a lilting Southern accent, she adorned a number of Sixties movies including two with Elvis Presley but never made it to the big time due to missed opportunities and her strict moral convictions.

**You May Remember Her Most From:** *Dracula vs. Frankenstein* (1971) as a mini-skirted hippie who is saved from being gang-raped but ends up a victim of the demented Dr. Frankenstein.

**Her Groovy '60s Credits:** Ann Morell's screen debut was in the sci-fi film *Beyond the Time Barrier* (1960), which was filmed in her native Texas, followed by a bit role in the forgettable talking duck comedy *Everything's Ducky* (1961). For the next couple of years, Morell worked steadily, alternating between decorative roles and ethnic parts due to her dark exotic looks while posing for pinup and cheesecake photos like every obedient glamour girl did during the Sixties. In the Robert Goulet comedy *Honeymoon Hotel* (1964) she was a newlywed, in *John Goldfarb, Please Come Home* (1965) she was a belly-dancing veiled harem girl, and in *Red Line 7000* (1965), directed by Howard Hawks, she was the "Girl in the Café" jilted by two potential suitors after sultry French babe Marianna Hill saunters by. In between movies, Morell also kept busy on television being romanced by Gene Barry in a few episodes of *Burke's Law* and, with her hair in braids, playing an Apache squaw in "Now Join the Human Race" on the western *Branded* opposite Burt Reynolds as her husband Red Hand who illegally flees with his wife and baby from the reservation and is pursued by a bloodthirsty major. Back on the big screen, Morell (playing one of the many sexy denizens of a dude ranch for models) snuggled up to Elvis Presley in *Tickle Me* (1965); next she was a curvaceous brunette itching to work as Elvis' secretary for his helicopter tour business in *Paradise, Hawaiian Style* (1966). She lost the job to British blonde beauty Suzanna Leigh in the movie while in real life she was nominated for "Star of Tomorrow" at the Hollywood Deb Star Ball in 1967 and lost out to Sivi Aberg. On TV, Ann's varied roles ranged from a sexy barber on *It Takes a Thief* in "38-23-36" and a Latin American revolutionary on *Mission: Impossible* in "Commandante" to appearing as herself on *Rowan & Martin's Laugh-In* and *The Dating Game*.

**The Beginning:** Of Greek, Sicilian, and American Indian descent, Ann Morell was born and raised in a strict religious household in Texas. She began winning a string of beauty contests at the age of fourteen. Her titles included "Miss Flame of Dallas," "Miss Spirit of Southwest," and "Miss Ruby Lips." She was sponsored by the publisher of *The Oak Cliff Tribune* who paid for her first dancing and modeling lessons at age sixteen. Her foray

Ann Morell and the Pink Panther (ca. 1964). *Courtesy of Ann Morell.*

to Hollywood was bankrolled by Texas oil man Bill Burke, who invested $12,000 to help maker Morell a star.

**The '70s & Beyond:** After being cast as a sexy Italian belly dancer in the spy spoof *The Phynx* (1970), Ann Morell finally landed a co-starring movie role: the Grade-Z production *Dracula vs. Frankenstein* (1971), directed by Al Adamson. Sporting some of the shortest mini-skirts ever worn on screen, she played a former biker chick turned hippie who aids buxom Vegas lounge singer Regina Carroll search for her missing sister at a carnival freak show. As the put-upon ingénue, Morell is almost gang-raped by Russ Tamblyn and his motorcycle gang and becomes the final victim of crazed J. Carrol Naish as a wheelchair-bound relative of Dr. Frankenstein and Lon Chaney, Jr. as his assistant. Ann's last movie before retiring was as a Depression-era prostitute who befriends Barbara Hershey as *Boxcar Bertha* (1972), produced by Roger Corman and directed by Martin Scorsese. Unfortunately, most of her scenes were cut and the film did not generate any more roles for her as her life took a new direction as wife and mother. She returned to show business as owner of Super Star Fire Records from 1979 to 1989 and produced her son Nico Princely's Top 20 Record "Roller Skate Rider" in the early Eighties. Throughout the years, the enterprising Morell worked as a doctor of holistic medicine, certified nurse assistant, certified phlebotomist, certified private training instructor, and esthetician member of the Academy of Anti-Aging Medicine. In 1992, she founded The Great Spirit Center, a public benefit charity dedicated to getting single parents out of poverty. Her determination to help others better themselves earned her the JC Penney National Award for Charity Service in 1994 and 1995. Today Ann Morell commutes between her residences in Las Vegas and Sherman Oaks, California. She continues helping others with The Great Spirit Center and is writing her memoirs.

## *Ann Morell speaks out on...*

**Her early days in Hollywood:** I never intended to be an actress. I was extremely beautiful and won a number of beauty contests and was brought to Hollywood by Lucille Ball and Desi Arnaz. I was under contract to 20th Century-Fox and MGM. There was a guy at I think MGM named Guy McElwaine who was really pushing me to become a star. He really liked me and was one nice guy. But I have a conflict with morality and the way the star system works. My focus is on doing good for people and setting a fine example by making things better. Money comes and money goes but your soul lasts forever. I have always been religiously oriented. In Hollywood I would go to all the parties arriving thirty minutes late and leaving thirty minutes early. I never took drugs or drank alcohol. I always had a good time and had lots of friends. I really didn't start to act thinking I was going to become the biggest star and want to do this and that. I was always grateful when I got work. I'd think, "What is this part going to do for me? Is it going to make me a little money? Is it going to be a good example? Am I going to entertain people?" I'd always think, "What effect is this going to have?" before I accepted a role. If I'd think it wasn't going to have the effect I was looking for (to bring laughter, happiness or joy to the audience's heart), I'd just tell my agent, "I don't want to do that." I felt movies should be entertaining as there is enough aggravation in the world.

**Staying true to her convictions in Sixties Hollywood:** My moral convictions might be the reason I am still on this earth, while others that I knew are gone and left at an early age. There is one way to live and that is God's way. Earth is for a relatively short period while eternity is forever and all that we do on Earth is left behind and soon forgotten.

**Cheesecake:** Hugh Hefner wanted me to appear in *Playboy*. They offered me a lot of money but I turned it down because it didn't fit with my morality. I think the body is a beautiful form to be used to give glory to God and not for debased reasons. When I first started out in Hollywood I did do some cheesecake shots. I remember one photographer took these great shots of me wearing hose with garters under a red dress blowing up.

*Tickle Me*: I knew Elvis before he became *Elvis*. He liked me and always called me his dream girl. Jocelyn Lane was quiet and didn't say too much to me because Elvis and I were always together. He treated me like I was the star of the movie. But I didn't know if the other girls were jealous or not. I was just a young kid and green—all smiles and God.

**Red Line 7000**: Howard Hawks was a wonderful man and a really nice guy. He loved me and would have built me into a star. I think he was ready to do more movies with me but there was a producer at MGM who gave me a hard time and was after me.

**Sixties Divas:** Shirley MacLaine was feisty and didn't want me on *John Goldfarb, Please Come Home*. Doris Day was another one. I never had any trouble with the girls my age playing the smaller roles. It was always the stars who'd be jealous because I was really pretty. I had problems with Connie Stevens and Marlo Thomas too. Both of them wouldn't let me work on their TV series. That girl Marlo was something else, I tell you. But I never got upset with these people. I would just pray for strength to go on.

**Working with Robert Wagner on** *It Takes a Thief*: Robert Wagner was handsome and charming. I was in awe of him. He was flirty, congenial, and very appealing to me but I was much younger than him. I don't recall ever dating him. I used to be invited to all of the parties and I would always have a nice celebrity date. Robert apparently liked me. He had me work with him twice. I had a page out of my old phone book somewhere with his number on it. It was in a frame until I moved and so many of my pictures, and memories on paper, were taken or lost.

**Reasons she appeared in** *Dracula vs. Frankenstein*: When I used to take those B-movie roles, I was given a script to read. I read the screenplay and it was okay. Then while working on the set, the script writer would change dialogue. Most of the time, the ideas for change came "after" the star or actor was established in the role. At that point, you either had to do it or in many cases "just walk off the set" and if you were important enough, there would be a discussion and/or debate and you could take a stand and remain in the picture. Another reason is that when you film a movie, you do it in scenes or segments. Until the film is edited and ready for rushes, you have not seen the film as a "story or role"—even today, I still have not seen this movie. When I worked as an actress, I seldom watched myself. I was young and impressionable and always eager to learn from those who were ahead of me. I would listen to their critiques and learn from that.

Al Adamson [the director] was a sweetheart and I had no trouble working for him. He was very nice. Russ Tamblyn was a friendly guy but J. Carrol Naish and Lon Chaney, Jr., were really nice to me. They thought I was just a kid and were very kind. I was an extrovert on stage and on PR tours but on the set I was an introvert and quiet so I really didn't get to know many people well.

**Missed opportunities:** I walked off the set on several movies. On one movie they wanted to put me in a coffin. It was nowhere in the script. I refused to do it and was taken off the picture. I was in *The Cincinnati Kid* with Steve McQueen when Sam Peckinpah was directing. He got fired for the things he tried to do. For instance, we were shooting late one night and he wanted me to wear a mink jacket with no clothes on and flash McQueen. I objected and called the Screen Actors Guild. When they hired a new director [Norman Jewison] I was let go because they thought I was difficult and I got a lot of bad press. Hollywood could be a real rat race. You are part of that Hollywood scene or you're not. I lost a lot of roles due to my integrity and morality. I never read any of my publicity because I didn't want to get a big head and lose sight of who I really am.

I was cast in *Viva Las Vegas* but I couldn't do it. I was raised in a family that said dancing was a sin. I had a cameo part and had to dance with Elvis. I actually broke down and started crying on the set. I said, "I can't do this." The director said, "Yes, you can." I just couldn't do it so they gave the part to someone else. I was just not ready for big success because I was not groomed for big success. I think I was groomed to be a minister or a teacher, but I had a lot to learn before that could manifest. Over the years, I have really had challenges that I have had to overcome and now have grown to have the ability and experience to share with others. One is that I have discovered that "Life is Ageless and Age is Lifeless." That is my registered motto for my teachings in Healiopathic Medicine and Rejuvenation NetWork System, the young and healthy lifestyle.

*Boxcar Bertha*: I was dating Paul Rapp who introduced me to Roger Corman. He cast me and I had a really good part in this but Barbara Hershey fought me constantly. She threw a fit about my wardrobe and everything else.

Publicity photograph of Ann Morell in the spy spoof *The Phynx* (Warner Bros., 1969). *Courtesy of Ann Morell.*

Martin Scorsese was just a young guy starting out and tried to do his best. He was okay with me. We filmed this in Camden, Arkansas, and that's when I realized that these small towns are not as nice as you think they are. That was my first lesson knowing that the city was a better place than the country. I met weird people there.

**Favorite Role:** I played an Indian named Snow Child in the western series *Branded* that starred Chuck Connors. I really liked that part. Burt Reynolds was my husband. He was okay to work with but he was one of those guys who had a big ego and liked to be recognized. I always gave people what they wanted. If he wanted to be recognized, I'd recognize him. I was never in competition.

In 1998, I saw Burt Reynolds on the corner of Ventura Boulevard and Laurel Canyon. I went up to him and said, "Burt! My long lost husband! I'm your squaw!" He said, "I wondered where you were! Whatever happened to you?" We exchanged numbers but I've lost track of him again.

**Quitting show business:** I stopped acting when I had a child. When my son was twelve years old, David Mirisch said to him, "Your mother could have become the biggest star but she decided to quit." I wanted to be a good role model for my son. I think fame is good if you are going to use it to help others and are going to be visible to help causes. But if you just want to be a star for vain glory to boost your own ego, then I do not think it is that big a deal.

**Her life today:** In October 1992 I founded a public charity called The Great Spirit Center in California. Our mission is to help single-parent families to get off of welfare and out of poverty. My motto is "Poverty is a social disease and it can be cured" when we all work together with one goal—to help one another. This is important and I hope to get established in Las Vegas, Phoenix, and perhaps Dallas. Then maybe people from New York will call to help, as I am sure they really need us there. Our website is www.thegreatspiritcenter.org. I am also a doctor of healiopathic medicine, which I discovered in the 1990s. That site will be an online college at www.healiopathicmedicine.com. In the meantime, I work with those patients who want to remain youthful, healthy and live a good lifestyle. That site is Rejuvenation NetWork System and www.rejuvenationnetwork.com is the web address.

I am also seeking agent representation to see if I can pick up a few acting roles to help the charity. Hopefully, I can land some nice parts or commercials as what I do is not just for me, but for others who need the assistance that I am able to communicate and do for them; especially two seldom remembered segments of our society, Single Parent Families with Dependent Children and those people who are between 50 and 62 who do not qualify for any kind of financial or health care. They are sick and cannot work, and either deteriorate to a point of existing—sometimes on the street—or die.

# Cynthia Myers

A sultry, wide-eyed, busty brunette, she parlayed her extremely popular reign as a Playboy Playmate into becoming a Russ Meyer leading lady but then opted for a family life rather than an acting career.

**You May Remember Her Most From:** *Beyond the Valley of the Dolls* (1970) as the aspiring bi-sexual rock star who meets a fatal end.

**Her Groovy '60s Credits:** At age eighteen, Cynthia Myers, a 5-foot-4, dark-haired beauty with a tantalizing 39-24-36 figure, became *Playboy*'s final Playmate of 1968. As Miss December, she graced the cover as a Christmas tree come to life (bet Santa never had it so good) and posed nude kneeling on a white rug alongside a teddy bear. She immediately became one of the most popular pinups for the GIs stationed in Vietnam and the magazine received the second largest amount of fan letters regarding her centerfold. (Strangely, she failed to be selected Playmate of the Year; that honor went to Connie Kreski.)

*Playboy*'s Miss December 1968 Cynthia Myers.

Movies beckoned and Myers played a bit role as one of the marathon dancers in the Depression-era drama *They Shoot Horses, Don't They?* (1969) starring Jane Fonda and Michael Sarrazin. She also made appearances as herself alongside Hugh Hefner in his syndicated variety series *Playboy After Dark* in 1969. That same year, Myers was brought to the attention of director Russ Meyer who was searching for three newcomers to play the leads in *Beyond the Valley of the Dolls*, which was billed as the first rock-sex musical. Since she was a 39DD cup, the bosom master flipped over her and cast her as Casey, the guitar-playing lost soul of the group—a powerful senator's daughter who, having been used and abused by men, falls in love with lesbian clothes designer Erica Gavin. After the Carrie Nations hit it big about ten minutes after arriving in Los Angeles from playing a senior prom back East, Myers and her band mates Dolly Read and Marcia McBroom become immersed in decadent Hollywood complete with drugs, sex, debauchery, sex, violence, and even more sex. Myers sleeps with the band's former manager David Gurian who is trying to prove his manhood after being called a "fag" by Edy Williams' porn star Ashley St. Ives. Myers winds up pregnant, angering her girlfriend, who immediately suggests an abortion. She goes through with the abortion but pays for her wanton ways when at the film's climax she has her pretty little head blown off by John Lazar's crazed Z-Man, who reveals a set of knockers to rival any Playboy Playmate as he goes off the deep end as Super Woman, also slaughtering Gavin, Michael Blodgett as a studly gigolo, and his German manservant. Myers gives a sympathetic performance a la Sharon Tate in the original and doesn't let her male fans down by exposing her breasts and shapely derriere in love scenes with both Gurian and Gavin. To help promote the movie, Myers joined Dolly Read and a host of bit players who posed semi-nude for the *Playboy* pictorial "The Dolls of *Beyond the Valley*."

**The Beginning:** Cynthia Myers was born on September 12, 1950, in Toledo, Ohio. By the time she was thirteen, she began to form curves galore. When she was fifteen she was prodded by friends to submit photos of herself in a swimsuit to *Playboy*. She was told to come back when she was legal, and she did.

**The '70s & Beyond:** Despite the notoriety *Beyond the Valley of the Dolls* brought her, Cynthia Myers' only other film appearance was in *Molly and Lawless John* (1972). This violent western starred a young Sam Elliott as a jailed gunslinger who sweet-talks lonely sheriff's wife Vera Miles to help him escape and to flee with him to Mexico. Along the way Miles delivers a baby whose mother dies in childbirth. When she realizes Elliott is only using her, she plots her revenge. Myers has a small role as the town's whore and Elliott's former flame who spends the night with him in a cabin while Miles is left outside to fend for herself. The movie has not much to recommend it. As for Myers, though she first appears wearing a robe with her cleavage clearly displayed, the rest of her scenes feature her clothed or wearing backless outfits to the chagrin of the male audience members.

Shortly after, Cynthia retired from show business to further her education and to care for her family. In 1994, she was persuaded to appear at a celebrity autograph convention. A hit with the fans, she began making personal appearances across the nation and disrobed once again for *Playboy* (the May 1996 issue). In 1999, she was voted one of the magazine's Top 100 Sex Stars of the Century and the following year she placed tenth in its poll of the Top 100 Centerfolds of the Century. A hot commodity once again, she made appearances in the videos *Playboy: 50 Years of Playmates* (2004) and *Strip de velours* (2005) and provides commentary on the deluxe DVD edition of *Beyond the Valley of the Dolls* (released in 2006) where she hints at a lesbian relationship with former co-star Erica Gavin. Her most recent film is the documentary *Bosommania: The Women* (2007) about legendary director Russ Meyer.

# Inga Neilsen

She was dubbed on the Internet as "A Nordic Goddess Supreme, the World's Greatest Glamazon"—and clearly deserves the title. Standing 6-foot-3 in heels, this striking blue-eyed blonde had curves galore and was built to be ogled on the big screen in spy spoofs and musical extravaganzas. Her body was not all she offered as she was an accomplished singer and had comedic talent, holding her own opposite some of the decade's top comedians.

**You May Remember Her Most From:** *A Funny Thing Happened on the Way to the Forum* (1966) as the voluptuous Roman courtesan Gymnasia or *Funny Girl* (1968) as the Winter Bride, the most dazzling of Ziegfeld Girls.

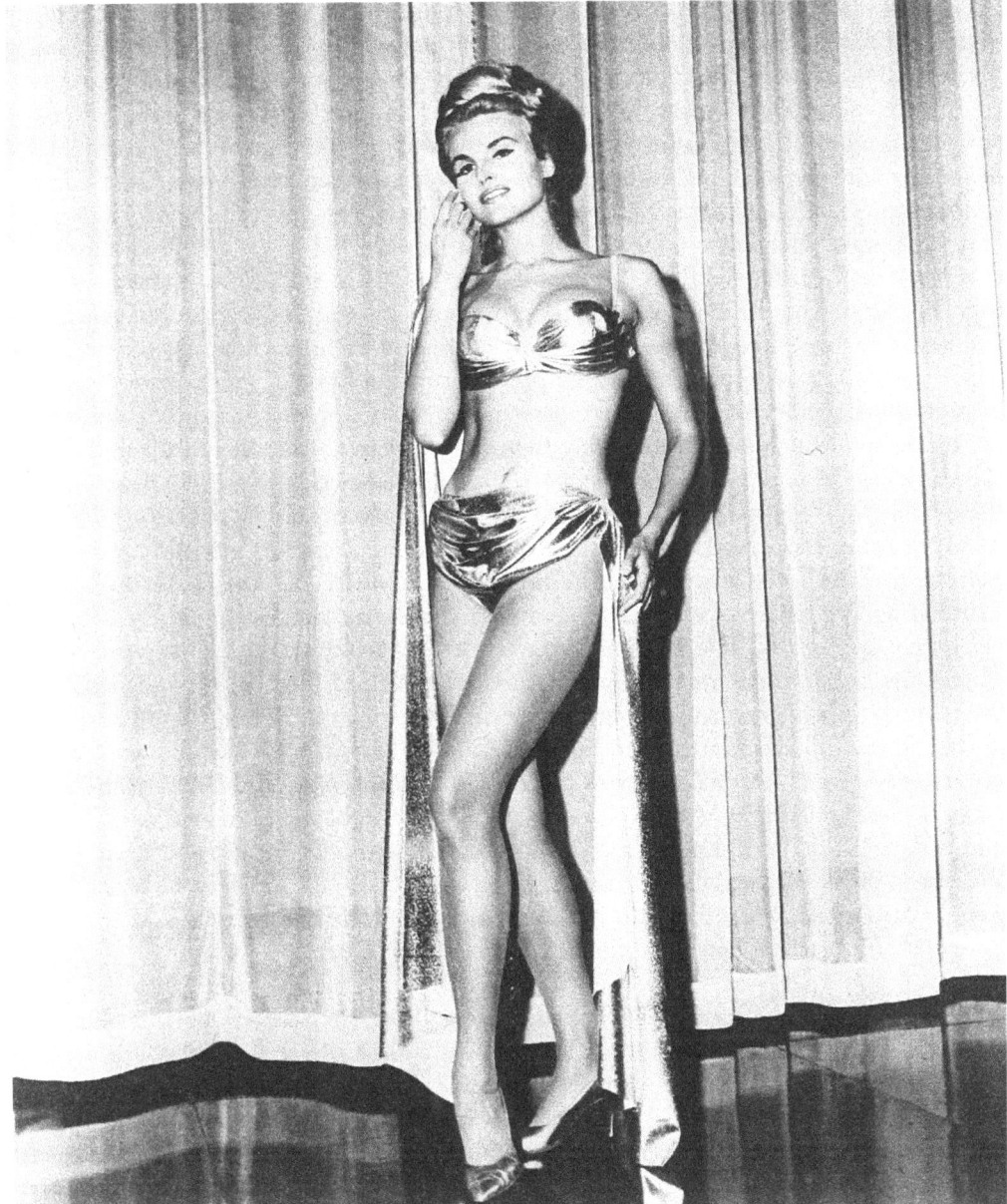

Inga Neilsen in costume from *The Silencers* (Columbia, 1966). *Courtesy of Inga Neilsen.*

**Her Groovy '60s Credits:** Inga Neilsen made her screen debut playing one of madam Shelley Winters' call girls in the trashy *A House Is Not a Home* (1964). Her next big screen role in *The Silencers* (1966) was due to a prior appearances on *The Dean Martin Show*. In this funny take-off on secret agents starring Martin as reluctant playboy–super-sleuth Matt Helm, the glamourous blonde literally redefined the meaning of statuesque with her role as a statue clad in a gold lamé bikini come to life with a showgirl walk in the film's elaborate nightclub act sequence. Inga gets a solo dance routine as she wiggles her way through the audience towards the stage, losing bits of her skimpy costume along the way.

Neilsen's years of dance training helped her to win the role of Gymnasia, the romantic interest for conniving slave Zero Mostel in *A Funny Thing Happened on the Way to the Forum* (1966). Trying to find his young master's true love among Phil Silvers' courtesans, enterprising slave Zero Mostel flips for Inga who is simply charming as the towering, voluptuous mute. The feeling is mutual and the beauty joins him in his zany plot to unite his master with the slave girl he covets who was sold to a Roman general. More Glamazon roles quickly followed for Neilsen in the spy spoofs *The Ambushers* (1967) as a man-flipping Slaygirl adorned in Oleg Cassini fashions and *In Like Flint* (1967) as a guard in cahoots with Jean Hale and the three top female leaders in the fashion industry to take over the world. This fabulous face is first distinguishable from the rest of the gals as the guard who uncovers Lee J. Cobb's disguise as a woman and throws him into the cell holding Andrew Duggan as the imprisoned president of the United States. Later Inga and Thordis Brandt lead the other girls in Operation Smooch: They distract the MPs patrolling the rocket silo launch area by emerging from the jungle with their hands up and waving their bras in surrender. When they approach the bemused guards, the slinky Amazons kiss them before overpowering the startled chaps with karate chops. *Funny Girl* (1968) featured Neilsen as the standout amongst the many stunning Ziegfeld Girls and the one chosen to open the lavish production number "His Love Makes You Beautiful" as the scintillating Winter Bride who "is typified with Christmas frost and fairies," catapulting her to gay icon status. The alluring Inga was the perfect choice to embody the part of Miss America in the parade scene in *Hello Dolly* (1969) and then spent most of the next few years on television amusingly playing the Amazonian dumb blonde foil to such comics as Arte Johnson, Dick Martin, and Jonathan Winters in numerous sketches on the variety series *Rowan & Martin's Laugh-In*, *The Carol Burnett Show*, *The Dean Martin Show*, and *The Jonathan Winters Show*. Neilsen also made guest appearances on episodic TV programs during this period playing a glamourous bank robber teamed with busty June Wilkinson in "Nora Clavicle and Her Ladies' Crime Club" on *Batman* and a sexy party guest on *Occasional Wife*. She also had co-starring roles in two failed TV pilots, *Holly Golightly* with Stefanie Powers in the title role and *Li'l Abner*.

**The Beginning:** Of Swedish and Polish descent, Inga Neilsen was born on July 1 in Chicago. At the age of seven she moved to Beverly Hills where she was raised by relatives. Sprouting quickly, the lanky child towered over her classmates and began taking voice and dance lessons at the American School of Dance in Hollywood. At age twelve, but passing for sixteen due to her height, she landed a part in *Scaramouche* (1952) and danced a minuet with the film's leading man, Stewart Granger. In high school, the versatile teen choreographed shows and sang in the school's choir. An injury sidelined her ballet aspirations so she began singing and dancing in Las Vegas revues at the Sahara Hotel, which led to a hugely successful solo tour of the Far East billed as Miss Chicago (she wasn't). Neilsen was a hit, especially in Tokyo where she literally stopped traffic on the street due to her stunning looks accentuated by her blonde hair and long lithe legs that just wouldn't quit. Returning to Vegas, Inga was once again employed at the Sahara as the featured singer working with comedian Shelley Berman. After performing with Ben Blue at the Desert Inn, she was selected to be *the* Ziegfeld Girl in *The Ziegfeld Follies* at the Thunderbird Hotel produced by Monte Prosser. She was with the revue for nine months. Wanting to stay close to her husband and family, Inga, a trained actress, gave up her successful singing career to act.

**The '70s & Beyond:** During the Seventies when nudity became the norm, Inga Neilsen refused to bare her bosom and saw the offers to work decline. On the big screen she turned up as a nurse in *Evel Knievel* (1971); one of Lynn Redgrave's ladies-in-waiting in Woody Allen's *Everything You Always Wanted to Know About Sex\* But Were Afraid to Ask* (1973), a murder victim in *Grave of the Vampire* (1974) starring William Smith as a heroic reluctant bloodsucker, and as a beautiful, bountiful nurse who clobbers Marty Feldman over the head with her medical bag in Mel Brooks' *Silent Movie* (1976). In between she was still being cast for decorative purposes as "beautiful woman" or "Swedish bombshell" on the TV shows *Banacek*, *Temperatures Rising*, *The Odd Couple*, and *The Invisible Man* before playing the ultimate Glamazon role of Wonder Woman's (Lynda Carter) friend and rival, Rena, in *The New, Original Wonder Woman* (1975). Though the perfect choice for the role, poor Inga is saddled with an unflattering red wig and outfitted in what looks like yellow Baby Doll pajamas. She is then defeated by Carter in a tournament to see which Amazon has the physical strength to reign supreme as Wonder Woman.

Still working in the Eighties and Nineties, Neilsen made two guest appearances on the Ted Knight sitcom *Too Close for Comfort* and continued acting in courtroom dramas and TV commercials. Prodded by her friends and husband, Inga returned to live performing in 1999 as the featured singer for three seasons in *The Fabulous Palm Springs Follies*. In 2003 she released her first CD, *Love Me with All Your Heart*. Performing with the Lee Lovett Quintet, the still beautiful Inga impressively belts out a variety of pop, blues and oldie standards in her rich and powerful low contralto voice. And she can also be seen briefly in a featurette about the making of *In Like Flint* on the special edition DVD set, released in 2007.

## *Inga Neilsen speaks out on...*

**Why she stopped singing:** Before I left on tour [of the Far East] I met a lifeguard named Richard Orr on Venice Beach and we were married before I journeyed east. I stopped touring when I became pregnant and had my son David. Wanting to remain close to home, I decided to concentrate on acting.

**Her height:** In the Sixties I was six feet tall and always wore three-inch heels. I loved being tall and I worked a lot because of my height. There weren't too many tall women who could dance and sing. Julie Newmar was one and I was often in competition with her for roles. My height has always been a plus for me. But it did have its drawbacks. They never wanted to put me with an actor that I was taller than. Often I didn't get those parts.

*A House Is Not a Home*: I had a speaking part in this and Raquel Welch was an extra. We shared a dressing room. I remember she wore a red dress in this. Whenever she would walk across the set she'd stop traffic. She had it even then. Raquel was very feisty and determined and told me that she was going to be a star by the time she was twenty-one. Edy Williams was very sexy and beautiful. She was extremely nice but a bit naïve. We stayed friendly after making the film and would call each other now and then but I lost touch with her.

*The Dean Martin Show*: This propelled me into feature films. I was always the comic foil. I would do little shticks of five or ten lines. When I first did the show I wore a bikini and they would write all over my body. This led me to the Matt Helm movies. Mel Frank saw me on the show and auditioned me for *A Funny Thing Happened on the Way to the Forum*.

Inga Neilsen poses as an Amazon guard plotting to take over the world in *In Like Flint* (20th Century–Fox, 1967).

**Dean Martin:** Dean was always so kind to me. In the way Hollywood used to be, every good-looking woman was hit on. I was propositioned by many men but never by Dean Martin. He was a quiet man and always a gentleman. I never saw him loaded either.

*The Silencers*: I had to wear a bikini in my scene. We rehearsed the scene for about ten days. On the day of the shoot, the director Phil Karlson told me that they wanted me to take off my top. There were about 200 extras in the audience. I think I must have turned scarlet red. I finally agreed to take it off only if they would tape up the front of my body. I didn't want to hold up production but it wasn't in my contract to do this. It worked out as I took off the bra and kept moving so all you saw was my bare back.

**Getting the role of Gymnasia in *A Funny Thing Happened on the Way to the Forum*:** My agent sent me to audition for the producer Mel Frank at the Beverly Hills Hotel. I remember thinking, "I never auditioned in a hotel room before. This is rather strange." I was dressed in a suit and went in to meet him. He said to me, "If you don't mind, I would like to see you without your suit on." I said, "I beg your pardon?" He replied, "In your underwear." I told him if he wanted to see me in a bathing suit, I would go home and come back again. That is what I did. He then wanted me to be a redhead and I told him no because I am naturally blonde. I was a bit feisty with him but I still got the part.

**Playing a mute:** I pat myself on the back for my talent but then I get hired because of what I looked like rather than what I really can do. That happened a lot to me where I was hired for a look only. They cast me because I am tall and could move well due to my dance training. It was a bit frustrating. Nicolas Roeg was the cinematographer on this. I remember him saying to me, "Inga, you don't have to open your mouth. Your face and smile say it all." It was a nice compliment.

I went on to play Gymnasia three times onstage. The last time was in 1993 with Avery Schreiber. I kept thinking, "How many years am I going to keep doing this?"

**Doing her own stunts in** *A Funny Thing Happened on the Way to the Forum*: It was a fun movie and I enjoyed making it. I did a lot of my stunt work. I fell out of the tree and I did all the stuff with the horses. They had two stunt doubles for me but one day the director Richard Lester came to me because he wanted my legs in the tree. He asked me, "Inga, do you mind climbing the tree? Your double does not have legs like you." I was so naïve, wanting to impress him, that I did the entire stunt—twice. I also crossed from one chariot to the other while one was pulled by horses and the other by camera car on a narrow road overlooking a cliff.

**Zero Mostel:** Zero was a very talented man but he had roaming hands. I loved working with him, though, and learned a lot. I sensed that there was competition between him and Phil Silvers as to how much film was spent on each of them.

*In Like Flint*: When you bring a group of girls together, everybody wants the lines. I was never assertive to push my way into something. The director liked me and gave me the lines, I think because of my audition and prior credits. I was friendly with all the girls because I never competed for lines. I know some of them did things to come in favor of the director. I didn't because I never felt it was necessary for me. James Coburn was a loner and really didn't mingle with the rest of us. Jean Hale is a sweetie. We lived in the same neighborhood and she was the type you could run into in the grocery store and stop to chat with.

*The Ambushers*: This was fun. I loved working with Jan Watson. Columbia sent us on a publicity tour all over Europe. It was first class all the way.

**Auditioning for** *Funny Girl*: I am a very down-to-earth person but when I was doing *A Funny Thing Happened on the Way to the Forum* in Spain I had my own apartment and each day I was chauffeured to the set where I had my own makeup person and wardrobe mistress. I felt like a star! When I came home, my agent told me that they were auditioning for *Funny Girl* and that it was a cattle call. I told him I didn't do cattle calls because I started to get a big head. He convinced me to go and there had to be close to 300 women auditioning. Every beautiful girl in Hollywood seemed to be there. I was interviewed by the choreographer, Herb Ross. He started pulling girls out of the line and when he narrowed it down he wanted to see how we could walk down a flight of stairs in high heels and a bikini. When it was my turn I heard him say, "Look at those legs." I think my legs got me the job and the fact that he had seen me in *Forum*.

**Barbra Streisand:** I love Barbra Streisand and think she is fantastic. She was always very friendly to me and suggested me to Gene Kelly for a part in *Hello Dolly*. On *Funny Girl* I don't think she had any say in casting or editing but if she didn't like the way a scene was lit, the next day they would re-shoot it. She was very fussy about her hair and makeup. One day I came into costume and my hair was done a certain way. She stared at my hair for the longest time across the room. The next thing I knew, my hair came down and her hairstyle became what I originally had. Nothing was said, of course.

In *Funny Girl* (Columbia, 1968) Inga Neilsen wowed the audience as the glamorous Winter Bride. Pictured (*left to right*) Virginia Ann Ford, Mary Jane Mangler, Bettina Brenna, Barbra Streisand, Neilsen, unidentified actress, Thordis Brandt, and unidentified actress. *Courtesy of Inga Neilsen.*

**The Winter Bride:** Herb Ross chose me to be the Winter Bride. I think he really liked me. Bettina Brenna and I were the tallest but she was a bigger-boned person than me. I think they liked my legs even though they used a close-up of my face when I recite the lines from the poem.

**The Other Brides:** I wasn't friendly with any of the girls except for Thordis Brandt and Mary Jane Mangler. I remember Alena Johnston was a beautiful, quiet girl who stayed pretty much to herself. I think she was the youngest of us. Bettina Brenna and I didn't know each other that well. Of the brides, I was the only one who was married. Most of them were jet setters. One gal was dating Tony Franciosa and another one was dating a judge. I really didn't get to know them as I came to work, did my job, and left.

**Typecasting:** I was always cast as the tall, dumb blonde sexpot wearing either short tight dresses or bikinis. I was making good money so I just went with it. After a while people thought I was really like the parts I played. On *The Carol Burnett Show* this AD [assistant director] always talked down to me like I was really dumb when he gave me direction. After that I appeared on *The Lohman and Barkley Show* where I made recurring appearances as a singer performing with an orchestra. This AD saw me so when I went back to the *Burnett* show a few weeks later he treated me very differently and said to me, "I didn't realize you had all this talent." It is a funny thing when people think you are a dumb blonde and you're really not.

**Carol Burnett**: Carol Burnett is the nicest woman in show business. She always remembered your name and would talk with you. After I did my first show with Carol she never had me audition again because she liked me. She would just tell the director Dave Powers to ask for me. I did many of her shows.

**Nudity in film:** Somewhere in the early Seventies when nudity became the norm, I started losing work because I refused to do it. I even turned down *Playboy*. When I did *Funny Girl* they chose a number of us to feature in a pictorial. I wouldn't sign the release and told them that if they wanted a picture of me that they could photograph me wearing a costume. They went on to shoot some other girls and parts of their clothing were removed and so on. I refused to do nudity because I was married and had a small child.

*Everything You Wanted to Know About Sex\* But Were Afraid to Ask*: I worked two days on this. Woody Allen was very distant and kept to himself. I didn't receive much direction from him.

*Funny Lady*: I was the only girl in *Funny Girl* asked back to do *Funny Lady* but most of my scenes were cut. Carole Wells and I were dressed identically in silver lamé gowns and we did a mirror image piece on one of the production numbers that never made it into the movie.

*Grave of the Vampire*: I did this only because I knew William Smith and thought he was the nicest guy. I was working less by this point and thought I would pick up some extra cash. It was done locally and I never got to see it but one Halloween my son came running in to me and said, "Mom, I just watched you die on television."

*Silent Movie*: Another actress had played my part of the nurse. I don't know who it was. They let her go because they weren't happy with her. They brought me in and what she did in a week I did in a day. Mel Brooks gave me no direction at all. He explained the scene and I don't know what possessed me but I started by hitting Marty Feldman over the head with my purse and Mel loved it. That worked real well. Marty was a funny man but during breaks he seemed to be nervous and chain-smoked.

**Juggling acting and a family:** My husband is a retired schoolteacher and we have been married for forty-five years. I guess you might say we have a storybook marriage. He allowed me to do what I wanted to do. The only thing he didn't like was when we were first married and I was touring the country. He told me I had to choose between the club gigs or being married. I let the music go and that is when I started doing television. He is very proud of me and I think he is proudest that, when I started to get less and less work, I started my music back.

**Resuming her singing career:** In 1997 I ran into an ex-showgirl friend of mine who asked me if I was still singing and I told her I hadn't sung in years. I went with her to an adult night class and sang a song. I was hooked again. I was the featured vocalist for three seasons in *The Fabulous Palm Springs Follies* from 1999 to 2002 and have performed in clubs throughout Southern California. My arranger on my CD called *Love Me with All Your Heart* is Lee Lovett who worked with Motown. I got very good feedback and am doing quite well. The CD is available on Amazon.com and is played on local radio stations in Southern California, Georgia, and Ohio.

# Alberta Nelson

The Eve Arden of the motorcycle set, this hazel-eyed blonde Glamazon never got her man as the rough-and-tumble, wisecracking biker chick in the Frankie and Annette beach movie extravaganzas. Adept at slapstick comedy, she alternated her film appearances playing sweet good girls on TV, most notably on *The Andy Griffith Show*.

**You May Remember Her Most From:** *Beach Blanket Bingo* (1965) as she and fellow biker chick Myrna Ross kidnap Linda Evans' singing sensation Sugar Cane, whom their leader thinks is nifty.

**Her Groovy '60s Credits:** Alberta Nelson began the decade with a Broadway flop: playing a servant in the 1961 play *Once There Was a Russian* co-starring Walter Matthau, Roger C. Carmel, and Julie Newmar, a drama which closed opening night. With nothing to lose, Nelson journeyed to Hollywood where she was cast in minor dramatic roles in episodes of *Thriller* and *The New Breed*. She played a doctor in "Love Is a Sad Song" on *Dr. Kildare* before Harvey Lembeck chose her to be his comic foil in *Beach Party* (1963). The first official beach movie starring Frankie and Annette, it combined the Malibu surfing scenes of *Gidget* with the beachgoing teenage vacationers of *Where the Boys Are*, added a number of songs and a hilariously bungling motorcycle gang, and started a whole new genre. Frankie, his girlfriend Dolores, and their friends share a beach shack during spring break where their main concerns are surfin', dancin', and romancin'. Their idyllic life is interrupted by Harvey Lembeck as the inept Eric Von Zipper and his motorcycle gang The Ratz and Mice who "hate those beach bums." Nelson and redheaded Linda Rogers were the Mice, the only two girls in the gang. Even early on in the beach party cycle it looks as if Nelson's character is resigned to the fact that Lembeck will never have eyes for her. Here he lusts after Annette but when she rebuffs him he turns to platinum blonde sexpot Eva Six. Despite always being passed over, Nelson is a good sport and joins the gang for the end-of-the-movie pie-throwing melee against the surfers. Her character began as the dependable yes-girl but as the bikers started to have more prominence in the films due to their popularity, Nelson delivered more wisecracks in her trademark screechy Brooklyn-style manner. In *Muscle Beach Party* (1964) the biker gang is replaced by a group of bodybuilders led by Don Rickles who tangle with the surfers over their beach turf. Alberta is the only biker from the first movie brought back. She and Amedee Chabot play fitness nuts who hang around the musclemen. Nelson hardly has any lines in this beach caper and is only there for decorative purposes.

Lembeck, Nelson, and crew became a fixture in the rest of the series as they were determined to drive those surf bums off the beach in *Bikini Beach* (1964), *Pajama Party* (1964), *Beach Blanket Bingo* (1965), and *How to Stuff a Wild Bikini* (1965). The only difference here was that in the latter two movies Linda Rogers was out and Myrna Ross was the new biker chick. Now called Puss (to Ross' "Boots"), Nelson had more of an opportunity to display her comedic talent as she and Ross kidnap Lembeck's latest crush, singer Linda Evans, in *Beach Blanket Bingo* and join Lembeck in two musical production numbers in *How to Stuff a Wild Bikini*. The service comedy *Sergeant Dead Head* (1965) featured Nelson as a WAC and in the spy spoof *Dr. Goldfoot and the Bikini Machine* (1965) starring Vincent Price in the title role, Alberta is the only robot not bikini-clad. Instead,

Biker chick Alberta Nelson looks on helplessly after her fearless leader Harvey Lembeck (*center*) as Eric Von Zipper gives himself "The Finger" once again in *Bikini Beach* (AIP, 1964) with Andy Romano (*at right*).

as the newly created No. 12, she emerges from the mad doctor's bikini machine dressed in black with a man's voice. She is immediately rejected by Price but not before this Glamazon beats the stuffing out of his assistant, Jack Mullaney. Her last appearance with Harvey Lembeck as befuddled bikers was in *The Ghost in the Invisible Bikini* (1966), which gave her the distinction of being the only actress to appear in all seven beach movies. In this one the ragtag motorcycle gang was out to steal a fortune hidden in a creepy old mansion where heirs Tommy Kirk and Deborah Walley have to survive the night to inherit the loot.

With the beach party movies dead at the box office, Nelson returned to television in 1966. Looking quite lovely despite the heavy eye makeup, Nelson played the concerned teacher of Dick Van Dyke's son (a nine year old who has been lecturing his classmates on where babies come from) in "Go Tell the Birds and the Bees" on *The Dick Van Dyke Show* and a former classmate of Don Knotts' Barney Fife who at their high school reunion meekly revealed that she had a crush on him in "The Return of Barney Fife" on *The Andy Griffith Show*. Impressed, the producers of the series brought Alberta back later in the year to play Flora Malherbe, a somewhat naïve, warm-hearted waitress sweet on George Lindsay's Goober. She played the role in three episodes and in "Emmett's Retirement" on *Mayberry, R.F.D.* in 1969.

**The Beginning:** Alberta Nelson was born on August 14, 1937, in Erie, Pennsylvania. After graduating from Andrews High School in Willoughby, Ohio, where her family was living at the time, she began studying nursing. The acting bug bit her when she returned to Pennsylvania and she landed the lead role in *The Seven Year Itch* at the Erie Playhouse. She then headed to New York to study acting. With a shapely 36-25-36 figure, she got some work as a model, which led to an appearance on *The Dave Garroway Show*. Small roles followed for her on Broadway including one line as a party girl in *The Gang's All Here* and various roles in *The Wall* in 1960. The later was set in Warsaw in the early 1940s and starred George C. Scott. It was a modest hit, running for 167 performances.

**The '70s & Beyond:** Alberta Nelson's final acting role was a real stretch and as far from her role in the series of beach party movies as you could get. She was cast as a psychiatrist who discusses case histories and how they relate to her domestic situation with Anita Eubank as her hippie daughter in *The Wild Scene* (1970). Unfortunately, this scene wasn't so wild and quickly sunk into obscurity. The following year Nelson married Herbert Gilman. It was her second marriage. She retired from show business and moved with her new husband to Millcreek, Pennsylvania. They had three children and Nelson spent her free time gardening and doing needlework until her death from cancer on April 29, 2006. She was sixty-eight years old.

# Warrene Ott

Extraordinarily beautiful with jet black hair, a distinctive name, and a hint of acting talent, she unfortunately came to Hollywood at a time when producers only cared how well a girl stuffed a wild bikini. She was never able to land that one role that would propel her to that next level in Hollywood so she floundered between minor decorative roles and supporting parts in low-budget movies, as blonde, redhead or brunette.

**You May Remember Her Most From:** the cult horror movie *The Witchmaker* (1969) as a witch who needs young women's blood to maintain her youth and beauty.

**Her Groovy '60s Credits:** Warrene Ott snagged a contract with Columbia Studios, who made the alluring brunette a blonde to play good girl Betty Cooper in the unsuccessful TV pilot *Archie* (based on the popular comic strip). She played bit roles on such TV series as *Bachelor Father*, *The Many Loves of Dobie Gillis*, and *Sky Riders* before making her film debut in *The Phantom Planet* (1961), a Grade-Z production about an astronaut (Dean Fredericks) who crashes on a planet where the inhabitants are only six inches tall. To save on special effects, he is shrunk to their size after passing through the planet's atmosphere. Ott has one line as a jury member who finds the Earthling guilty of assault. A more glamourous bit came her way next as one of the beautifully draped fashion models who pose for married photographer Bobby Darin in the comedy *If a Man Answers* (1962). Continuing with the glamour girl roles she played a beauty pageant contestant on the TV anthology series *Alcoa Premiere* ("Whatever Happened to Miss Illinois?") and a sexy senorita who accompanies Spanish playboy Tony Franciosa to a party where he flirts with tourist Pamela Tiffin in *The Pleasure Seekers* (1964). In between, Warrene is terrorized by a tiger set on her by crazed zookeeper Michael Gough in the low-budget *Black Zoo* (1963). Returning to television, Ott appeared in episodes of *Hawaiian Eye*, *Kentucky Jones*, *The Bill Dana Show*, and *Bewitched* as a sexy blonde secretary in "That Was My Wife." She returned to the big screen in two low-budget ventures. In *Rat Fink* (1965), she played the adulterous wife of a music agent involved in a torrid affair with rock singer Schulyer Hayden, who is clawing his way to the top. Their volatile relationship ends with a violent argument high up on a balcony where Hayden falls to his death after causing so much misery to everyone around him. The film's exploitative poster ad exclaimed, "A Rat Fink likes women, bars, and expensive cars. How do you describe a movie like this… You don't… You see it! *Even if we could… we wouldn't dare!*" More bizarre was the cannibalistic gore fest *The Undertaker and His Pals* (1966), which mixed laughs with lots of blood. Two bikers kill pretty young women and serve them up at their Greasy Spoon Café while their pal who owns a funeral parlor makes money off the families burying the remains. Top billed, Ott has a dual role as a kooky blonde sexpot named Friday and her more sophisticated sister Thursday. Friday sashays into the office of private detective Rad Fulton and lies down on his desk, offering him her typing skills. He sends her off to have lunch at the Greasy Spoon where she winds up on the dinner menu as the hamburger special; her twin sister soon comes looking for her missing sibling. Equally as amorous as her twin, Thursday gets miffed when the virile, studly gumshoe falls asleep on her. Later he abandons her on a deserted highway where she almost becomes lunch meat.

It was back to bit roles for Warrene in a brief vignette playing a wife who shoots her cheating husband dead "because he was a louse" in the comedy *A Guide for the Married Man* (1967). She then made her first of three appearances on *The Beverly Hillbillies* in "The Marriage Machine" followed by "Something for the Queen" in 1968 as a harried stewardess serving the London-bound Clampetts. Ott then journeyed to Iran to co-star in *The Invincible Six* (1968), a low-rent rip-off of *The Dirty Dozen*. She made headlines because her house was robbed of $250,000

**Warrene Ott (ca. 1965).**

worth of furs, cash, and jewelry in the hours between her farewell party and her trip to the Middle East. In the movie, Ott played the daughter of the chief of police in a village where Stuart Whitman and his gang of jewel thieves hide out. The ragtag group reluctantly comes to the town's aid when there are set upon by bandits searching for a treasure map supposedly hidden in the village by their fallen leader. Though Ott was well cast as the Persian beauty, she was overshadowed by the under-costumed Elke Sommer. In *Where's It At* (1969), she and Edy Williams played Las Vegas showgirls who work for casino owner David Janssen. Her last movie *The Witchmaker* (1969) took her to the swamps of Louisiana as a witchy hag transformed into a raving beauty by warlock John Considine, who needs to sacrifice thirteen women to obtain their blood to keep his love young and fresh.

**The Beginning:** Warrene Ott was born in Pittsburgh, Pennsylvania, on January 23, 1942. Her father was a Navy commander stationed at Pearl Harbor at the start of America's involvement in World War II and that is where his daughter's unusual name originated. After leaving the service, Ott relocated his family to Los Angeles where he and his wife operated a convalescent home. Talented Warrene could do it all and she danced with the Starlight Opera Company in San Diego, sang with the San Francisco Opera Company, did summer stock, and performed numerous times with the USO. During her later teen years, Warrene began landing minor TV roles.

**The '70s & Beyond:** Warrene Ott began the decade with her third and final appearance on *The Beverly Hillbillies* in "Farm in the Ocean," playing the sexy wife and secretary of doctor Richard Deacon in 1970. In February 1974, Ott married Angelo Robert Vitale in Las Vegas. After quitting show business, she worked as an immigration officer/specialist for the INS. She passed away on January 1, 1995, in Los Angeles. She was fifty-two years old.

# Beverly Powers

A bosomy brunette, this former stripper had identity issues throughout the Sixties—sometimes billed with her stage name of Miss Beverly Hills and sometimes with her real name of Beverly Powers. But whatever moniker she went under, you were assured to see lots of cleavage in her many roles that usually took advantage of her striptease prowess.

**You May Remember Her Most From:** the Elvis Presley hillbilly hoedown *Kissin' Cousins* (1965) as the leader of the Kitty Hawks, a gaggle of sexed-up Daisy Mae types out to trap themselves a man.

**Her Groovy '60s Credits:** Beverly Powers made her film debut as (what else?) a stripper in *Breakfast at Tiffany's* (1961). She then joined Pamela Curran playing victims of a notorious serial killer in "Yours Truly, Jack the Ripper" on *Thriller* in 1961. More bit roles followed in *Days of Wine and Roses* (1962) and the comedy *Critic's Choice* (1963) as one of the many girls squired by ladies man Rip Torn, who is directing Lucille Ball's play. A

Beverly Powers (*second from right*) as the leader of the man-chasing Kitty Hawks joins Elvis Presley (*far right*) for a hillbilly hootenanny in *Kissin' Cousins* (MGM, 1964).

bigger role came her way as an eager widow with cleavage galore in the hilarious horror spoof *The Comedy of Terrors* (1963) starring Vincent Price as a desperate funeral home director who murders wealthy gentlemen to drum up business for his failing establishment.

Powers next made her first of three appearances with Elvis Presley. *Kissin' Cousins* (1964) offered her the biggest role as the leader of the Kitty Hawks, man-chasing hillbilly maidens out to snare husbands. When G.I. Presley arrives at their mountain retreat with his fellow military men, the gals are in hog heaven. Every time she spots an eligible man, Powers lets loose with a sort of pig-call that tells the Kitty Hawks to come a-running. Their chasing pays off and Powers snags herself a general by the film's end. Beverly also turned up in Elvis' biggest hit *Viva Las Vegas* (1964) albeit in an unbilled role as a showgirl. She had a small dramatic role as the girlfriend of Robert Conrad's Pretty Boy Floyd in the violent *Young Dillinger* (1965) before being cast as yet another stripper in the Bob Hope comedy *I'll Take Sweden* (1965). As Electra, whose bosoms light up, she tries to make Hope part of her act when he accidentally wanders onto the stage searching for his wayward daughter Tuesday Weld and her boyfriend, Frankie Avalon. Two more minor unbilled roles came next—an "orgy dancer" who pops out of a coffin to entertain some military officers in *The Loved One* (1965) and a saloon hostess in the western

*The Last Challenge* (1967) starring Glenn Ford and Angie Dickinson. Beverly finally landed her first and only lead role in the grade Z Filipino production *Brides of Blood* (1968) starring John Ashley. She does well playing the acid-tongued busty blonde wife of scientist Kent Taylor. Dressed as if she was going to attend a tea party rather than an expedition, Beverly is almost raped by one of the local deck hands on board the steamer taking them to Blood Island but gives in to her passion. She flaunts her wanton ways in the face of her possibly impotent husband and is punished when in an act of lunacy she roams the jungle clad in a low-cut negligee looking to seduce the virile host Mario Montenegro. Her night of fun turns into a nightmare when he morphs into a mutant monster who rapes and then tears her into pieces.

Back in Hollywood, Powers was once again relegated to bit roles, playing a party girl in the science-fiction film *The Power* (1968) and a receptionist in *The Split* (1968). She reunited with Elvis Presley in *Speedway* (1968). Lucky Beverly gets to kiss both Bill Bixby and the King all in the film's first five minutes; the movie opens with a shot of Powers as "Miss Charlotte Speedway 100" smooching Bixby's amorous playboy, thinking he is race car driver Steve played by Elvis. Wearing a low-cut mini-dress to accentuate her positives, she is seen waving to the fans in the pace car at the start of the big race, which is won by Elvis. Naturally, she congratulates him by planting a big kiss on his lips. Powers ended the decade with supporting roles in the western *More Dead Than Alive* (1968) as a saloon girl who befriends reformed gunslinger Clint Walker and the comedy *Angel in My Pocket* (1969) as a befuddled burlesque queen who awkwardly auditions, stripping to church music being played on an organ by the oblivious Reverend Andy Griffith, who is looking to convince the theater manager to donate it to his church. In the latter two movies she was billed as Beverly Powers and used her real name throughout the rest of her career, which included making a number of appearances on *The Red Skelton Show* between 1968 and 1970.

**The Beginning:** Beverly Jean Powers was born in Southern California and graduated from Van Nuys High School. Powers is her married name as she wed Los Angeles tree surgeon William Powers at a young age. The brunette beauty with the tantalizing 37-24-34 figure then became a striptease artist using the name Miss Beverly Hills. Working mainly in Las Vegas, her act entailed dancing glamorously, dressed in showgirl-type gowns, and gradually removing her clothes until she is clad in a two-piece bikini; during the final minutes on stage, she doffs her top (she always had pasties on underneath). Becoming well-known, Powers was provocatively photographed for a number of men's magazines of the time including *The Dude* and *Knights* before giving acting a try.

**The '70s & Beyond:** Beverly Powers had a minor role in the underrated drama *J.W. Coop* (1972), directed by and starring Cliff Robertson as an ex-con who revives his rodeo career and hitchhikes from contest to contest accompanied by hippie Cristina Ferrare. Powers played a bigoted big-haired barmaid who won't serve Robertson's African-American friend. After making an unbilled cameo as her alter ego Miss Beverly Hills the stripper in the forgettable comedy *Get to Know Your Rabbit* (1972), Beverly met her second grisly on-screen death in *Invasion of the Bee Girls* (1973) where Earth women are being turned into queen bees who kill their lovers after mating. Powers is a bored housewife who, after morphing into a Bee girl, seduces her scientist husband, who strangles her during lovemaking when realizing what she has become. Her last movie credit was the low-budget *Sixteen* (1973) where she played a trashy exotic dancer at a carnival who seduces teenage John Lozier in an effort to get her hands on his family's newly gotten money. Beverly continued acting on television and, after guest starring in episodes of *McMillan and Wife* and *Fantasy Island*, called it quits in 1979. Today, they don't ask Beverly Powers to take it off any longer—she is a minister now. Based in Maui, she heads The Living Ministry, a non-denominational, non-profit ministry which she founded; "[Its] purpose is to spread God's Light and Kingdom to the far corners of the world through the services it offers to visitors and residents alike." In association with that, Powers also created A Wedding Just for Two, which funds the ministry from the income earned. As of 2006, she has performed over 1,600 weddings.

# Anne Randall

A sexy mini-skirted blonde in the mode of Alexandra Hay and Melodie Johnson, Playboy's Miss April 1967 descended on late Sixties movie audiences and epitomized the new breed of independent, free-spirited women.

**You May Remember Her Most From:** the classic sci-fi flick *Westworld* (1973) as a medieval wench who is the first robot to blow a fuse.

**Her Groovy '60s Credits:** Blossoming into a stunning blonde with a shapely figure (35-23-35) and a sweet girl-next-door persona, Anne Randall worked as a Playboy Bunny before becoming a Playboy Playmate as Miss May 1967 in a pictorial entitled "Queen Anne." She posed topless in two photos, including the centerfold, but most of the pictures featured her in clothes clowning around with her two brothers, playing ping-pong and shooting pool. Her Playmate profile was more down-to-earth than some. Her turn-on was "my boyfriend" and she listed "margaritas" as the one thing she'd sit still for. A minor role in "Everywhere a Sheik, Sheik" on *The Monkees* as a harem girl in 1967 led to her film debut in *The Fakers*. But the movie wasn't released until 1970 as *Hell's Bloody Devils* with newly shot footage of a biker gang thrown in to expand its marketability. Receiving "introducing" billing, Randall played an underage temptress and daughter of Kent Taylor, the leader of a neo–Nazi group involved in a counterfeit scheme. Not wanting to let down her many admirers from *Playboy*, Randall has a brief nude scene as she tries unsuccessfully to seduce undercover agent John Gabriel and then prances around the rest of the movie in very short mini-dresses. Minor roles followed: playing the girlfriend of Donald Sutherland in the caper flick *The Split* (1968) and a model in Jacques Demy's *The Model Shop* (1969). In the western *A Time for Dying* (1969) she was the new girl in town who marries ill-fated farmboy-turned-gunslinger Richard Lapp, who gets involved with the James Gang led by Frank James (Audie Murphy in his last movie appearance). Though Randall had too modern a look, she gave a spirited performance but it went unnoticed as the film had major distribution problems.

**The Beginning:** Anne Randall was born Barbara Burrus on September 23, 1944, in Alameda, California, of Irish, Yugoslavian, and Cherokee descent. At the age of fourteen she became a regular on *KPIX Dance Party*, a local teenage musical series in San Francisco hosted by Dick Stewart, whom she would later marry. She twisted, shimmied, and shook on the program from 1959 to 1961 while attending Loyal High School in the city's Haight Ashbury section. During this period she developed an interest in acting but didn't think to pursue it as a career until she enrolled in San Francisco City College to study drama. She also became reacquainted with Dick Stewart at this time; he was now divorced from his wife and the two began dating. When he relocated to Los Angeles, Randall followed.

**The '70s & Beyond:** Television kept Anne Randall busy with a guest appearance in "The King of Empty Cups" on *The Mod Squad* as a strung-out murderous hippie and in the TV movie *Banyon* (1971). Back on the big screen, *The Christian Licorice Store* (1971) featured Randall as "Texas Girl," a beauty queen who hooks up her curvaceous derriere to Beau Bridges as a hot-shot pro tennis player who becomes enmeshed in a decadent Hollywood lifestyle that ultimately corrupts him. The film was not a hit so it was back to the boob tube as Randall spent time on the daytime drama *Days of Our Lives* as fashion model Sheila Hammond (1971–1972) and then was one of the Hee-Haw Honeys on that hit hillbilly hoedown *Hee Haw* (1972–1973). Trying to capitalize on the notoriety these series brought her, she went the drive-in exploitation route playing lead roles in *The Doomsday Voyage* (1972) and *Stacey* (1973). The former, which sat on the shelf for two years, was a leisurely-paced action film that reunited Anne with John Gabriel playing a political assassin, on the run after murdering a corrupt politician, who stows away in NYU student Randall's cabin on a freighter captained by her father Joseph Cotten. With his daughter being held hostage, Cotten tries to abide by her abductor's wishes but the crew soon learns of the fugitive's presence and in a surprise ending Randall is gratuitously killed off with her corpse found in the cabin's shower. *Stacey*, directed by Andy Sidaris, was less serious and much more exploitative and fun as a lusty, busty Randall starred as "The Centerfold Private Eye," hired by a dying rich old woman to go undercover to find out which of her nutty family and staff deserve her fortune. Though the assignment keeps her busy, Randall still finds the time to hit the sheets with her amorous boyfriend and race her yellow Corvette. The film, a sort of white man's blaxploitation movie, with Randall filling in for Pam Grier, features nudity, incestuous sex, drugs, violence, and funky Seventies fashions. What more can you ask? Due to *Stacey*, Randall, posing seductively with a cigar in her mouth, became the cover girl for the November 1973 issue of *Playboy* touting the "Sex Stars of the Year," one of whom was Anne. In between drive-in fare, Randall turned up in a funny bit as a stewardess in Brian DePalma's absurdist comedy *Get to Know Your Rabbit* (1971) starring Tom Smothers as a tap-dancing magician and then as a policewoman who tries to stop persistent reporter Darren McGavin from barging into the office of the chief of police in the TV-movie *The Night Strangler* (1973). Anne's last theatrical feature was the sci-fi classic *Westworld* (1973) written and directed by Michael Crichton, where she played a sexy wench in the resort's Medieval World and the first robot to malfunction, striking guest Norman Bartold as a knight trying to seduce her. Trouble ensues when further electrical glitches send the robots on a murderous rampage. Randall rode out the remainder of the decade playing various type roles on television in *Love, American Style*; *Cannon*; *The Streets of San Francisco*; *Barnaby Jones*; *The Rockford Files*; and *Switch*. Her last credit was doing a voice over in *J-Men Forever* (1979), a spoof of superhero movies featuring clips from old serials spliced together and over-dubbed. With the acting roles coming fewer and farther between, Randall became an entrepreneur and concentrated on TV commercial work. In the early Nineties, Anne and her husband relocated to Sun City, Arizona, where she now spends her time as a community activist. *Playboy* did an update on Anne in their monthly

**Anne Randall as a sexy robotic wench in *Westworld* (MGM, 1973).**

feature "Playmate Revisited" in the June 1998 issue though she did not pose for any new semi-nude photographs. Anne Randall and her husband have remained friendly with Hugh Hefner to this day and are often guests at the Playboy Mansion.

## *Anne Randall speaks out on...*

*Playboy*: After I moved to Los Angeles I got a job as a Bunny at the Playboy Club, which I thought was fun. It was at this time when they approached me to be a Playmate.

I thought it might be good publicity. While doing a play, I invited agents from William Morris to come see me right at the time my *Playboy* issue came out. They were interested in representing me because I was in the magazine.

The nudity they showed in *Playboy* at the time didn't bother me. If it was like today, I do not think I would have done it. I only exposed my breasts and nothing too suggestive. Out of eight pages including the centerfold, there were only two semi-nudes of me. I never did any publicity for *Playboy* because I just signed to be in the magazine and did not sign a promotional contract. I immediately began working as an actress and didn't have the time (or the interest) to do this. For me, being a Playmate was a character job—I considered myself a character actress. I liked *Playboy* because it was the girl-next-door. But let me tell you, some of these guys just don't forget you ever—*ever*!

**Hugh Hefner:** He is one of my and my husband's closest friends to this day. Though we live in Arizona now, we go back about every six weeks to LA and spend time at the Playboy Mansion. Hefner has been extremely generous to us and I am close friends with Kimberly Hefner. We are like family there. He is just terrific and I have nothing but wonderful things to say about him.

**Typecasting:** In the movies, they were asking me to do more than I wanted to do. Nudity is fine but they pushed for more. I *am* the girl next door—I really am. Playing the sexpot for me was character acting. As an actress I made myself into whatever they wanted for the part. I was competing with other actresses for roles.

**Why she loved to act:** On *The Mod Squad* you wouldn't even recognize me. I played a drugged-out hippie killer. When I auditioned for this, they liked my reading but said I looked too much like Peggy Lipton. I suggested that I could do it with no makeup and my hair in an Afro. They agreed and that is how I dressed the part. This was one of my favorite roles because I enjoyed doing it. It was a fun part to play. Acting gives you the opportunity to do things that you would never do in real life. In character I smashed a cream puff in this woman's face and called her a fat pig. That is something I would never do in real life. It would be horrible. After we did the scene, the actress, instead of wanting to beat me up, came over to me and said, "Great job!" That

Anne Randall, *Playboy*'s Miss May 1967. *Courtesy of Anne Randall.*

is what I liked about acting—it is all make-believe. You can do really rotten things and nothing happens to you.

*Hell's Bloody Devils*: This was one of my first movies and I was really grateful to get the job. Al Adamson was really nice to me and very decent. I liked working with John Gabriel. He was a wonderful person. I was very friendly with his wife too. I had a very brief nude scene in this. I was never raised to believe that my body was shameful so it didn't bother me.

**Being a working married actress:** I was married throughout the whole time I was an actress, which I am glad for. I didn't have to go from relationship to relationship on movie to movie. You see that a lot. I never did that and am still married to the same man [since 1967].

*The Model Shop*: This was wonderful and one of my favorite memories! Jacques Demy [the director] was a very nice man and easy to work with. I worked with Gary Lockwood and found him to be very professional. By that, I mean, he didn't hit on me. I didn't get to know him and I really can't remember any kind of exchange with him.

**Sharon Tate:** I remember hanging out on the set with an unknown actress who was visiting Jacques Demy and his wife. I thought she was absolutely stunning and a sweet person. She had a beautiful face and a great body—very tan with smooth skin. She was wearing a flimsy mini-sundress and sandals with bare legs and no bra. I thought, "She's going to be a huge sex symbol!" Her name was Sharon Tate. Sharon was there all day and we got to know each other. She was *so* nice and *so* beautiful.

*Rosemary's Baby*: I did a screen test to become a contract player at Paramount Pictures. (I didn't get one since they discontinued the contract player system after this period.) The director was Roman Polanski. He was auditioning actors for the male lead in *Rosemary's Baby*. They tested actresses by having them play Mia Farrow's part, killing two birds with one stone. The studio wanted me to be "beautiful" with a "great body." So, that's how I was costumed. However, the scene we did was the one where Mia Farrow was about to have the Devil's baby, when she had dark circles under her eyes and a major pain in her huge, about-to-give-birth belly. It must've been an extreme disadvantage for the actor working with me to suspend belief when he was instructed to "feel the baby kicking" on totally hard-body abs and deliver lines like, "You don't look so good." When I was doing the scene, I feared I was coming across as suffering from a gas attack! This test could've been used in a Pepto Bismol commercial! The actor I performed with was Roger Smith, who had just married Ann-Margret. I hung out with the other contenders—Burt Reynolds and the one who got the role, John Cassavetes. They all treated me very well.

Afterwards, Roman Polanksi invited my husband and me to a party he was throwing at his beach house. I got to see Sharon Tate once again. She remembered me from *The Model Shop* and was just so gracious to us. It was not too long after she was murdered along with my husband's barber, Jay Sebring. I still remember where I was when I heard the news. I cried as if I lost my best friend and I only met her twice, that's how endearing she was.

**The film business:** At the time I became an actress, I was naïve about the whole thing. I thought if you were in a movie, then you would be discovered. You'd become a star and every single movie you did would be perfect. I had no idea you could make a movie and nobody would ever see it or it would never be released or it be terrible and you'd look like a fool. I was extremely young and innocent and just didn't know.

*A Time for Dying*: This starred Audie Murphy and was directed by Budd Boetticher. It is one of the few movies of mine available on DVD. I thought it was a nice little movie. But Richard Lapp [the leading man] and I didn't get along very well. He gave me a little bit of advice, which I thought was "interesting." He said, "If you want a lot of close-ups, then blow your lines in the two-shots and long shots. Then they have to use your close-up." Another tip he gave me was, "Make faces in the long shots and everybody will look at you." He did that and if you look at his face he looks like an idiot. Needless to say, I didn't follow his guidance.

**Audie Murphy:** He died in a plane crash—I had a very pleasant experience working with him. He played Jesse James and I thought he gave a great performance. I had a manager at the time who years later went to one of these western conventions and the door prize question was "Who was the last leading lady in an Audie Murphy western?" It was me and he was the only person who knew it and won a TV.

**Why *A Time for Dying* wasn't a hit:** Budd Boetticher was always one to do favors for people. He hired somebody to be the script girl who was the daughter of a friend of his that just died. She didn't take notes very well and after filming was completed, it turned out the movie was too short. Per Budd, it was too difficult to get more money to shoot more scenes to extend the running time so they had difficulty distributing it because of the length [67 minutes].

***The Christian Licorice Store*:** This was directed by James Frawley and starred Beau Bridges. I played a Texas beauty queen and we had a nude scene on a trampoline in this but I don't remember how much you see because it was at night. Beau was great and very professional. Jim Frawley was not great to work with. I had to bring my husband onto the set because Jim got a little mean with me. I never wanted to work with him again. Now I probably would work with him because he wouldn't be interested in me now!

***Days of Our Lives*:** Working on a soap opera was interesting for me because of the way they shoot it—like a stage play. It was much more exciting than moviemaking and you get some rehearsal, which was nice too. But as for the acting part of it, I didn't like doing it because there was a lot of nothing happening—just talking. I left because if remember correctly—I also worked on *General Hospital*—I got fired. In those days I wore a fall because I had short hair. They wanted me to take the fall off but I couldn't because I had had my hair bleached and it was all broken. They then sent me a script for the next show and I started to memorize the lines when I got a phone call telling me I wasn't in it.

***Hee Haw*:** This was a great experience for me. It's the only show I did that impressed my daddy who was born in Oklahoma and loved *Hee Haw*. When I was introduced from the stage of the Grand Ole Opry as a *Hee Haw* cast member, I didn't realize what it meant at the time. But, my daddy did. I was cast [in the show] by director Bill Davis. I worked one season with him and found it to be creative and fun.

**Being fired from *Hee Haw*:** When I showed up for the second season, I discovered that Bill Davis had moved on. His replacement abused me on the set and made me cry, causing me to run out, humiliated. This abusive director called a meeting at the end of the day's shoot. We talked it out and he told me he had thought I was "stuck up." He told me he was the lighting man from the previous season and I never looked at him or said hi. I explained that I didn't look at anyone or say hi because I was legally blind (20–650!) and couldn't wear my "jar-bottom" glasses or contact lenses while working. Unless I talked to someone up close, I never saw them at all. I thought we made up, but I noticed I was placed on the periphery of the group and given less to do. Then, I heard his wife, whom I never met, didn't like me. While in Hawaii on vacation, I got a call from my agent that I had been canned. My daddy never watched that show again after that. That's down-home country loyalty for you.

**Her *Hee-Haw* co-stars, Marianne Gordon and Barbie Benton:** For about a year or so, I was close to cast member Marianne Gordon, who was married at the time [eventually divorcing to become Mrs. Kenny Rogers]. Marianne was frequently depressed. I had to cheer her up all the time, which was fine with me. However, when the tables turned, I naively expected she would reciprocate in kind. It didn't happen. Instead, when I was crying over the director's abuse, Marianne said, "Anne, yer depressin' me! Yer my friend because you make me *laugh*!" When we got back to LA, we went to lunch and Marianne was unusually cheery. I said, "Marianne, why are you so happy?" She said, "Because I heard they're firing someone from *Hee Haw*." I asked, "Why would that make you happy?" She said, "At first, it didn't because I didn't want it to be *me*. But, then, I realized it wasn't goin' to be *me* gettin' fired; it was goin' to be *yew*!"

Barbi Benton [Hugh Hefner's live-in girlfriend at the time] and I sang duets on the show. Our collaboration resulted in my husband and me getting invited to the Playboy Mansion where we are part of the Hefner Family to this day. During a passing conversation at the mansion, Barbi asked me why I thought I got fired. Not wanting to unload on her and risk "depressin' her" like I did Marianne, I merely said I didn't know. She said, "I know! How much fan mail did you get?" She was good at jabs like that. I came back with, "I'm glad I was the one who got fired because I can get other work."

***Stacey*:** At the time I was still friends with Marianne Gordon whose husband was friends with director Andy Sidaris. They were planning to do *Stacey* and Marianne got me an interview. That is how I got the part. Andy was really a character and would swear on the set. He'd tell me, "This is going to be the best fuckin' movie you are ever going to be in."

**Her *Stacey* co-stars:** I didn't have much to do with Anitra Ford but I guess she was okay. We didn't become friends. My memory about Christina Raines was that she held up production. She didn't show up on the set and claimed to be sick but she really went to a rock concert.

I wasn't real thrilled with *Stacey*. It was silly and I looked real stupid in it. After the movie, I got an audition for *Charlie's Angels* because of the description of *Stacey*—I don't think they actually saw the movie. I went in for the audition and read the scene and saw that it was me wrestling an alligator. I got up and left without auditioning. I thought, "I am not going to wrestle an alligator!" I think they picked the right girls and don't think I would have gotten it anyway.

**Pitfalls of Hollywood:** Getting wed at age 22 was the best thing I ever did. As a married woman, I avoided the many pitfalls of show business. I had a protector. As a young "bimbo," being pursued by casting directors, film directors, and producers is part of the business. They were less likely to attempt it with a husband around. However, I *still* got molested by them. But at least I didn't get involved in fake romances—dealing with the disappointment of getting repeatedly dumped like they do to young women in Hollywood. "They use women like Kleenex." That was a line they gave me on the TV show *Divorce Court*! It's funny what the brain retains.

***Westworld*:** It is one of the few movies I made that when watching it I thought, "I like this movie." I was surprised how popular it became. It was the only movie that I was in that became such a smash at the box office. Michael Crichton, who wrote and directed this, was absolutely brilliant. I loved and admired him. For my part they were looking for a girl to be sexy. That was it. I wore sexy clothes and my hair long to try out for it. I didn't have to read for Michael because all he did was talk with me. And I got picked for the part. I understand that is how he cast people because he figured if you already have gotten work, you would not freeze on the set and should be easy to direct. I just had a wonderful experience working with him. I didn't work with any of the stars because my character worked in Medieval World. My scenes were with character actor Norman Bartold who was a really nice guy.

**Steve Martin:** After I got fired [from *Hee Haw*], I guess Bill Davis felt sorry for me because he hired me as a Dolly Parton look-alike backup singer for a comedy sketch on *Cher*. It was fun dressing up like her! Steve Martin was the guest star. I didn't know who Steve Martin was at the time. He hadn't done, "Well, excuuuuz meeee!" yet. Instead, he did the bit, "I'm glad to be here." He'd move to another spot and say, "I'm glad to be *here*." Then move, again, "I'm glad to be *here*." He was darling and very professional.

**Why she stopped acting:** As I got older I started to realize that I just wanted to do commercials and not do anything else. I left my theatrical agent and it was very difficult to get another agent though I tried. I really didn't care at this point anyway. I did keep my TV commercial agent and kept working for years. But at some point you reach the age where you are too old for Taco Bell and too young for Polident. When I was at this juncture in my career, one morning I was looking outside my window and watched people going to work and I thought, "I'm going to give that a try and see what is out there for me." I went to a temp agency and began working at $5.00 an hour. I learned to use a computer and then started to work as a legal secretary. I eventually had my own clientele of people who I worked for and could work whenever I wanted to. Then my husband wanted to retire and the last commercial I got was an industrial promo film for Sun City West [in Arizona]. We went out there and put money down on a nice modest condo right on the golf course in Sun City.

**Her life today:** Five years after moving to Sun City I started having problems with the Home Owners Association. I then discovered these inequities in HOAs all over the country and I have become an activist. Now I am working to change legislation and in the last four years we've made some major changes. In retaliation, I've been barred [by Sun City's HOA] from using the recreation center and all its activities, and kicked out of meetings. They have filed false charges against me in order to keep me from overseeing what they are doing. Prior to moving to Sun City I was neither political nor an activist—never thought of it in my life. It does not come easy to me and is very scary. I am standing up against very powerful people. I have not beaten them yet. But I have about 3,000 people on my list backing me. A lot of people though are afraid to stand up to them because these people have the power to bar you from using the swimming pool, for instance. It is amazing to me that people will give up their freedom because they don't want to give up swimming or playing golf!

# Jacki Ray

Arguably one of the most beautiful girls to appear in a Sixties spy movie—a sort of Barbie doll come to life—she was a highly successful model with a handful of credits but chose modeling over acting before becoming Mrs. Tom Selleck.

James Coburn as agent Derek Flint contemplates his next move in *In Like Flint* (20th Century–Fox, 1967) with (*left to right*) Mary Michael, Jacki Ray, Diane Bond, Inga Neilsen, Kay Farrington, and Jean Hale.

**You May Remember Her Most From:** *In Like Flint* (1967) as one of a trio of bikini-clad beauties who decorate super agent Derek Flint's penthouse before they are tricked into vacationing on an island paradise being used as a front by a group of Amazonian women planning to take over the world.

**Her Groovy '60s Credits:** Jacki Ray was an extremely successful model so it is no surprise Hollywood came a-calling. Unfortunately it was for a part in Walt Disney's forgettable *The Gnome-Mobile* (1967) starring Walter Brennan and the two children from *Mary Poppins*. In a minor role without any lines, Ray played Poppy, a gnome maiden who vies with other young lovelies for the attention of Tom Lowell's strapping gnome named Jasper. The wood nymphs clad in their Daisy Mae–type outfits then chase the poor fellow through the forest, desperate to catch him in a ritual similar to Dogpatch's Sadie Hawkins Day. Much better was the role of Denise in the hit spy spoof *In Like Flint* (1967) starring James Coburn as suave secret agent Derek Flint. Less subservient then the original Flint girls from *Our Man Flint*, the *In Like Flint* girls still assist the suave secret agent but are tricked into accepting a tropical vacation at Fabulous Faces Spa where Ray then spends the remainder of the movie clad only in a bikini. When the Amazons discover that their brainwashing technique is not working on Ray and the other girls, they freeze them in the Cryogenic Lab. After they are rescued by Coburn, the girls join up with the Amazons to defeat the evil president and his men who betrayed their cause. Ray didn't capitalize on the success of *In Like Flint* and instead devoted her energy to modeling. Her face adorned numerous magazine covers including *Pageant*.

**The Beginning:** A native of Burbank, California, the slender 5-foot-5 blonde of German, Irish, and Welsh descent was born in 1945. Blossoming into a stunning young adolescent, she began modeling at age fifteen. While attending Valley College majoring in Theatre Arts, she was elected Homecoming Queen in 1964. Possessing a highly enticing look that combined all–American sweetness with a hit of sexiness on top of a curvaceous 35-23-34 figure, Ray's face became familiar to TV audiences as she began appearing in ads hawking beer, suntan oil, soda pop, and skimpy bikinis.

**The '70s & Beyond:** In 1970 Jacki Ray married a struggling young rugged actor named Tom Selleck. In 1973 she turned up briefly in the family comedy *Frazier the Sensuous Lion* (1973) starring Michael Callan as a lonely college professor who befriends a talking lion and on TV she was in "The Endless Moment" on *Marcus Welby, M.D.* as a fashion model. After the birth of her son Kevin Selleck, Ray stopped working to raise him. In 1980, Tom Selleck hit it big playing Hawaii-based private eye Thomas Magnum in the hit series *Magnum, P.I.* Soon after, Ray resumed her acting career and, now billed as Jacquelyn Ray, snagged film roles in two obscure sci-fi films. *The Killings at Outpost Zeta* (1980) was a cheap rip-off of *Alien*, with Ray as part of a space crew sent to explore the mysterious goings-on at an outpost inhabited by blood-devouring rocks. In *Beyond the Universe* (1981) she played a duplicitous nurse caught between good and evil factions trying to save the dying Earth. On TV, she made two guest appearances on *Magnum, P.I.* In "J. 'Digger' Doyle" she was a rifle-toting bad girl who kidnaps John Hillerman and injects him with truth serum to learn where his billionaire employer is hiding his latest manuscript. In "Birdman of Budapest," billed as Jacquelyn Selleck, she played the icy secretary of a deadbeat condo builder who owes Magnum $800 for services rendered. She also turned up in episodes of *Dallas* and *Mickey Spillane, Private Eye*. The Sellecks divorced in 1982 and Jacki Ray disappeared from the Hollywood scene.

# Dolly Read

A buxom, blue-eyed, auburn-haired knockout, she gained fame for her nude appearances in *Playboy* and on film but was best known to TV audiences as a frequent game show celebrity and wife of comedian Dick Martin.

**You May Remember Her Most From:** *Beyond the Valley of the Dolls* (1970) as the groovy lead singer of the Carrie Nations who is briefly led astray by a debauched Hollywood crowd.

**Her Groovy '60s Credits:** Under her real name of Margaret Read, Dolly made a brief appearance in Hammer Films' classic fright fest, *The Kiss of the Vampire* (1963).

Dolly Read (*left*) in a publicity photo for *Beyond the Valley of the Dolls* (20th Century–Fox, 1970) with (*clockwise from top*) Marcia McBroom, Cynthia Myers, and Erica Gavin. *Billy Rose Theatre Division, The New York Public Library for the Performing Arts, Astor, Lenox and Tilden Foundations*

In this atmospheric vampire tale set in the early 19th century, she played one of the many disciples of Bavarian vampire Noel Willman, who abducted newlywed Jennifer Daniel as she and her husband passed through a creepy village. Clad in white, Read and her fellow bloodsuckers meet a grisly end at the mouths of bloodthirsty vampire bats at the film's climax. Read returned to modeling and then became one of the original Playboy Bunnies at the London Playboy Club. While training to be a Bunny at the Chicago mansion, Read consented to become a *Playboy* centerfold as Miss May 1966. Read had a curvaceous (37-24-37) body built for the pages of the magazine. Her turnoff was "getting up in the morning" and her perfect meal was "Chinese food and coffee." Becoming a favorite of *Playboy*'s readers, Read began working at the Chicago and New York Playboy Clubs.

On the big screen she was seen briefly as herself in *Tonite Let's All Make Love in London* (1967), a documentary on the swinging British scene notable for its film footage of Pink Floyd. Read's first real acting role was that of a sexy maid who tries to seduce the older Bee Tompkins who only has eyes for her ex-lover Sue Bernard (now married to a man) in the lesbian drama *That Tender Touch* (1969). That same year, director Russ Meyer was casting for his first major theatrical film, *Beyond the Valley of the Dolls* (1970), written by Roger Ebert. Though British, Read had an innocent fresh-faced quality that snagged her the role of Kelly MacNamara, the all-American girl leader of a rock trio (re-named The Carrie Nations) who travel across country to decadent Hollywood where they experience fame, fortune, and heartache. Success goes straight to Kelly's pretty head as she dumps her loyal high school sweetheart, falls in with the pot-smoking Hollywood in-crowd, and begins a romance with actor-gigolo Michael Blodgett, who cajoles her to go after a bigger share of her inheritance held by rich Aunt Phyllis Davis. Kewpie-face Read projected a sincere naivety with her performance as she spirals down into the valley of the dolls but comes to her senses before it is too late. She also convincingly lip-synched all her songs including "Come with the Gentle People" (which were actually sung by Lynn Carey) and bared her breasts a number of times. The film aimed to be "a satire, a serious melodrama, a rock musical, a comedy, a violent exploitation picture, a skin flick, and a moralistic expose." Meyer expertly directed Read and her castmates to treat it as a serious drama and not a comedy, knowing full well he was aiming for camp, which he achieved. To help promote the film, Read did a cameo on *Rowan and Martin's Laugh-In* and posed again semi-nude for *Playboy* in July 1970 in a pictorial entitled "The Dolls of *Beyond the Valley*." Though *Beyond the Valley of the Dolls* turned a profit, most critics dismissed it at as garbage at the time of its release. It is now considered a cult camp psychedelic classic from the period.

**The Beginning:** Dolly Read was born Margaret Read on September 13, 1944, in Bristol, England. Her father was an engineer and her mother a housewife. She began modeling at a young age and when she progressed into adulthood she posed for pinups.

**The '70s & Beyond:** After her success in *Beyond the Valley of the Dolls*, Read should have gone on to a successful career in movies or at least women-in-prison exploitation films but instead she married comedian Dick Martin of *Laugh-In* fame in 1971 and put her career on hold. She became a staple of daytime television, making frequent guest appearances on the game shows *Match Game* and *Tattletales*. The Martins divorced in 1975 only to remarry three years later. Read tried to resuscitate her career in 1978 using the name Dolly Martin and turned up on episodes of *Charlie's Angels*, *Vega$*, and *Fantasy Island*. She gave up acting in the early Eighties and today resides with her husband in Malibu. In 1997, Read once again undraped for *Playboy* in its "Playmate Revisited" section in the April issue. Three years later she placed 79th in *Playboy*'s pool of the 100 Centerfolds of the Century. In 2006, Read offered commentary and appeared in a few featurettes on the deluxe box DVD set of *Beyond the Valley of the Dolls*.

# Jeannine Riley

A busty, brown-eyed blonde who resembled a cross between Carol Wayne and Deanna Lund, she usually was cast as the naïve hillbilly or slutty country girl on television and the big screen.

**You May Remember Her Most From:** TV's *Petticoat Junction* as the rural comedy hit's first Billie Jo from 1963 to 1965 or from TV's cornpone *Hee Haw* as the first in a long line of Hee Haw Honeys.

**Her Groovy '60s Credits:** After graduating from the Pasadena Playhouse where she studied all aspects of performing, the buxom 5-foot-6, 38-23-35 Jeannine Riley landed a contract at MGM. They were grooming her to be another Marilyn Monroe but Riley never even came close to being a Mamie Van Doren as the best the studio offered her were guest parts playing nurses on *Dr. Kildare* and the sitcom *Father of the Bride*. After her option was not renewed, Riley made her film debut in a bit role as "the girl" in *Five Finger Exercise* (1962). This was followed by supporting TV roles on *Route 66* as a conventioneer in "Lizard's Leg and Owlet's Wing" and *My Three Sons* as a coed vying to become the campus beauty queen in "The Beauty Contest" before she copped a lead role in the exciting B-movie *Strike Me Deadly* (1963), directed by Ted V. Mikels. She played the wife of park ranger Gary Clarke who witnesses a murder. When the killer proceeds to burn the body, he unintentionally starts a forest fire and pursues the fleeing couple through the deadly inferno.

Riley's wonderful screen presence could have led to more movie roles but she opted to play Billie Jo Bradley in a new series called *Petticoat Junction* from the creators of the hit sitcom *The Beverly Hillbillies*. The oldest of the Bradley sisters, Riley's Billie Jo was more worldly and a man chaser as she had left home for the big city to launch her singing career and recently returned. The show made good use of Riley's comedic and singing talents as the three sisters even appeared on *The Ed Sullivan Show* as the fictitious group The Ladybugs (the female counterparts to The Beatles). Riley left the popular show after two seasons to work in movies. In the press she was very outspoken, announcing she felt the series was holding her back and she desired to become an Academy Award–winning actress. Instead, she was one in a long line of actors who departed popular TV shows to see their careers stall. With no film offers, Riley returned to television and completely erased her good girl image in "The Many Colors of Courage" on *Convoy* where she was seen in a slinky negligee drinking a glass of Scotch. Additional sexy roles followed on *Occasional Wife*, *The Wild Wild West*, and two episodes of *The Man from U.N.C.L.E.* In the latter she played a bikini-clad spokesmodel for Spy Guy Lotion for Men, which is inscribed on her stomach, who gets tangled up with U.N.C.L.E. agents when they discover her roommate was actually one of an army of shapely robots in "The Sort-of-Do-It-Yourself Affair" and a hillbilly girl who finds a cache of exploding apples created by enemy THRUSH agents in "The Apple a Day Affair." In 1967, she starred in two failed TV pilots, *Li'l Abner* as Daisy Mae and *Sheriff Who* as a schoolmarm. Thinking her acting career was kaput she returned to her hometown of Fresno and opened a very successful dress shop called The Gunny Sack with her mother. Jerry Lewis lured her back to Hollywood for a co-starring role in *The Big Mouth* (1967). She played the shapely Bambi

**Jeannine Riley leaves her *Petticoat Junction* days far behind her as a busty barmaid in *Electra Glide in Blue* (United Artists, 1973).**

Berman, a hotel social director in league with a gang of jewel thieves who tries to work her feminine wiles on schnook Lewis to find the missing diamonds. In her next movie Riley was out of her depth playing a widow who runs her late husband's garage and falls head-over-heels in love with reckless stock car driver Nick Adams in the low-budget *Fever Heat* (1968). Not well-received, the movie went out on the bottom of a triple bill with *Red Line 7000* and *Fireball 500*. Jeannine redeemed herself and gave an amusing performance in the underrated comedy-drama *The Comic* (1969) as a bubble gum-chewing dumb blonde with dreams of movie stardom who is forced by her ambitious stage mother to marry retired silent film star Dick Van Dyke. Again, Riley stalled her movie career when she agreed to co-star in a new variety series called *Hee-Haw* in 1969. The chance to sing and dance was the selling point for her in this hillbilly rip-off of *Rowan & Martin's Laugh-In*.

**The Beginning:** Jeannine Riley was born on October 1, 1940, in Fresno, California. Her father was in the army and six-year-old Jeannine would entertain the troops on the base, singing and dancing. The family moved to Madera, California, located in the farm belt of the San Joaquin Valley, after her father left the service. While attending high school where she performed in all the school plays, she was also a champion swimmer, drum majorette, cheerleader, and Blossom Day Queen. All the attention led the pretty blonde to a regular role on a local TV show in Fresno and a gig performing in an underwater ballet at the Hacienda Hotel. Her ticket to Hollywood came via a two-year scholarship to the Pasadena Playhouse.

**The '70s & Beyond:** Jeannine Riley left *Hee Haw* in 1971 after two seasons. She returned to the big screen in *The Outfit* (1973) in a bit role as a prostitute and more memorably in the cult movie *Electra Glide in Blue* (1973) starring Robert Blake as a diminutive motorcycle cop of American Indian descent whose dreams of becoming a detective are realized when he rightly questions an "open-and-shut" suicide. However, now partnered with detective Mitchell Ryan, Blake's integrity comes into play during the investigation of a murder as his adoration of Ryan turns to revulsion. Riley gave a poignant performance as Ryan's embittered girlfriend who owns a dive bar where the walls are decorated with childhood pictures from her glory days in high school and as a young dancer who had dreams of going to Hollywood. In a drunken stupor she rubs her affair with Blake and his sexual prowess in Ryan's face. The movie actually opens with Riley and Blake in the sack. This should have led to more dramatic parts for Jeannine but she accepted a regular role in the abysmal 1974 syndicated comedy series *Dusty's Trail*, a sort of re-working of *Gilligan's Island* complete with that series' star Bob Denver. Instead of seven castaways stranded on a desert island, here we had seven members of a wagon train lost in the Old West. Riley had the Tina Louise role playing a glamourous saloon girl. Unfortunately for Riley, when the series was cancelled her acting career seemed lost as well. She made a few more TV appearances in episodes of *Nashville 99*, *James at 15*, and in the TV-movie *Like Normal People* (1979) before calling it quits. She resurfaced about ten years later on *High Mountain Rangers* in an episode entitled "Ambassador" and then essayed the small role of a landlady in the sci-fi movie *Timebomb* (1991) starring once hot Michael Biehn and Tracy Scoggins. It is her last known credit.

# Pamela Rodgers

A curvaceous, statuesque baby-face redhead with a button nose and little-girl voice, she always seemed on the verge of stardom but never made it to the big time.

**You May Remember Her Most From:** TV's *Rowan & Martin's Laugh-In* as the kewpie doll bikini-clad beauty who dances and shakes her groovy, curvy body as the camera zooms in on various slogans painted on her skin.

**Her Groovy '60s Credits:** Pamela Rodgers made her film debut in *Dr. Goldfoot and*

Pamela Rodgers as a porn starlet rocks Dick Martin's world in *The Maltese Bippy* (MGM, 1969).

*the Bikini Machine* (1965) where she pranced around in a gold lamé bikini as a newly created robot programmed by Vincent Price's Dr. Goldfoot to marry and kill a Spanish artist. She had even less to do as a Slaygirl in *The Silencers* (1966). That same year she kept busy playing bit roles in the Jerry Lewis comedy *Three on a Couch*, *The Oscar*, and the made-for-TV movie *The Doomsday Flight*. Rodgers received lots of screen time though not many lines playing a bikini-clad beach bunny in the enjoyable *Out of Sight* (1966), a combination spoof on beach and spy movies with a rock 'n' roll beat. But it was television that gave audiences their first taste of Rodgers' comedic ability when she was cast as the glamourous Timothy Morgan, a ditzy weathergirl and one of the zany tenants living in a New York City brownstone inherited by naïve Ohioan Will Hutchins (newly arrived in the big city) in the sitcom *Hey Landlord!* The series lasted only one season (1966–67).

Rodgers next joined the cast of *The Jonathan Winters Show* (1968–69). Each week she appeared clad in a short nightgown looking for "Uncle Johnny" and then going into a four-minute monologue on various topics. Rodgers could make the most innocent subject sound dirty with her kittenish voice and became an audience favorite. In 1969, the adorable redhead returned to the big screen in the bad movie we love, *The Big Cube*. She looked terrific as the free-spirited friend of unhappy Karin Mossberg, whose rich daddy has just married the stage's greatest actress (played by the slumming Lana Turner). Rodgers gives her pal some groovy advice: "Sweetness, baby, float with the tide. That's my bag. This is a pop art world." Rodgers has a LSD freak-out scene where she strips down to her panties and later seductively dances with newly married pusher George Chakiris despite the presence of his bride Mossberg.

More lightweight was the horror movie spoof *The Maltese Bippy* that same year. A bikini-clad Rodgers turns up in the opening scenes as an underage, dippy starlet playing the Queen of the Moon, who is being instructed by nudie filmmaker Dan Rowan to make love to Earthman Dick Martin (who keeps interrupting the scene with his strange urge to howl like a wolf—foretelling what is to come). Rodgers impressed Rowan & Martin so much they offered her a regular gig on their hit show, *Rowan and Martin's Laugh-In*. Touted as the "Quickie Girl," Rodgers became the show's resident naïve sexpot, usually turning up go-go dancing (bikini-clad with her body painted with gags) during the show's "It's a Mod, Mod World" segment and as correspondent "Pam—Our Man in Washington." Unfortunately, her reign on *Laugh-In* lasted only one season (1969–70).

**The Beginning:** Pamela Rodgers was born August 18, 1944, in Pasadena, California. After graduating from Milby High School, the 5-foot-8 teenage beauty was crowned Miss Texas, which led her to the finals in the Miss World pageant. She studied acting in New York while working as a fashion model, then relocated to Las Vegas to become a showgirl. This eventually led her to Hollywood.

**The '70s & Beyond:** Pamela Rodgers was able to parlay her newfound fame from *Laugh-In* into appearances on many talk and game shows of the early Seventies, most notably *Match Game* and *The Hollywood Squares*, as well as acting in a few episodes of *Love, American Style* including "Love and the Tattoo" in 1971 and "Love and the Disappearing Box" in 1972, usually cast as the sexy ding-a-ling. She never returned to the big screen but was able to scrounge up supporting roles in the TV-movies *Suddenly Single* (1971) as a sexpot on the make for recently divorced Hal Holbrook and the detective mystery *Jigsaw* (1972) as a murder suspect. A second marriage to a doctor (she was previously married to film producer Jere Henshaw) sidelined her career. She was preparing a comeback in 1976 when she married business tycoon Edward Fickett and abandoned her plan, settling for domesticity instead.

# Linda Rogers

A stunning, titian-haired, green-eyed beauty who in her heyday resembled Debra Messing of *Will & Grace*, she was arguably one of the sexiest starlets to ever don black leather or a bikini in a Sixties beach movie.

**You May Remember Her Most From:** *Beach Party* (1963) as a biker chick who gives Frankie and Annette a rough time.

**Her Groovy '60s Credits:** Linda Rogers' first acting job was on the TV sitcom *My Three Sons* in 1962, playing a shapely coed vying to win "The Beauty Contest." Her film debut was in *Beach Party* (1963) as one of the members of the Rat Pack, a motorcycle gang headed by Harvey Lembeck's clumsy Eric Von Zipper, whose mission in life was to run Frankie Avalon, Annette Funicello, and the rest of those lousy surf bums off the beach. Things come to a head at the local surfer hangout when Von Zipper makes a play for the dejected Funicello; when he tries to kiss her against her wishes, Robert Cummings' Prof. Sutwell comes to the girl's rescue. He uses some Zen Judo tactics ("the Finger") on the biker, putting him into "time suspension." The gang retaliates at the end as the film climaxes with a bar fight complete with flying cream pies. To promote the movie, Linda was sent on publicity tours, which included visiting Marines at Camp Pendleton and judging department store events. *Beach Party* became the sleeper hit of 1963 as it combined aspects of *Gidget* and *Where the Boys Are* and struck a chord with the teenage moviegoing public. She would reprise her role as one of the chopper-riding Mice in *Bikini Beach* (1964), which began on the sandy beaches of Malibu and ended on a dragstrip as Von Zipper briefly becomes allies with real estate tycoon Keenan Wynn to cleanse the sand of the surfers and in *Pajama Party* (1964) with Tommy Kirk as a Martian who crashes the beach party and falls for Annette. Both films ended with a surfer vs. biker melee where the pretty redhead was pummeled by the beach gang (*Bikini Beach*) or dunked in a swimming pool (*Pajama Party*). In black leather from head to toe, Rogers could not help but stand out from the rest of the biker gang due to her gorgeous mane of auburn hair. The viewer is automatically drawn to her but Rogers proved she was more than just a beauty and got off some glib wisecracks with flair. In between beach parties, Rogers played a student nurse under the tutelage of monster, (on and off the screen) Joan Crawford in the melodramatic *The Caretakers* (1963), set in a mental ward, and rich widow Beverly Powers' sexy maid in the horror spoof, *The Comedy of Terrors* (1964). Rogers then played one of the many models who are guests at a health spa-dude ranch in the Elvis Presley movie *Tickle Me* (1965).

The beach party in the snow *Winter a-Go-Go* (1965) offered Rogers her biggest role. As Penny, she is part of a group of college kids who helps William Wellman, Jr., get his just-inherited ski lodge running while pulling double duty as one of the scantily clad dancing Winter a-Go-Go girls complete with fur-trimmed leotards and fishnet stockings. During the course of the movie she vies with buxom blonde Nancy Czar and droll Julie Parrish for the attention of sexy playboy James Stacy. Unusual for a teenage beach party movie, the film ends with a wedding as the three man-hungry gals catch the bouquet and then try to nab the illusive Stacy. In *Wild Wild Winter* (1966) Rogers' character Tricia remained in Malibu as one of many bikini-clad beach girls romanced by lothario surfer Gary Clarke. He learns that hell hath no fury like a beach bunny scorned when an irate

**Linda Rogers poses in costume to hype *Winter a-Go-Go* (Columbia, 1965).**

Rogers discovers that the special surfing medal he gave her is a duplicate that he has given to ten other girls. To escape the irate surfer chicks, he accepts his friend's offer to join the ski team at his mountaintop college. This was Rogers' last screen appearance. A car accident in 1966 left her paralyzed from the neck down, derailing her promising career. She astounded her doctors and made a full recovery but decided not to return to acting.

Linda Rogers (ca. 1964).

**The Beginning:** Linda Rogers was born in San Diego, California. Coming from an affluent family, as a child she didn't want for anything. She began modeling as a teenager and appearing on stage, first at the San Diego Playhouse and Globe Theater and later at the La Jolla Playhouse where, appearing in a play with Marge Champion, she was spotted by Debbie Reynolds' agent Louis Shurr who wanted to represent her. Linda declined at first but, to escape the confines of an all-girl college, she headed to Hollywood to take him up on his offer.

**The '70s & Beyond:** Remarried, Linda Rogers worked as a talent agent for a short period. She currently lives in Las Vegas with her new younger husband and works for a medical school.

## Linda Rogers speaks out on...

*Beach Party*: This was my first movie. I arrived on the set and was put with Harvey Lembeck and his group of actors. I had so much fun on *Beach Party*. Harvey Lembeck was such a character. I loved him. I had to go on a PR tour with him all over the U.S. and he was such a joy to be around. He was very protective of me. I wasn't very aggressive and never went for the camera. I'd hang back when filming would begin. But Harvey would say, "Hold it. Linda, come up here." I always thought that was very nice of him. We socialized in groups off camera. I mostly hung out with the actors playing the bikers in between takes. When they were shooting the beach scenes, we'd have time off so we would be sitting somewhere or eating together. But I did get to know Frankie and Annette. Honestly, I thought Annette was very, very nice but just so timid. I'm not shy so I sort of mixed with everybody. Frankie was a doll with absolutely no ego whatsoever. I really enjoyed working with him. He was sweet.

**Robert Cummings:** He was also helpful to me and wanted to get me a better agent because he thought I shouldn't be in small roles. He said to me, "You shouldn't be an extra." I replied, "Am I an extra?" I was very fortunate to have Robert Cummings and Harvey Lembeck's guidance but I wasn't pushy enough to be an actress.

*The Caretakers*: This was a nightmare. I was very excited when I got this role as a nurse. It wasn't on the beach and I was looking forward to it. After all was said and done, I think I wound up in two scenes with two lines in the movie. Joan Crawford was just a terror on the set. She was sarcastic and nasty. It was unbelievable what that woman did. I'd get yelled at by her to move or she'd complain about my makeup. She'd position herself at the opposite frame from you or she'd lean over in front of you like she was looking at something. She was a pro at it. Most times I had to stop myself from laughing because she was so obvious. Poor Diane McBain had it worse than I did because she had a much bigger role. The director [Hall Bartlett] was no help because I think everybody was scared to death of Joan Crawford.

*The Comedy of Terrors*: I went on an interview for this. They asked me to scream and talked with me for about ten minutes. They told me I got the part and gave me instructions of where and when to show up. When I arrived on the set they had already begun filming so everybody was sort of familiar with each other. I did my usual standing back until I knew everybody. That whole cast was something else! They were all pranksters and loved to scare me. I just had a small role but Vincent Price and Peter Lorre had a ball teasing me. They'd put scary props in my dressing room. Vincent Price was absolutely enchanting! He would tell these stories and talk about cooking. He was a sweetheart and I really felt badly when he passed away. Peter Lorre was constantly playing tricks on me. He'd come up behind me and try to scare me with that voice of his. I loved him but he teased me so. I had scenes with me in a coffin and he'd tell me, "You know, once you get into a coffin, they say you only have so much time to live. Don't let them talk you into doing it." *He was terrible!* I laughed so hard making this film.

*Pajama Party*: *Pajama Party* was my favorite. It was the most fun I ever had working on a film. Also, I was more relaxed in front of the camera. The night before filming began I was at a party with the Beatles. John Lennon wanted to see me the next day but I had to be on the set at 5 a.m. When we were filming on the beach I looked up at this house and said, I think to Annette, "I want to live in that house." That's the house my first husband bought me when we got married a few years later.

**Jody McCrea**: The only actor I ever had trouble with was Jody McCrea—ai yi yi! We were sent on a PR tour together to promote *Pajama Party* and he drove me crazy. He was very grabby with his hands. I have a bad temper. We got into it on a plane and he left me alone after that.

*Tickle Me*: I just got home from Europe and my agent told me to show up to play a role in the new Elvis Presley movie. I thought, "Oh, no." I had dated Elvis prior to making the movie. But it worked out very well. We had a little dance scene together. I remember the director Norman Taurog saying, "I don't know what you guys have going on between you but Elvis, look here at the camera." I know they cut a lot of this scene out of the movie because we were teasing each other back and forth. Elvis seemed preoccupied when we made this and didn't seem as outgoing as he used to be when I dated him.

I thought Jocelyn Lane was absolutely gorgeous but she didn't want anything to do with the rest of us. Oh please, we were so beneath her! She especially didn't like me. Most people like me but she did not. In fact, I would tease Elvis about her. Jocelyn just ran around with her nose in the air. I agree with what Francine York once said—she was a little snit!

*Winter a-Go-Go*: My agent got me an interview for this with the director Richard Benedict. He got fresh and I ended up dumping an ashtray in his lap. I wasn't used to that at all. As you can tell, I just fell into these roles. My agents would tell me where and when to show up. I hardly ever interviewed so when I came across [Benedict] I was stunned. I never in a million years thought I'd get the part because I rudely told him off. He left me alone after that. But I know he would make remarks to the other girls.

Bill Wellman on the other hand was such a gentleman. He was not the actor type at all but more the business type, actually. He was an extremely nice guy. At the time I didn't know he was helping to produce *Winter a-Go-Go*. I don't know how he didn't tear his hair out because we were so unprepared for that movie. For that dance scene ["Do the Ski with Me"] we had about forty-five minutes to learn the routine. I'm going one way and Nancy Czar is going another. It was embarrassing. On the umpteenth take, the director said, "Just leave it in and we'll have a character make a remark about the girls needing more rehearsal." I thought, "Wow, this is a loose film!"

**Stardom**: I had no idea the *Beach Party* movies would become so popular—none of us did. I remember vividly a PR thing we did in San Diego. We drove in a limo up to a drive-in theatre and the kids surrounded the car. They were screaming and shaking the car back and forth. I said to myself, "What the hell am I doing?" It was really frightening. That stuck with me so when MGM talked to me about co-starring opposite Rock Hudson in his new movie, which I think was scrapped, it scared me. I went over to the studio and they were making all these plans about signing me to a contract, sending me out on a publicity tour, and photographing me. I still have the pictures they shot. They dyed my hair black to make me look older. It made me nervous because I always thought of acting as a hobby. It was fun but now I thought, "Geez, this could be real work!" I wasn't sure if I wanted acting to be a lifelong thing for me. My dad came with me and explained to them that it wasn't what I wanted, not just because of the work but how I saw how it affected some of my friends with acting taking precedence over everything, including their families.

You had to have the drive like Raquel Welch to make it. I didn't. My agents would arrange interviews for me and I would back out with any excuse I could think of. You really had to want it very, very badly, especially at that time. I turned down an interview for *Playboy* too, because I could just imagine my parents' reaction. It was something I never would do.

**Why she stopped acting:** I got in a car accident with Nancy Czar and suffered a skull fracture. I was in the hospital for a very long time and my brain had swollen. I lost my sight, hearing, and body movement for a period of time. It was the most frightening time in my life. When the swelling started to come down, things began coming back. When I got out of the hospital, I never called my agent because I didn't want to act any more. I spent time in Europe with a girlfriend of mine who was the cousin of the prince of Iran, who I had dated a few years earlier. When I came back to California I met a businessman whom I married. I never went back to acting but I worked as a talent agent for about three or four years. I was helping out a friend.

# Myrna Ross

A statuesque, dark-haired, blue-eyed, tough-looking Glamazon, she was the quintessential biker chick in the beach party movies, taking over from Linda Rogers, but oddly never appeared in a single late Sixties motorcycle drama.

**You May Remember Her Most From:** *Beach Blanket Bingo* (1965) as biker chick Boots to Alberta Nelson's Puss who snatch singer Linda Evans from her bed.

**Her Groovy '60s Credits:** Myrna Ross made her film debut as an extra in *Ocean's Eleven* (1960) followed by *Bells Are Ringing* (1961) and *Days of Wine and Roses* (1962), in which you'd be hard-pressed to spot her. Another minor role followed in *Ride the High Country* (1962) as a bordello girl who acts as one of Mariette Hartley's bridesmaids at her arranged wedding to James Drury. A talented dancer, Ross' big break should have come when she was cast in the role of burlesque queen Miss Mazeppa in the movie version of *Gypsy* but a car accident almost claimed her life and prevented her from taking the part. A few years later she had the opportunity to play the role on stage at the Santa Monica Civic Auditorium in a production starring Gisele MacKenzie. In 1962, Ross made the first of three appearances on TV's *The Joey Bishop Show* playing a clubwoman backing Joey's wife's run for the Assembly in "A Woman's Place." She also turned up in a skit opposite Danny Kaye on *The Danny Kaye Show* in 1963. *What a Way to Go!* (1964) featured leggy Ross, who stood 5-foot 7½ and sported a 37-23-27 figure, in an uncredited bit clad in a leopard-print bikini as one of the beautiful "Orgy Girls" whom widow Shirley MacLaine imagines frolicking on the private jet of playboy Robert Mitchum.

Harvey Lembeck (*front*) and his biker gang (*from left*) Allen Fife, Jerry Brutsche, Bob Harvey, Myrna Ross, Jerry Macchia, Alberta Nelson, and Andy Romano scrap the leather duds for business attire and perform "He Is His Ideal" in *How to Stuff a Wild Bikini* (AIP, 1965).

In 1965, Ross joined Alberta Nelson as the only two female gang members who are part of the motorcycle clique led by Harvey Lembeck's Eric Von Zipper. Replacing the more glamourous redhead Linda Rogers, Myrna brought a fresh, tough attitude to the role beginning with *Beach Blanket Bingo* as the jealous biker chicks kidnap their leader's ideal—Linda Evans as singer Sugar Cane, who almost gets killed when their plot goes awry. In *How to Stuff a Wild Bikini* (1965) Lembeck tries to be the boy next door and his gang go the same route, darning suits and dresses for a musical production number. Ross and Nelson showed more heart in the latter two beach movies with Ross drolly commenting "That ain't nice" regarding some of Von Zipper's schemes against the surfing crowd. While working at AIP, Ross received reams of publicity when the studio chose her to be "Goliath's Mate" and sent her on a cross-country tour to promote their new sword-and-sandal adventure *Goliath and the Barbarians*. Another publicity stunt had Ross walking up and down the streets of Hollywood with an ad promoting *The Mouse on the Moon* painted on her back. Her final beach movie *The Ghost in the Invisible Bikini* (1966) featured the bungling biker gang on the loose in a haunted house searching for a hidden fortune (the beach gang are also staying in the creepy mansion). In between beach movies, Ross played, without receiving screen credit, a hardened dame beaten up by drunken Ben Gazzara in *A Rage to Live* (1965). *The Swinger* (1966) offered her a more lightweight supporting role as the loyal and protective secretary to girlie magazine publisher Tony Franciosa. She tries to keep the persistent aspiring writer Ann-Margret from seeing her boss; later, when Franciosa realizes that her swinger persona is a fraud, Ross plots with him to expose the redhead. When his plan goes amiss and he winds up in jail, Ross dutifully rushes to his side with a tray of coffee and food. Ross does well and stands out as she is practically the only nubile starlet in the movie who doesn't reveal any skin. Back on television, she got to demonstrate her dancing prowess as the daughter of a Bedouin trader who has a KAOS bomb underneath her bed in "Appointment in Sahara" on *Get Smart* and her strength as an Amazonian bodyguard who flips playboy reporter Tony Franciosa and holds him down under her foot on *The Name of the Game*. Returning to the big screen, Ross deserved better than playing a bordello girl in the comedy *How Sweet It Is!* (1968) and a blink-and-you'll-miss-her bit in *Live a Little, Love a Little* (1968) starring Elvis Presley. A bigger role followed as "Miss Forever," a fashion designer's model, in *2000 Years Later* (1969). This comedy about ad man Terry-Thomas exploiting a Roman soldier who comes back to life from ancient times failed to find an audience and disappeared from theatres quickly. So did Ross as this was her last known credit.

**The Beginning:** Myrna Ross was born in 1938 in New York. She was one of five children and her father drove a taxi cab to support his family. Revealing a talent for singing and dancing, Ross attended the High School of the Performing Arts in Manhattan. Maturing into a ravishing beauty resembling model Suzy Parker, Ross entered and won the Miss New York beauty pageant and went on to the Miss America contest.

**The '70s & Beyond:** Married to men's fashion designer Stuart C. Nelson since July 1967, Ross gave birth to their daughters Tiffany Blake in June 1970 and Sabrina Blythe in February 1973. She retired from show business to devote time to her family. Her life was cut short when she perished in a plane crash on December 26, 1975, near Granby, Colorado. She was thirty-seven years old.

# Tura Satana

One of the most exotic glamour girls of the Sixties, she always seemed to be cast as voracious man-eaters in low-budget films and fantasy television shows. Her on-screen persona was so powerful that you could not help but be transfixed by her. Personal relationships vexed her and prevented her from becoming a star.

**You May Remember Her Most From:** *Faster, Pussycat! Kill! Kill!* (1966) as *the* bad girl of the Sixties—the ass-kickin', vile, leather-clad Varla.

**Her Groovy '60s Credits:** Tura Satana was spotted by director Billy Wilder while dancing at the Pink Pussycat Club and he cast her as Suzette Wong, an Asian hooker, in *Irma La Douce* (1963) starring Jack Lemmon as a Parisian policeman who leads a double life to keep streetwalker Shirley MacLaine (with whom he has fallen in love) away from her other clients. Satana got noticed in her small role and kept busy for the next three years playing minor exotic roles in films and on TV. Her dancing prowess got her cast as a stripper in *Who's Been Sleeping in My Bed?* (1963) and later as a go-go girl in *Our Man*

**Tura Satana as the evil Varla tussles with Paul Trinka in the climactic fight scene in *Faster, Pussycat! Kill! Kill!* (Eve Productions, 1966).**

*Flint* (1966). In "Who Killed the Paper Dragon?" on *Burke's Law* she was the demurely named dancer Peach Pedal, which was ironic considering Satana was a tough chick off the screen. She first got to portray that side of her personality as the heavy in "The Finny Foot Affair" on *The Man from U.N.C.L.E.* (an episode that also featured a very young Kurt Russell). She played the henchwoman to villainous Leonard Strong, who has created a chemical that accelerates the aging process and can wipe out the entire population.

She then was cast in the role of a lifetime—the man-hating viper Varla in Russ Meyer's *Faster, Pussycat! Kill! Kill!* (1966). The movie was ahead of its time and possibly made audiences (especially men) squirm in their seats as buxom Satana, Haji, and Lori Williams physically and verbally abused the males in the movie. To make the gals even more Amazonian, Meyer brilliantly positioned the camera close to the ground so he could film the girls from a low angle. Clad in a black catsuit with her cleavage prominently displayed, Satana was the trio's depraved leader who, after breaking the neck of her teenage male opponent in a car race, takes his nubile, prissy girlfriend hostage. The terrified teen is dragged along as the vixens plot to rip off the fortune of a crippled old man despite the presence of his two sons—one beefy and dumb and the other weak but suspicious. Satana oozes a sort of evil sexiness as the angry Varla and menaces, karate chops, and kills her way into B-movie infamy. Surprisingly, the film was a box office dud when released.

Viewers were treated only once more to Satana's delicious brand of wickedness: She played Rabbit, the leader of a gaggle of Amazons working for Michael Dunn in "The Moulin Ruse Affair" on *The Girl from U.N.C.L.E.* in 1967. In a form-fitting grayish leotard, Satana possesses superhuman strength and knows how to wield her power due to a pill developed by Shelley Berman's mad doctor. Unfortunately, Tura never appeared in another mainstream movie or TV show. In 1968 she turned up in director Ted V. Mikels' Grade-Z horror movie *The Astro-Zombies* playing a wicked Chinese dragon lady named Satana who works for a foreign power that covets mad doctor John Carradine's process for turning lawmen into programmable robots.

**The Beginning:** To say Tura Satana had a tumultuous childhood is an understatement. She was born on July 10, 1935, and grew up in Chicago. Before she was fifteen, she had been in numerous fistfights, raped, sent to reform school, and was married and divorced. Moving to Los Angeles, Satana worked as a cigarette girl at the Moulin Rouge and Trocadero nightclubs. She then briefly worked as an interpretative dancer before the lure of big money enticed her to become a stripper. Unbeknownst to the club managers who hired her, Tura was underage. After working the burlesque circuit around the country, she took a job stripping at the Pink Pussycat Club in West Hollywood.

**The '70s & Beyond:** Tura Satana remained off the big screen for a number of years and returned in a supporting role in Ted V. Mikels' *The Doll Squad* (1973), which the director claims was the inspiration for the TV show, *Charlie's Angels*. In a supporting role, Satana was part of an elite all-girl team of commandos led by Francine York who are picked by the CIA to stop a madman from sabotaging a top secret rocket launch. Satana's career was sidelined when she was shot by a former lover. She planned on acting again after she recovered but marriage to a Los Angeles police officer who despised show business led to her retirement. She worked as a dispatcher for the LAPD and then when her husband retired from the force they relocated to Las Vegas. When *Faster, Pussycat! Kill! Kill!* received a resurgence in popularity during the Nineties, Satana emerged from obscurity and began attending celebrity autograph conventions around the world. After the death of her husband in October 2000, Tura decided to give acting a try once again. She recreated her role of Satana in *Mark of the Astro-Zombies* (2002), a re-working of *The Astro-Zombies* by the same director Ted V. Mikels, and appeared as herself in the documentaries *Cleavage* (2002), *Go, Pussycat, Go* (2005), and *Bosommania* (2007) about the women who worked with Russ Meyer. Tura is the star of her own comic book series, entitled *Tura Satana*, by artist Mike Hoffman. In 2007 she completed her long anticipated autobiography, *The Kick Ass Life of Tura Satana* and played a judge in the women's prison flick *Sugar Boxx*.

# Christiane Schmidtmer

Germany's answer to Brigitte Bardot, this stunning, busty blonde had comedic talent but due to her figure (purportedly measuring 44-25-38) and accent she was typecast in Hollywood as Aryan bimbos and bad girls.

**You May Remember Her Most From:** the trash drive-in classic *The Big Doll House* (1971) as the lesbian warden with voyeuristic tendencies.

**Her Groovy '60s Credits:** Highly sought-after model Christiane Schmidtmer made her film debut as a beautiful newlywed in the German movie *Verspätung in Marienborn* (1963) which was released in the U.S. as *Stop Train 349*. A Cold War adventure, it starred the strikingly handsome Sean Flynn (Errol's boy) as an American soldier and Jose Ferrer as a reporter who are passengers on a train traveling west from Berlin and have to decide if they should turn over an East German refugee to the Russians. Schmidtmer next appeared in two more European productions, the bawdy *Fanny Hill* (1964), directed by Russ Meyer, where she played one of the brothel whores, and *DM-Killer* (1965) starring Curt Jurgens and Dahlia Lavi. Extremely popular in Germany where her fans nicknamed her "Liebesbombe" (Lovebomb), she was recruited by Hollywood and was cast in the Academy Award–winning *Ship of Fools* (1965) directed by Stanley Kramer. A sort of *Grand Hotel* at sea, the film is set in 1933 on an ocean liner sailing from Mexico to Germany. Christiane had a supporting role as the feisty, glamourous, Zaftig paramour of anti–Semitic German magazine publisher Jose Ferrer in the film's most interesting subplot. Schmidtmer, looking terrific bedecked in Thirties fashions, doesn't mind her obnoxious lover's hate speeches about Jews but when she discovers that he is married with three children she viciously bites his lip and leaves him. In her next movie, the bedroom farce *Boeing Boeing* (1965), Christiane got to lighten up and almost stole the film as an Amazonian German air hostess nicknamed "Miss Luftansa." Tony Curtis played a playboy pilot engaged to three stewardesses. Due to their travel schedule he is able to juggle them with the help of his disapproving housekeeper Thelma Ritter. But an aircraft equipment screw-up forces a schedule change and all three young ladies descend on him in Paris, where he recruits his reporter friend Jerry Lewis to help him out. Despite her fine performance (one critic dubbed her "the most exciting German import since Dietrich"), Christiane was relegated to television for the remainder of the decade though she came close to snagging the female lead opposite Elvis in *Paradise, Hawaiian Style* but lost the part to *Boeing Boeing* co-star Suzanna Leigh. In 1966, she portrayed the wife of a German general in "The Last Man" on the short-lived series *The Blue Light* starring Robert Goulet as an undercover American correspondent masquerading as a Nazi sympathizer. Her episode was one of a few that were culled together and released as the feature *I Deal in Danger* (1966). Soon after, her half-naked torso was on delectable display in the March 1966 *Playboy* pictorial "Trio con Brio," which saluted her, Italian Rossana Podesta, and British Shirley Anne Field. A bit more modest than the other girls, she only bared a portion of her breasts. That same year she was cast as the daughter of a German contact for the Americans in "Fortress Weisbaden" on *Twelve O'Clock High* and as the greedy fiancée of a diamond thief who has perfected a formula to make him move so quickly that he appears invisible in "The Night of the Burning Diamond" on *The Wild Wild West*. Realizing that her beau has turned maniacal, she balks and turns against him. On *Hogan's Heroes* Christiane was a beautiful German spy hired to wheedle secrets out of the American prisoners in "To the Gestapo with Love" in 1968. She was also a popular guest on talk and game shows of the era including *The Tonight Show*, *The Merv Griffin Show*, *The Dating Game*, *Funny You Should Ask*, and *Truth or Consequences*. She ended the decade with a supporting role in the German romantic comedy *Unser Doktor ist der Beste* (1969), which failed to find a U.S. distributor.

**The Beginning:** Christiane Schmidtmer was born Christel Schmidtmer in Zurich, Switzerland, on December 24, 1939. Her family relocated to Germany when Christiane was a young child. Her father Jakob Schmitmer worked for the government and disappeared in Russia as World War II ended. Raised by her grandparents outside of Zurich,

**Christiane Schmidtmer with Jose Ferrer in a publicity photo for *Ship of Fools* (Columbia, 1965).**

she developed an interest in acting and at age seventeen she went to Munich, Germany, where she appeared in a number of stage productions for children before turning to modeling. At 5-foot-6 with curves galore, the sexy blonde began getting lots of assignments including being a cover girl for Max Factor cosmetics while also appearing in German nudie magazines such as *Er*.

**The '70s & Beyond:** After making a guest appearance on the detective series *The Most Deadly Game* in 1970, Christiane Schmidtmer followed in the footsteps of other glamour girls and went the drive-in exploitation route. She played a nasty prison warden in Roger

Corman's cult trash classic *The Big Doll House* (1971), one of the most popular women's prison movies filmed in the Philippines. Of course, being German running an American prison on an island, you know Christiane is not going to play nice: The kinky warden likes to dress up in men's bondage attire and watches as the nubile female prisoners are stripped, whipped, and stretched on the rack. When the fed-up inmates including Pam Grier make their escape, they take her hostage. In the violent finale, the warden goes up in a ball of flames when a truck where she is being held prisoner is blown up. Schmidtmer recites her lines in a dull monotone and gives a wooden performance but drive-in audiences didn't flock to this for the acting, as the topless mud wrestling and naked floggings took center stage. In the suspenseful TV-movie *Scream, Pretty Peggy* (1973) Christiane played Bette Davis' deranged daughter who lives in the attic of the garage on the estate. Her sculptor brother Ted Bessell hires a new caretaker who quickly learns that there is something strange about the family, especially when the father of the former caretaker comes looking for his missing daughter. More TV roles followed on *Police Story* and *Hec Ramsey*. Back on the big screen Christiane could be spotted as one of the terrified passengers in *Airport 1975* (1974). She next turned up playing a nude model in *The Specialist* (1975) starring Adam West and Ahna Capri, and an adulterous pig-tailed waitress who surprisingly survives *The Giant Spider Invasion* (1975). In the latter, a black hole comes crashing down in a Wisconsin town and millions of spiders emerge, overrunning the town until they create one huge spider (actually a Volkswagen Bug decked out to look like a big spider) to finish off the townsfolk.

As Christiane's career began to wind down after she turned thirty-five, she played an uncredited bit role in *Swashbuckler* (1976), guest starred as a Nazi on *Wonder Woman* in "Judgment from Outer Space, Part 2," appeared in TV commercials, and landed a small part in the obscure light comedy *Half a House* (1979), which surprisingly received an Academy Award nomination for its theme song "A World That Never Was." Her final acting credit was as a nymphomaniac piano teacher in the German-Israeli co-production *Shifshuf Naim* (1981), released in the U.S. as *Lemon Popsicle III*, about three randy teenage boys in early 1960s Israel. Schmidtmer retired from show business shortly after this and became a highly successful real estate agent in the Los Angeles area. In the early Nineties she purportedly married producer-director Howard Avedis. If so, it would have been her first trip to the altar as she had turned down a number of proposals over the years because she did not want to have children. In 2000, she left Hollywood for good and moved to Heidelberg, Germany. She passed away on March 30, 2003, from injuries suffered in an accident.

# Linda Gaye Scott

The epitome of the sun-drenched California blonde surfer girl, this sophisticated beauty started out playing out-of-this-world sex kittens with a mean streak on a number of fantasy television shows before morphing into a big-screen hippie chick.

**Linda Gaye Scott in *Little Fauss and Big Halsy* (Paramount, 1970).** Billy Rose Theatre Division, The New York Public Library for the Performing Arts, Astor, Lenox and Tilden Foundations

**You May Remember Her Most From:** TV's *Batman* as the Riddler's catsuit-clad moll Moth or from *Lost in Space* as an intergalactic Delilah who clips the hair and strength from a Samson-like Dr. Smith, who has ingested a mysterious potion.

**Her Groovy '60s Credits:** Linda Gaye Scott made her film debut in the obscure adventure film *Man in the Water* (1963). She was billed as Linda Scott but needed to add a middle name as singer Linda Scott already had that name registered with the Screen Actors Guild. Linda's second feature was the equally forgettable *Run Home, Slow* (1965).

This offbeat western starred Mercedes McCambridge as a hard-boiled old broad out to avenge the death of her tyrannical father at the hands of fed-up townspeople. She enlists the help of her two brothers, dim-witted Gary Kent (married to his slinky cousin Scott) and hunchback Allan Richards. They rob a bank and murder the entire family of the man they hold responsible for the death of their pa. The duplicitous Scott seduces her brother-in-law and plots to run off with the stolen loot while making their doomed escape across the desert. The film is most notable for the music score provided by twenty-year-old Frank Zappa.

Between 1965 and 1967 Scott became a lovely fixture on television. She at first was featured in a number of lightweight roles such as a bodacious beach babe who makes time with Gidget's surfer boyfriend in "The War Between Men, Women, and Gidget" on *Gidget*, a harem girl of an evil sultan who is in possession of a bottle with an entrapped Ray Walston in "Bottled Martian" on *My Favorite Martian*, a ditzy hairdresser trapped on a Caribbean island with U.N.C.L.E. agents Robert Vaughn and David McCallum who are investigating voodoo practices in "The Very Important Zombie Affair" on *The Man from U.N.C.L.E.*, and the object of desire of bumbling Ensign Pulver in "The World's Greatest Lover" on *Mister Roberts*. The bad girl roles began with *Batman* in "The Ring of Wax" and "Give 'em the Axe" when Scott was cast as the Riddler's moll, Moth. Though she had little more to do then to help the nefarious ghoul try to melt the Dynamic Duo over boiling wax in their quest to plunder the lost treasure of the Incas, she was a knockout in her form-fitting purple jumpsuit with a matching cape to give her an insect-like look. On *Lost in Space*'s "Collision of the Planets" she was an intergalactic Delilah-like hippie who along with her three cohorts are assigned to blow up the planet the Robinsons are stranded on. The space family's only hope is Dr. Smith who has gained enormous Samson-like strength complete with thick curly green hair—but the buffoon succumbs to the wiles of the seductive Scott, who is itching to shear those locks. On *The Green Hornet* the crimefighting duo try to figure out if Linda's beautiful Varna is really an intergalactic visitor in the series' final episode "Invasion from Outer Space." During 1967, Scott also had a recurring role on the sitcom *Occasional Wife* playing Miss Wilson, ambitious junior executive Michael Callan's helpful but ditzy secretary.

In 1968, Linda returned to the big screen playing minor roles in *The Party* as a bikini-clad starlet working on a movie with inept Indian actor Peter Sellers and in the groovy youth flick *Psych-Out* where she received "introducing Linda G. Scott" billing in the opening credits. Scott played a newlywed into communal living who puts the moves on hippie Jack Nicholson (who is aiding deaf runaway Susan Strasberg find her missing brother amongst the long-haired, peace-loving flower children of Haight-Ashbury). He rebuffs Scott and she spends the rest of the movie playing tambourine in his rock band.

**The Beginning:** Another socialite in the vein of Pamela Curran, Linda Gaye Scott is the daughter of advertising millionaire Milton Bradley Scott and grew up in ritzy Bel-Air, California. Not much is known about her early years except that she attended finishing school in Lausanne, Switzerland.

**The '70s & Beyond:** Linda Gaye Scott began the decade playing another hippie chick, this one sporting a tight tube top accentuating her bountiful bosom, who is picked up by womanizing motorcycle racer Robert Redford in *Little Fauss and Big Halsy* (1970) and accompanies him to a race. Redford's partner Michael J. Pollard expertly tunes his cycle for a second-place win. He celebrates by bedding Scott and another racetrack tramp.

Redford cruelly tempts the innocent Pollard with a chance to score with the two sleeping beauties but then changes his mind, deciding not to share, and the cyclists head on to the next track, leaving Scott in the dust. The film's publicists pushed Scott as the find of the year and touted this as her film debut, discounting her four earlier screen projects. She followed this with two guest appearances on *Bonanza* in 1971 before returning to the big screen in the comedy *Hammersmith Is Out* (1972) starring Elizabeth Taylor, Richard Burton, Beau Bridges, and Peter Ustinov, who also directed. In this reworking of *Faust*, Bridges is a neglectful nurse in a nut house; Svengali patient Richard Burton promises to make the richest man in the world and pairs him with Taylor, a golddigging blonde floozy who slings hash at the local diner. Scott has a small role as one of the bimbos Bridges sets his sights on to replace Taylor, whom he wants to dump. In the classic sci-fi film *Westworld* (1973) she has a featured role as a saloon girl robot who beds resort guest Richard Benjamin before the robots run amok at the futuristic resort. Neither motion picture did anything for her career so she was relegated again to television, playing a supporting part in the TV-movie *Rolling Man* (1972) starring Dennis Weaver, a luscious nurse in "Love and the Woman in White" on *Love, American Style*, a dowdy Irish maid working for has-been actress Janet Leigh in "Forgotten Lady" on *Columbo* (the only episode where the crime goes unsolved), and a minor role in the TV-movie *Cops and Robin* (1978). Her final acting credit was a bit on *Archie Bunker's Place* in "The Boys' Night Out," playing "Woman #3" who meets up with Archie and friends when they go out on the town to celebrate their years of friendship. Soon after, Linda Gaye Scott disappeared from Hollywood. Her present whereabouts are unknown.

# Lisa Seagram

A sultry siren with impeccable cheekbones, long dark hair, and a curvaceous figure, she started off in sophisticated roles before literally cutting her hair short and loosening up in a string of mid–Sixties fantasy and adventure films and TV shows, usually cast as the duplicitous vixen or wanton woman.

**You May Remember Her Most From:** TV's *Batman* (1966) as Lila the Lilac, who is partners in crime with Milton Berle's Louie the Lilac.

**Her Groovy '60s Credits:** Lisa Seagram made her acting debut as a college coed in the forgettable teenage comedy *Love in a Goldfish Bowl* (1961) with Tommy Sands and Fabian. More minor roles quickly followed in *Man-Trap* (1961), *Bachelor in Paradise* (1961) as Bob Hope's shapely French secretary, *Too Late Blues* (1962), and *Come Blow Your Horn* (1963) as a sophisticated New York party guest. In the Doris Day-James Garner spoof of TV commercials *The Thrill of It All* (1963) she was an actress playing a French peasant who throws a glass of wine in the face of Carl Reiner's German officer. Her early TV work included guest stints on *The Gallant Men* in "Fury in a Quiet Village" as an Italian peasant, *McHale's Navy* in "Is There a Doctor in the Hut?" as a glamourous movie star,

**Lisa Seagram as one of Polly's Girls (hookers all) in *A House Is Not a Home* (Embassy, 1964). Courtesy of Lisa Seagram.**

*Gunsmoke* in "My Sister's Keeper" as a saloon girl, and six appearances on *Burke's Law*. Back on the big screen she was a randy secretary in the so-bad-it's-good box office smash *The Carpetbaggers* (1964), based on the novel by Harold Robbins. As the flirtatious assistant to the bank officer who loans George Peppard's Jonas Cord $500,000 to get into the plastics business, Lisa does her best to convince Jonas to take her along with the money. *A House Is Not a Home* (1964) featured Seagram pulling out all the stops as an ill-fated harlot who beds a myriad of men working for Shelley Winters' Polly Adler, a real-life New York bordello keeper in the Twenties and Thirties. Lisa followed this playing a lusty cocktail waitress who tries to pick up attorney Mike Connors in *Where Love Has Gone* (1964).

With her dark sultry looks accentuated by elegant high cheekbones, Seagram was a natural for TV fantasy shows and appeared in a number of them including *Bewitched* as Miss Jasmine, a perfume spokesmodel and wicked witch who is determined to steal Darrin from Samantha in "It Takes One to Know One" and *Amos Burke: Secret Agent* as a Spanish princess involved in a government coup in "Deadlier Than the Male." *The Girl from U.N.C.L.E.* featured Lisa as bad girl Miss Karum, a member of a cult of Middle Eastern assassins, who kills a scientist with a scratch from her poisonous fingernail to obtain his reincarnation serum that can bring their evil leader back to life in the body of her descendant in "The Garden of Evil Affair." Seagram continued her wanton ways in "Louie the Lilac" on *Batman* in the infamous hippie episode portraying redheaded Lila to Milton Berle's Louie the Lilac, who plans to take over Gotham City by altering the minds of the flower children with his Lilac Spray and feeding the Dynamic Duo to a man-eating lilac plant. Back on the big screen, Seagram appeared as a fashion model awakened from a deep sleep by a smack on the behind from Richard Harris' secret agent in the mod spy spoof *Caprice* (1967) and then played an ambitious secretary who plots with TV producer Pat Harrington to exploit an ancient Roman who materializes in the present in *2000 Years Later* (1969). By the time of the satiric comedy's release, Seagram had already packed it in and relocated to Rome, joining the ranks of female stars Carroll Baker, Mimsy Farmer, and Pamela Tiffin who had already tried their luck in Italy. Seagram landed many a movie including the spaghetti western *El Puro* (1969) where she played a saloon owner opposite American actor Robert Woods and *Yellow: Le Cugine* (1969). Most of her films were geared to Italian audiences and never released in the U.S.

**The Beginning:** Of Mediterranean descent, Lisa Seagram was born in the Bedford-Stuyvesant section of Brooklyn, New York. Her father was Harry Brower, a highly decorated detective in the New York City police department who aided in the arrest of members of Murder, Inc. An extremely intelligent child, Lisa was sent to a special school where she studied art (she was drawing on the walls of her mother's house since kindergarten). After graduating college, Lisa took a job as a graphic artist, illustrating medical books. When Lisa became bored with the work, a friend recommended that she try modeling, and she quickly began working in the garment district. She started acting when a stranger suggested she should because she "looked like an actor," which led to three years of studying drama with renowned teachers Paul Mann, Herbert Berghof, Uta Hagen, and Bill Hickey. Seagram soon nabbed a minor role in the John Cassavetes film, *Shadows* (1959).

**The '70s & Beyond:** After wrapping up her movie career in Italy with *La Cugina* (1974) as a murderess and *La Studentessa* (1976), among others, Lisa Seagram returned to California in the late Seventies. Remarried with another daughter, she decided to concentrate on her domestic life. When her daughter became school age, Seagram decided not to pursue her acting career and instead went into commercial real estate; she sold the Biltmore Hotel in downtown Los Angeles. In the Eighties, Seagram founded Actors 2000 in Hawaii where she taught acting and helped newcomers avoid the pitfalls of show business. Her school was immediately successful and Seagram acquired a number of clients.

**Publicity photo of Lisa Seagram as a model in *Caprice* (20th Century–Fox, 1967).**

She even produced, directed, and wrote a movie about it called *Paradise Pictures* (1997). Highly respected, when she decided to relocate the company to Los Angeles, 22 of her students packed their bags and accompanied her. In 2001 she co-produced a short called *You Never Know* about a straight guy who kisses his best friend the night before his wedding and begins to question his sexuality. Today, Lisa Seagram still runs Actors 2000 and has been specializing in helping former actors return to show business.

## Lisa Seagram speaks out on...

**Why she almost did not become an actress:** I was studying acting and I hated it. However, Herbert Berghof, my teacher at the time, told me to give it one more try and gave me a scene from *Desire Under the Elms*. I rehearsed with my partner and we brought the scene into class. It was a love scene where we had to jump onto a bed on stage. We did and the bed broke. Instead of everyone laughing, the audience gasped and I thought, "Ooh, I like this."

**Her decision to give Hollywood a try:** I was at El Morocco with some friends. A stranger at the next table (who I later learned was the vice-president at RCA) asked me what I did. I told him I was a fashion model in the garment district and was studying acting. He told me that I should be in Hollywood. When I disagreed, he said, "The movies are in Hollywood and you belong there." I went the next day. I was divorced with a two-year-old child who I left with my mother. I told [my mother] with my heavy Brooklyn accent, "If I don't make it in a week, I'll be back." I didn't know my accent was unusual even though I had taken speech for many years.

**Her first time on a studio back lot:** I went to Paramount Pictures because it was under the same astrological sign that I was. At the gate I asked the guard who was the head of the studio because I wasn't aware that you had to go through a casting director. He told me that Marty Rackin was the president and he pointed out the building where his office was located. I walked up to his receptionist and said, "Hi, I'm Lisa Seagram from Noo Yawk to see Mr. Rackin." When she asked if I had an appointment, I said, "No but he'll see me." She laughed and called Mr. Rackin. With a surprised look on her face she said, "Go on in."

I sashayed into Mr. Rackin's office and walked up to his desk and said with my heavy accent, "Hi, Mr. Rackin. I'm Lisa Seagram from Brooklyn and I'm here to give Paramount the first chance." Of course, he fell off his chair laughing. He said, "You have a lot of guts. I like that. I was brought up by Damon Runyon so I know what you are talking about." He then said, "A girl got sick on Stage 9 where Jack Sher is directing a film called *Love in a Goldfish Bowl* with Fabian and Tommy Sands. Go ask for Jack and tell him Marty Rackin said you have the part." I said thanks and walked out of his office.

*Love in a Goldfish Bowl*: Two days after meeting with Mr. Rackin I was in wardrobe and on the set. My mother came out to LA with my daughter, who I enrolled in nursery school. The one thing I remember about this movie is that I had to dance and I had to lie on a chaise lounge with custard on it from a wild party the kids threw the night before. There was a nanny goat that leaped on top of me, I guess for the custard, and really hurt me. I had a lot of bone bruises and contusions. I thought, "This is really hard work!"

**Turning down studio contract offers:** Paramount and later Universal offered me a contract. I passed on both of them. I had just come to Hollywood and I had no idea what was going on. I was very fortunate nevertheless.

*Man-Trap*: This was directed by actor Edmond O'Brien. It was one of the first movies I ever did. I remember standing there looking at the camera smiling—what I thought was the camera. O'Brien came over and tapped me on the shoulder and said, "Little girl, if you want your mother to recognize you, you're going to have to look in the camera." I replied, "Isn't that the camera?" He said, "No, honey, that's a light."

**Making the adjustment from stage to screen acting:** I studied acting for three years in New York but I had no clue about making films. The external technique for film acting is quite different from stage acting. I also had no idea what I sounded like or looked like on film. In the first few movies that I did, I would ask the cameraman if I could look through the camera and I would ask the soundman to let me listen to what he hears. This helped me tremendously.

**Her Brooklyn accent:** After I did three or four films at Paramount I got the lead in a TV show at Warner Bros. called *The Gallant Men*. I had to play an Italian peasant. The first time I heard my accent was when I watched the episode on television. I did half–Italian and half–Brooklyn. It was a nightmare and I was humiliated. When I woke up the next morning my voice had dropped about four octaves. I had studied speech for three years but it just didn't take until I saw that show. I later developed the skill to do a general "European accent" that of course only exists in Hollywood. I somehow mastered it and made a living for about two years doing accents.

*The Carpetbaggers*: I loved it! Every time I walked onto the set, George Peppard said [*in a sing-song voice*], "Lisa Seagram! Lisa Seagram! Lisa Seagram!" It was a lovely experience and everyone was wonderful to work with. I really had a very smooth, enjoyable career. I had very few hassles and they were nothing major. It was probably the easiest thing that happened to me in my life.

*A House Is Not a Home*: There were two lead prostitute roles in this played by Meri Welles and me. The rest of the girls such as Raquel Welch, Edy Williams, and Sandra Scott were featured extras. This was a phenomenal experience for me. I really had to help carry a lot of the film and up to that point I hadn't really understood the responsibility of that. Shelley Winters went to my junior high when she was Shirley Shrift. She was older than me... *a lot older*. I didn't realize how much older until after she passed away. She never told anyone her age. Shelley was a great lady and I put her on a diet. The first day she had the caterer wheel in a big cart of celery and carrots—nothing fattening at all. The second day they wheeled it in again. On the third day it never came. She held the diet for two days. Shelley would come into my dressing room and bring me music so I could prepare for a scene. I said, "Shelley, the music that you prepare with is different from my music because our characters are so dissimilar." She was so nice and very helpful but would insist, "No, you've got to listen to this."

**Favorite actors she worked with:** There were very few people in my career that in any way disturbed me. Some were really neat and nice such as Gene Barry. I made many appearances on *Burke's Law* and his wife was from my old neighborhood. Gene was wonderful and such a huge supporter. Also, *Burke's Law* was just such a calm and fun set to work on. Red Buttons was an absolute doll and I did an episode of *Wendy and Me* with George Burns who told me that I had the best comedy timing since Gracie Allen. I considered that my greatest compliment.

I worked with former silent screen star Gilbert Roland in an episode of *Gunsmoke*. He was such a gentleman. Carl Reiner too was absolutely fun to work with.

**Juggling being an actress and a mom:** It wasn't difficult at all because I was a different kind of mother than other actresses. Some referred to their children as their sisters or brothers. They didn't admit to having children and I didn't understand why. They explained to me that if you have a child, people think you are old. I said, "I don't care what people think about my age. I have a child and I am not going to call her my sister." I would take my daughter with me to play tennis at Jack Ryan's house every Sunday and I was the only one with a child she owned up to. I did have to hire a fulltime housekeeper because I worked so much. But it was a pleasure because I was home four full months out of the year. I was able to spend all that time with her.

*Bewitched*: I had a problem with the director [William Asher] while working on *Bewitched*; otherwise it was terrific. Elizabeth Montgomery was wonderful and Agnes Moorehead was a great lady. Dick York was just delightful. I had a great time and loved it.

**Her recurring role as Edythe Brewster on *The Beverly Hillbillies*:** This was great fun. Donna Douglas as Elly May was throwing animals at me all the time. I really conquered my Brooklyn accent on this because I had to be this haughty, high-class society woman. Buddy Ebsen and Irene Ryan were phenomenal. I had a ball working on this.

*Batman*: *Batman* has seemed to have survived the ages, which is shocking to me because it seemed like such a silly show at the time. I liked Adam West. He was very easy to work with. Milton Berle was a one-liner guy and never stopped with the jokes. He was very funny and you felt like your face was breaking off from laughing so much. It was great but we had to act too.

**Missed opportunities:** There were two roles that I wanted and didn't get. I was up for and close to getting the role of Jennifer in *Valley of the Dolls*. Sharon Tate got the part and some time later she was murdered with my friend Jay Sebring. After that happened I never had a bad thought about another person. I was given the lead role in *Fantastic Voyage* and certain circumstances beyond my control led to Raquel Welch being cast in the part instead. That is all I can say.

*2000 Years Later*: I am a natural brunette. When I got the part in this movie they said they wanted me to be a redhead so I thought they were going to give me a wig. The first day on the set they came at me with this color and I had never dyed my hair before. They wouldn't agree to a wig so they colored my hair a Lucille Ball red. But what I discovered was that when I was a brunette I had to be lit very carefully because it threw shadows on my face. As a redhead it didn't. So when I was done with the film I stayed a redhead but with more of a golden shade.

Terry-Thomas and Edward Everett Horton were brilliant and great fun to work with. I think this was one of Horton's last movies before he died. I knew of Myrna Ross through a friend of mine because she too modeled in the garment district in New York. But she really didn't have much of a role in the movie and I didn't get to know her. Sadly, she was killed in a plane crash sometime after finishing the film. This was a very funny movie but I think it was ahead of its time. The director [Bert Tenzer] had a hard time with it.

**Relocating to Rome:** I had become involved in a meditative philosophy and the Master was in India. I went there to meet him and on the way back I stopped in Rome and fell madly in love with the city. I returned home and decided that I had enough of Hollywood because in my estimation I wasn't climbing any higher. I felt that my career had reached its plateau and in Hollywood when that happens the only way is down. Since I had such a wonderful career, I didn't want to go through that experience. I decided that I wanted to investigate Rome even though I had never been out of the country before. I lived and worked there for seven years and it was just wonderful. It was one of the most incredible times of my life.

**Making movies in Europe:** The most fun on Earth is to go on location with an Italian crew. They were just wonderful. In Hollywood, they were still filming a lot of outdoor scenes on soundstages because they couldn't control the sound. In Italy, they shoot with no sound because they have co-productions in French, German, and Italian and nobody speaks the same language. Consequently, you film on location, which was the

**Seagram in Europe (ca. 1973).** *Courtesy of Lisa Seagram.*

first experience I had with that, with people who do not speak English and had to mouth the words so later they could dub in the English words. It was ludicrous because you had to control yourself from laughing like crazy because some of the actors couldn't control the words. I dubbed my own voice and I also dubbed into English many other actresses.

**Actors 2000:** After working in real estate for seventeen years, I decided to go back into show business but not as an actor. I wanted to help other people have as smooth a ride as I had, and I am doing that. I am working with newcomers and resurrecting careers that had died. Some of these actors are bigger than before even if they have had a ten- or fifteen-year lag. It is just thrilling for me to help people. I teach as well as manage and am having a wonderful time.

**Her biggest success story in terms of her clients:** I had many students but the one who stood out was a little girl named Q'Orianka Kilcher. Her mother, Saskia Kilcher, was my student first. Q'Orianka at the age of four was an opera singer. She had an amazing voice. At six she was one of the stars in my film *Paradise Pictures*. I directed it and she understood what I said more than any of the adults in the movie. This kid was born to be an actor. When I came back to LA from Hawaii (my daughter who is a set dresser moved back to California with her husband), 22 students came with me including Q'Orianka, her mother, and brother. Cut to 2005—Q'Orianka was Pocahontas in *The New World*. She did a gorgeous job in the movie and she was only fourteen.

# Bobbi Shaw

A buxom blue-eyed, rosy-cheeked blonde, she was *the* sexpot of the AIP beach party movies, usually clad in only a fur-trimmed bikini.

**You May Remember Her Most From:** *Beach Blanket Bingo* (1965) as the Swedish bombshell who is continually chased by dirty old man Buster Keaton.

**Her Groovy '60s Credits:** Prior to arriving in Hollywood, Bobbi Shaw performed as a singer and dancer in Las Vegas musical productions of *High Button Shoes* and *Anything Goes*. An American International Pictures talent scout spotted her and the company signed her to a seven-year contract. Her first movie appearance was in *Pajama Party* (1964) playing a Swedish knockout (with an eye-popping 38-22-35 figure) who, along with bungling Indian chief Buster Keaton, is hired by con man Jesse White to help fleece rich Elsa Lanchester. To achieve their goal, Shaw has to entice information from volleyball-playing Jody McCrea as Lanchester's dim-witted nephew whose girlfriend Annette Funicello has fallen for Martian Tommy Kirk. Problem is, Shaw doesn't speak English and answers every question with, "Yah! Yah!" Impressed with the laughs that they brought to *Pajama Party*, AIP paired Keaton and Shaw again in *Beach Blanket Bingo* (1965). But this time they were only used as a running gag as Keaton's dirty old man could be seen chasing the nubile bikini-clad bombshell around the beach and the airport as the beach gang took up skydiving. The duo also turns up dancing during the film's end credits. Sans Keaton, Shaw played a Swedish ski instructor enamored of Frankie Avalon in *Ski Party* (1965). Even in tight ski clothes, Shaw is still a knockout (*Yah! Yah!*). She has a very funny scene when she decides to give up on the Swedish way of free love and adopt the prudish ways of American girls, much to the amorous Avalon's dismay. In *How to Stuff a Wild Bikini* (1965), Shaw was reunited with Keaton as she played a sexy native girl to his potion-mixing witch doctor on an island where naval reserve officer Frankie Avalon is stationed. This role required nothing more than for Shaw to look sexy in a sarong and long dark wig. She next donned the tightest of military uniforms as a sexy WAVE in the juvenile comedy *Sergeant Dead Head* (1965) starring Avalon as an astronaut who has swapped brains with a chimp after their return from space.

Bobbi finally got to drop the Swedish accent and the fur bikini in *The Ghost in the Invisible Bikini* (1966), playing a greedy, wisecracking carnival girl once again in cahoots with Jesse White and Basil Rathbone to knock off Tommy Kirk and Deborah Walley (heirs to a fortune who must survive a night in a creepy old house complete with Susan Hart as the title character). This was Shaw's last film for AIP. A talented comedienne, she, Rob Reiner and Richard Dreyfuss headed up Los Angeles' first improvisational comedy troupe, The Session. They performed in Hollywood and at the Playboy Club in New York as well

**Bobbi Shaw (ca. 1964).**

as making recurring appearances on *The Steve Allen Show*. They eventually had their own club on the Sunset Strip.

**The Beginning:** Bobbi Shaw was born Barbara Shaw, of Danish and Russian descent, in 1943 in New York City but grew up outside of Philadelphia. After high school, she studied Theatre Arts and Psychology at the University of Miami. While in school, she was crowned Miss Miami Beach. Shortly thereafter she dropped out of college and headed west.

**The '70s & Beyond:** Bobbi Shaw returned to moviemaking in the Seventies playing colorfully named characters beginning with her role as Twila Zornes in the obscure rural shoot-'em-up *The Devil and Leroy Bassett* (1973). She then co-starred with the Carradine brothers (David, Keith, and Robert) in *You and Me* (1975) playing a character named Wynona. In *Pipe Dreams* (1976) Shaw was cast as Slimy Sue, a hooker peddling her flesh in Alaska who befriends newcomer Gladys Knight as a woman escaping an abusive relationship. Today, Bobbi Shaw (who is married to writer Larry Chance and has two children, Allison and Richie) is one of Southern California's most respected acting coaches and runs Expressions Unlimited in Los Angeles. Her students have included Brad Pitt, Jennifer Aniston, Drew Barrymore, and Giovanni Ribisi. She has also invested a lot of time in The Abused Children's Foundation where she incorporates theatre games and on-stage improvisation to help children heal emotional scars. In 2006, Shaw began turning up on TV as herself, coaching wannabe actors on the reality series *The Starlet*, *Faking It*, and *Fight for Fame*.

# Eva Six

A glamourous, buxom platinum blonde bombshell from Hungary, she looked like Marilyn Monroe, talked like Zsa Zsa Gabor, and craved publicity like Jayne Mansfield but she never rose above being a poor man's Mamie Van Doren.

**You May Remember Her Most From:** *Beach Party* (1963) as the lusty barmaid (nicknamed the "Hungarian Goulash") who tries to entice surfer Frankie Avalon away from his girlfriend, Annette Funicello.

**Her Groovy '60s Credits:** Christening her Eva Six (purportedly because it was as close to "Sex" as they could come), Eva's agents brought her to the attention of American International Pictures, who hyped their 40-22-38 discovery as Hollywood's newest glamour girl and heir to the throne vacated by the deceased Marilyn Monroe. Appropriately, the busty blonde, nicknamed Eva Forty-Six, was chosen to be 1963's Miss Golden Globe (and boy did she have a pair of them) even before any of her films were released. But astonishingly AIP hid her flaxen tresses under a dark wig to play a very unglamourous Filipino freedom fighter in the World War II adventure *Operation Bikini* (1963). Six aids seamen Tab Hunter, Frankie Avalon and others in finding their submarine captured by the Japanese. She and Hunter wind up in a wrestling slapfest when he prevents her from helping a friend shot by the enemy. Later, an apparently forgiving Six awakens him for a midnight massage, literally ripping his shirt off his torso as she rubs his muscles. Alas, their romance is ill-fated as the nude bathing island girl is gunned down by the Japanese—but it is not the last we see of her. Eva with her natural hair turns up in the film's end credits (shot in color) as she and another bikini-clad cutie frolic on the sand, extolling the joys of Bikini Island. It was this image that was used on the film's poster to make people think it was a beach movie. It was no surprise that she wound up working again with Frankie Avalon

Eva Six (ca. 1963).

(though they purportedly clashed on the set over scene-stealing) in *Beach Party* (1963). This time, however, she got to play the voluptuous siren as a platinum blonde. Eva is quite amusing as a sexy barmaid, nicknamed "The Hungarian Goulash," who puts the moves on surfer boy Frankie Avalon, who has just broken up with his girlfriend, Annette Funicello. Avalon sings to Six as she seductively dances around him and later the duo make out on the beach in full view of Annette and friends. Six makes sure to ruin Frankie and Annette's almost-reconciliation but when the surfer finally wises up and returns to his girl, a jilted Six joins forces with the surfers' worst enemy, biker leader Eric Von Zipper (Harvey Lembeck). During a wild melee between the beach denizens and the motorcycle gang, Six throws the first custard pie and is quickly creamed by a retaliating Annette.

*Beach Party* was Six's swan song at AIP. In her next movie, Eva has nothing more to do than stand around on a riverboat looking absolutely stunning in her form-fitting white gown, playing crooked banker Victor Buono's trophy wife in the Frank Sinatra–Dean Martin western *4 for Texas* (1963) but she was overshadowed by international sex symbols Ursula Andress and Anita Ekberg. This was Eva Six's last screen appearance as her promising career quickly fizzled out, though she continued to act in her native Hungary. She tried performing on stage but bailed out on the French farce *In One Bed* co-starring Jules Munshin while on tour in Pittsburgh. She then made headlines when in 1964 she crashed her car into a light pole in Miami Beach and in 1966 when she was convicted of careless driving in Budapest after she injured a motorcyclist. Luckily for her (but unlucky for her fellow drivers), she received a suspended sentence and did not have to do any jail time. She disappeared from the Hollywood scene soon after.

**The Beginning:** Born Eva Klein in Budapest ca. 1937, the daughter of a Jewish father and Catholic mother, Eva escaped the Nazis after the death of her father when her mother changed the family name to Kennedi. As a child, she acted, sang, and danced in all the school plays. She made her film debut at age ten and became a national folk dance champion by the time she was fifteen. More Hungarian movies came her way before she quit at age seventeen to marry Roy Schmidt, a well-known architect. With the Communists coming into power, the couple fled first to Austria and then Los Angeles in 1956. They had a daughter named Linda Marie and then separated in 1960. Eva worked for a time selling barbeques in Las Vegas, where she struck up a friendship with Frank Sinatra; he encouraged her to go back into show business. Instead she opened a delicatessen in Hollywood where she kept getting mistaken for Marilyn Monroe. That was the impetus for her decision to try acting again.

**The '70s & Beyond:** Her whereabouts today are unknown.

# Sharon Tate

A radiant, buxom blonde sex kitten with a sweet persona, she quickly progressed from minor roles to leads and was on the cusp of becoming an internationally known sex goddess when she was brutally murdered.

**You May Remember Her Most From:** *Valley of the Dolls* (1967) as the ill-fated, top heavy starlet who took the blue pills.

**Her Groovy '60s Credits:** Sharon Tate headed for Hollywood following the advice of actor Richard Beymer, whom she met while working as an extra on *Hemingway's Adventures of a Young Man* (1962) in Italy. After working as a model in print and TV ads, she was discovered by Filmways Studios executive Martin Ransohoff, who signed her to a seven-year contract. Sensing that she had superstar potential, Ransohoff kept his discovery under wraps but to get her experience of acting in front of the camera made her don

**Sharon Tate (ca. 1967).**

a brunette wig to play the recurring role of Janet Trego, one of Mr. Drysdale's secretaries on *The Beverly Hillbillies*. Tate was originally signed to play eldest daughter Billie Jo on *Petticoat Junction* but she was let go when it was discovered she posed semi-nude for a magazine. On the big screen, Tate appeared without receiving credit as a "Beautiful Girl" in *The Americanization of Emily* (1964) and as one of artist Elizabeth Taylor's Big Sur beatnik friends in *The Sandpiper* (1966). In between, Tate could be seen as a THRUSH bad girl who (along with Kathy Kersh) gives chauvinistic agent Robert Vaughn a thrashing in "The Girls of Nazarone Affair" on TV's *The Man from U.N.C.L.E.* Ransohoff finally unleashed the blonde sexpot onto the moviegoing public in the occult thriller *Eye of the Devil* (1966) as warlock David Hemmings' sister, a bewitching witch who changes a dove into a toad and gets a well-deserved flogging from wine grower David Niven. To give his starlet that extra push, he produced the ten-minute featurette *All Eyes on Sharon Tate*. The promising starlet never looked more gorgeous as the cameras followed her from the studio to photo shoots to celebrity-filled parties.

Back on the big screen, *The Fearless Vampire Killers* (1967), a spoof of Hammer Films' vampire movies, directed by Tate's future husband Roman Polanski, featured Sharon, wearing a red wig, playing an innkeeper's beautiful, buxom, virginal daughter who becomes the main course of vampire Ferdy Mayne. Tate looks delectable, especially in her bathtub scene (still photographs of a topless Sharon were shot by Polanski for publication in *Playboy* magazine's March 1967 issue to help promote the movie). Her next two films solidified her status as a sex kitten and pinup. In *Don't Make Waves* (1967), a satire on the Southern California lifestyle, she played a vapid surfer-skydiver (named, appropriately enough, Malibu) who leaves her good-natured bodybuilder boyfriend Dave Draper to live with con artist pool salesman Tony Curtis. With her hair wet and matted down to her head, Tate makes a memorable entrance a la Ursula Andress in *Dr. No* as she pulls an injured Curtis from the surf after he gets clobbered on the head by her surfboard. But it was *Valley of the Dolls* (1967), about three young women's rise and fall in show business, that made Tate a star and an icon among gay men. In this camp classic, while Patty Duke hammed it up and Barbara Parkins listlessly glided through the movie, Sharon, looking radiant, was vulnerable as a desperate starlet who does nudie European "art" films to pay her husband's medical expenses. Thinking her beauty and body are her only marketable assets, when she learns she has breast cancer she commits suicide by overdosing. She gave another standout performance in the comical role of a bungling spy posing as a tour guide in the last Matt Helm spy caper *The Wrecking Crew* (1969) starring Dean Martin as the super sleuth, sent to Denmark to track down count Nigel Green who stole a billion dollars in gold. Tate looks stunning in her micro-minis and even has a catfight with Nancy Kwan's evil enemy agent. Her last screen appearance was in the Italian slapstick comedy *12+1* (a.k.a. *The Twelve Chairs*) playing a beautiful art dealer who has brokered the sale of thirteen antique chairs for schnook Vittorio Gassman, unaware that his late aunt hid her fortune in one of them. She joins him on his quest throughout Europe to track down the chair with the money in it. Tate was a vision of loveliness and has a few topless scenes to boot.

**The Beginning:** She was born Sharon Marie Tate on January 24, 1943, in Dallas, Texas. Since her father was in the military she spent most of her childhood on the move. A beautiful child, she racked up a number of beauty pageant wins including Miss Tiny Tot of Dallas at six months old, Miss Richland, Washington, and Miss Autorama. When Tate was sixteen years old, her father was assigned to Italy where the blossoming teenager was voted her high school's Homecoming Queen and played bit roles in Italian films such as *Barabbas* (1961) before going to Hollywood.

**The '70s & Beyond:** There are no post–glamour girl years for Sharon Tate. On August 9, 1969, Charles Manson's hippie followers butchered an eight-months-pregnant Tate, hairdresser Jay Sebring, heiress Antoinette Folger and two others at her rented home on

Cielo Place in Beverly Hills. Her family to this day fights for victims' rights and speaks out against parole for all the convicted Manson followers who participated in Tate's murder.

## Margaret Teele

An angelic blonde with porcelain-doll features, she tried to buck the glamour girl parts without success.

**You May Remember Her Most From:** TV's *The Andy Griffith Show* playing a teenage tease in the classic episode where Don Knotts' Barney Fife made one of his return appearances to the show.

**Her Groovy '60s Credits:** Margaret Teele studied acting at the Pasadena Playhouse and Desilu's Acting Workshop and began modeling. A bit in *The Human Duplicators* (1965) was followed by playing a Slaygirl in *The Silencers* (1966). She has no lines and doesn't appear on screen until the tail end of the movie where she is seen standing around a rotat-

Publicity photo from *The Silencers* (Columbia, 1966) with (*standing in back row*) Susan Holloway, Margaret Teele (wearing man's shirt), unidentified actress, and unidentified actress, and (*clockwise on bed from left*) Mary Jane Mangler, Margie Nelson, Larri Thomas, Jan Watson, Dean Martin, Barbara Burgess, and Marilyn Tindall.

ing bed as Dean Martin lies between a bevy of Slaymates in a promo for the upcoming sequel *Murderers' Row*. A strict Catholic, she asked not to be scantily clad. The producers obliged and gave Teele a man's red shirt to wear over her skimpy outfit; however in the world of Sixties glamour girls, modesty was not a desirable trait so she was not invited to promote the movie on the European tour and was not asked back as a Slaymate in the sequel. Another small role followed in the futuristic comedy *Way... Way Out* (1966) as one of the many female admirers of playboy astronaut Jerry Lewis. Next Teele kept popping up as Jacques Bergerac's hot-to-trot frustrated paramour who constantly phones him ("I'm waiting for you, Jacques, dear") to see when he is going to come by her room in the bizarro sex comedy *Mother Goose a-Go-Go* (1966). She turned down a cover spread for *Playboy* (no surprise there), campaigned mightily to work with Elvis Presley (she never did), and began guest starring on television. She played minor roles on *Gomer Pyle, U.S.M.C.*; *Captain Nice*; and *Batman* before landing the female lead in 1966's "It Takes Only One to Suffer" on the comic western *The Rounders* starring Ron Hayes and Patrick Wayne as two modern-day womanizing cowboys. Teele played the romantic interest of Hayes as he chucks his freewheeling ways to run a gas station. Her most fondly remembered role was in "A Visit to Barney Fife" on *The Andy Griffith Show* where she played Agnes Jean Parker, an amorous sex kitten who is captivated with Don Knotts' Barney. (When her ma states that they think of him as family, Agnes coos, "I don't.") Pal Andy Griffith comes to visit Barney in Raleigh and helps the bungling detective realize that he is living amongst a family of thieves who have been robbing local supermarkets. Teele's last screen credit was playing a nurse in the Jerry Lewis comedy *Hook, Line and Sinker* (1969)—or, as it was dubbed by the critics, *Hook, Line and Stinker*. The movie sunk at the box office and took Teele's career with it.

**The Beginning:** Margaret Teele was born on November 15, 1942, in Joliet, Illinois. She arrived in Hollywood at age eighteen from Green Bay, Wisconsin, after working as a model.

**The '70s & Beyond:** Margaret Teele gave up her fight to obtain better roles and settled down to a life of domesticity with her GI boyfriend upon his return from Vietnam. Out of the limelight for years, Teele is currently on the sidelines of show business once again as her daughter Jenna Drey has taken center stage as an up-and-coming pop singer. Jenna's first single "Just Like That" was adopted by the Boston Red Sox as their battle song and her next record "Killin' Me" was a Top 20 hit on the Billboard Charts in 2006.

# Marilyn Tindall

A lithe blonde beauty, she was more famous for being a beauty queen and the first swimsuit cover girl for *Sports Illustrated* than for being an actress.

**You May Remember Her Most From:** playing one of secret agent Matt Helm's Slaymates in *The Silencers* (1966), *Murderers' Row* (1966), and *The Ambushers* (1967).

A bevy of decorative Slaymates from *Murderers' Row* (Columbia, 1966) featuring (*left to right*) Mary Jane Mangler, Rena Horten, Luci Ann Cook, Marilyn Tindall, Dee Duffy, Jan Watson, Dale Brown, Mary Hughes, Lynn Hartoch, Amedee Chabot, and Barbara Burgess.

**Her Groovy '60s Credits:** Marilyn Tindall began her brief movie career as a Slaygirl with *The Silencers* (1966) starring Dean Martin as amorous secret agent Matt Helm. Wearing a low-cut one-piece swimsuit and matching cap, she is the second Slaygirl who pops into the fantasy of the sleeping Matt Helm. Though she is holding a fishing reel, passionate Matt has another sport in mind and it doesn't involve flounder. She reappears at the very end with Martin and the other Slaygirls in a promo for *Murderers' Row* (1966). Tindall once again is used only as window dressing in the sequel. She first appears wearing a black trenchcoat along with the other Slaygirls, now Slaymates, who are mourning the supposed death of Matt Helm at his favorite watering hole. As Miss May, she reappears at the fadeout, with flowers in her hair and on her bikini, along with the calendar girls who surround Helm's indoor pool after Dean Martin's Helm and Ann-Margret take the plunge from his circular bed into the water. Marilyn traveled the world helping to promote the Matt Helm movies and appeared in pinup photos in numerous European magazines such as *Ciné Monde* in France and *Ses* in Turkey. The third Matt Helm adventure, *The Ambushers* (1967), was Tindall's big screen swan song. After appearing with the other girls throughout the opening montage clad in mod Sixties designs, prowling for men as the title tune is sung over the credits, Tindall is one of the Slaygirls at ICE's rehabilitation center, getting a refresher course on the newest weapons developed by the spy organization. As the instructor demonstrates a device that dissolves metal electronically by aiming it at the belt buckle of a male mannequin, she and the other Slaymates (scantily clad in short shorts) watch with detached amusement. Later she and the other Slaymates show up undercover at a fashion show in Mexico to aid Dean Martin.

In January 1967, Tindall became the first cover girl for the *Sports Illustrated* debut swimsuit issue. According to the magazine, she was hired due to her "California look" and photos of her in bikinis designed by Bill Blass, Rikki, and others were shot by Jay Maisel on the cliffs surrounding Arizona's Apache Lake. Insecure about her looks, Tindall refused to appear without mascara despite the protestations of the makeup artist. She finally relented on day three, and Maisel snapped the photo of her that was chosen for the cover. Wearing a Dacron knit red bikini, sultry Tindal gazes off to her left, holding her long blonde hair with her right hand while standing in front of a jagged rock formation. Though the first swimsuit issue did not achieve the worldwide popularity it has today, the notoriety it brought Tindall kept her as one of the most in-demand swimsuit models for a few more years. One of her most famous print ads had her in a zebra print bikini holding a movie camera, enticing men to enter "The Vivatar Movie Camera Contest" in 1969.

**The Beginning:** Marilyn Tindall was born and raised in Los Angeles, making her a true California girl, but this lovely blonde never dreamed of acting or modeling even though her father worked in security at Paramount Studios. After graduating from Hollywood High School, she took a job as a secretary for the Los Angeles Department of Water and Power. A dare by a co-worker in 1962 led her to enter a local beauty pageant, which she won. The radiant beauty queen went on to enter nine more pageants. She placed first runner-up in the 1962 Miss California contest and assumed the crown when the winner upped and married her boyfriend. Tindall then went on to the Miss USA pageant where she finished in third place. Standing 5-foot-7½ and measuring 37-22-37, she began modeling, which led to commercial appearances as the Amazonian foil a la Inga Neilsen for such comics as George Burns for El Producto Cigars and Jimmy Durante for Kellogg's Corn Flakes.

**The '70s & Beyond:** Marilyn Tindall made a few minor TV appearances such as a USO performer in "Is This Trip Necessary?" on *Make Room for Granddaddy* in 1971, then retired from modeling and acting after marrying insurance executive Robert Percival. The couple resided for a number of years in Newport Beach, California, and they have a daughter named Chelsea who was born in 1979.

# Corinna Tsopei

A sultry Greek beauty queen with exquisite cheekbones, she alternated between minor decorative and ethnic roles in film and television. But her family life took precedence, hindering her acting career.

**You May Remember Her Most From:** *A Man Called Horse* (1971) as an Indian squaw who falls in love with white man Richard Harris.

**Corinna Tsopei (ca. 1968).** *Billy Rose Theatre Division, The New York Public Library for the Performing Arts, Astor, Lenox and Tilden Foundations*

**Her Groovy '60s Credits:** A talent scout brought former Miss Universe Corinna Tsopei to the attention of 20th Century–Fox and the studio signed her to a contract. The budding starlet was accepted into the Fox talent program where her classmates included Jacqueline Bisset, James Brolin, and Linda Harrison. But whereas her fellow students were handed lead roles, Tsopei toiled in bit parts. Her film debut was playing a scantily clad model in the spy spoof *Caprice* (1967) starring Doris Day and Richard Harris. She was one of a bevy of beauties seen briefly walking down Wilshire Blvd. at the start of the comedy *A Guide for the Married Man* (1967) and then was in the background answering phones during Patty Duke's star-making telethon number early on in *Valley of the Dolls* (1967). She finally landed a role with more than a few lines in the surf movie *The Sweet Ride* (1968). The first shot of Tsopei is of her shapely derriere while playing tennis as one of tennis hustler Tony Franciosa's many girlfriends. Later, at the country club, she is seen nagging Franciosa to play tennis with her while surfer Michael Sarrazin pleads with him to help find the culprits who beat up Jacqueline Bisset. In between movies, she did a few TV shows, most notably playing a mute silver-skinned ice queen given shelter by the Robinson family from the alien bandito on the hunt for her in an episode of *Lost in Space* and as an Indian maiden on *Daniel Boone*. Marriage to Beverly Hills plastic surgeon Dr. Steven Zax sidelined Tsopei until the early Seventies.

**The Beginning:** Corinna Tsopei was born on June 21, 1944, in Athens, Greece, the daughter of an army major. Blossoming into a dark-haired beauty, she became her country's first woman to be named Miss Universe, winning the crown in 1964. After a year-long reign, which included an appearance on the 1965 Golden Globe Awards, the 5-foot-7 beauty with the curvaceous 36-24-36 figure moved to New York to study English and became a very successful fashion model.

**The '70s & Beyond:** In 1971, Tsopei surprisingly copped the female lead in *A Man Called Horse*, reuniting her with Richard Harris. She was enchanting as Running Deer, a member of a Sioux tribe that has captured Harris' English lord. To prove his manhood he is put through a series of their Indian trials. As he is accepted and rises in rank to chief, he falls in love and marries the sultry Tsopei. Despite the film's success, Tsopei retired from show business to concentrate on raising her sons Andreas, Stefano, and Giorgos though she was coaxed to do the film *Psihi kai sarka* (1974) in her native Greece. Divorced from her former husband, Tsopei is now remarried to producer Freddie Fields and resides in Los Angeles. She has been a judge for a few Miss Universe pageants and devotes her time to a charity that helps children afflicted with leukemia.

# Victoria Vetri

She toiled in Hollywood for a few years as dark-haired Angela Dorian and was voted Playmate of the Year in 1968 but it wasn't until she went blonde and reverted to her real name that she gained brief fame and was able to progress to lead roles—albeit in exploitation movies.

**You May Remember Her Most From:** *Rosemary's Baby* (1968) as Mia Farrow's ill-fated neighbor who suspiciously falls out the window of her apartment.

**Her Groovy '60s Credits:** Due to her Italian heritage, Victoria Vetri (using the nom de screen Angela Dorian) began landing supporting ethnic roles on television. She played an Indian maiden in "Johnny Brassbuttons" on *Cheyenne*, an Italian peasant girl in "Next of Kin" on *The Gallant Men*, and a Mexican in "The Zebedee Titus Story" on *Wagon Train*. She made enough of an impression to be voted a Hollywood Deb Star in 1962. On the big screen, after losing out on parts in *West Side Story* and *Lolita*, she landed a bit role in *The Pigeon That Took Rome* (1962) starring Charlton Heston. She was then cast as the confidante of Mayan princess Shirley Anne Field in *Kings of the Sun* (1963) starring Yul Brynner as an Apache chief whose tribe tries to live in peace with George Chakiris' fleeing Mayan people in what was to become the southwest U.S. For the next four years Vetri kept busy on TV playing a variety of lead guest roles, most notably in "The Indian Affairs Affair" on *The Man from U.N.C.L.E.* as a go-go-dancing college student and daughter of an Indian chief (both of whom on kidnapped by enemy agents); "I'll Be a Mummy's Uncle" on *Batman* as villain King Tut's belly-dancing moll Florence of Arabia; and "The Crittendon Plan" on *Hogan's Heroes* as a sexy resistance fighter who aids Bob Crane's Hogan in blowing up a German tunnel. She returned to the big screen in the western *Chuka* (1967), cast in the ingénue role of Mexican countess Luciana Paluzzi's niece, promised to a man she doesn't want to marry. Traveling by stagecoach, the women are stranded in a cavalry outpost manned by an army of misfits who enlist the aid of hired gun Rod Taylor to battle an attacking tribe of Indians. The fort is overrun and Taylor and Vetri are the only survivors.

Thinking it would give her career a boost, the shapely brunette with the 36-21-35 figure doffed her top as *Playboy*'s Miss September 1967. Her ambition was "to have my pick of acting roles" and her major turnoff was "women who wear hair curlers in public." Despite her vapid answers, she was voted Playmate of the Year for 1968, proving that nobody read the magazine, they just ogled the pictures; Dorian's were very sultry and sexy. Prior to posing for *Playboy*, she played the small part of Mia Farrow's chatty neighbor who plummets from an eleventh floor window in *Rosemary's Baby* (1968). It was the film's director Roman Polanski who advised her to drop "Angela Dorian" and revert to her real name. In the movie he even had Rosemary mistake her for actress "Victoria Vetri." The brunette beauty took his advice, then dyed her hair blonde and followed in the footsteps of Raquel Welch by donning a skimpy loincloth bikini as the lead in the Oscar-nominated *When Dinosaurs Ruled the Earth* (1970) for Hammer Films. (Purportedly director Val Guest was not thrilled that the Playboy Playmate was foisted on him by the American distributors.) The movie was filmed in 1968 but not released until two years later. As the only flaxen-haired beauty amongst a bunch of bosomy brunette cavegirls, Vetri is chosen to be sacrificed to the Sun Gods but she is washed out to sea when a fireball is hurled from the sun, forming the moon; she is saved by muscular caveman Robin Hawdon. She goes to live with him amongst his fishing tribe only to anger jealous cavegirl Magda Konopka and her former tribesmen. Throughout the rest of the movie Vetri catfights with her rival in the surf, is almost bitten by a giant snake, is gobbled up by a carnivorous plant, makes love with Hawdon, and befriends a baby dinosaur and its mother. Despite Guest's reservations, Vetri does a competent job and looks fetching as the playful cavegirl. She truly is one of the unheralded blonde sex goddesses of the Sixties. Unfortunately, she never followed up with anything substantial and seemed to be caught between two worlds, alternating between

**Victoria Vetri strikes a fierce pose to publicize *When Dinosaurs Ruled the Earth* (Hammer Films, 1970).**

straight "Angela Dorian" roles on TV and exploitative "Victoria Vetri" parts in film. Her most notable TV role was that of a publicity-hungry starlet whom youngster Brandon Cruz brings home from his movie studio tour to stay with him and his widower dad Bill Bixby in "Mrs. Livingston, I Presume," the premiere episode of *The Courtship of Eddie's Father* in 1969. She ended the decade in the made-for-TV movie *The Pigeon* (1969) playing a rebellious runaway whom private detective Sammy Davis, Jr., is hired to protect.

**The Beginning:** Of Italian descent, Victoria Vetri was born on September 26, 1944, in San Francisco, California. Her father was a successful restaurateur and her mother was a former Broadway actress and pinup girl; both of them emigrated from Italy. While majoring in art at Los Angeles City College, Vetri took a shine to acting. Thinking her real name was inappropriate for a movie actress, she chose Angela Dorian, which she borrowed from the ill-fated cruise liner with the half-alike name.

**The '70s & Beyond:** Victoria Vetri continued working on the small screen, co-starring in the made-for-TV movies *Night Chase* (1970) and *Incident in San Francisco* (1971) and then portraying a dying mobster's granddaughter who becomes a pawn in the takeover of his business in "Squeeze Play" on *Mission: Impossible*. She then made the leap to exploitation fare, co-starring with Playboy Playmate Claudia Jennings and Aimée Eccles in *Group Marriage* (1973), a boudoir farce complete with many topless scenes of the delectable Vetri. Her last feature, the cult exploitation T&A flick *Invasion of the Bee Girls* (1973), cast Victoria in the damsel-in-distress role as a mousy lab assistant who discovers scientist Anitra Ford is transforming women into Queen Bees who get the urge to mix with the local yokels before killing them. Burly William Smith is the virile Federal agent hired to investigate. Victoria's shapely nude body is clearly on display when captured by the Bee Girls but she is rescued by Smith before they have a chance to swath her in honey. This may have proven too sticky a situation for Vetri, who retired from show business after one last TV appearance in "Bonus Baby" on *Lucas Tanner* in 1975. In 1984, she was working as a waitress and bartender when she was lured by *Playboy* to pose again for their pictorial "Playmates Forever! Part Two." And in 2000, she placed 56th in *Playboy*'s 100 Centerfolds of the Century.

# Jane Wald

A petite beauty with honey brown hair and penetrating brown eyes, she sported a curvaceous 38-22-35 figure that most men wanted to ogle. She wanted respectability as an actress but unfortunately the buxom brunette was only hired to fill a bikini or prance around in a towel on the big screen.

**You May Remember Her Most From:** *Under the Yum Yum Tree* (1963) as one of voyeuristic landlord Jack Lemmon's many nubile tenants.

**Her Groovy '60s Credits:** Relocating to Hollywood in 1959, Jane Wald's first film appearance was in the avant-garde drama *Weekend Pass* (1960). She played a dance hall girl opposite Paul von Schreiber's naïve sailor on leave. The film never found a distributor despite being shown at the Cannes Film Festival. She then began appearing on television in episodes of *Surfside 6*, *The Many Loves of Dobie Gillis*, *Hawaiian Eye*, and *The Tab Hunter Show* as a gold digger after millionaire Richard Erdman's money. Wald's movie career officially started with a splash (literally) as she is seen soaking in a bathtub in *The Three Stooges in Orbit* (1962). She covered up, albeit with a towel, for her roles as one of lecherous landlord Jack Lemmon's va-va-voom tenants in *Under the Yum Yum Tree* (1963)

**Jane Wald (1965).**

who likes to shower with her basement bathroom window wide open, and as one of coed Sandra Dee's Paris roommates in *Take Her, She's Mine* (1963), emerging from her morning toilette when Dee's harried father James Stewart barges into the apartment looking for his daughter and mistakes the gals for hookers. Wald was bikini-clad in *Honeymoon Hotel* (1964) but finally got to wear some clothes on screen in the Shirley MacLaine comedy *What a Way To Go!* (1964), giving an energetic performance as artist Paul Newman's kooky French beatnik friend who creates her artwork by shooting paint balloons onto her canvas. Another abysmal comedy, *John Goldfarb, Please Come Home* (1964), starred Shirley MacLaine as a reporter and Richard Crenna a former football player coerced to coach a Middle Eastern sheik's football team. Hired for her figure, Jane was indistinguishable from many of the other chiffon-clad starlets (including Eve Bruce, Ann Morell, Teri Garr, Shelby Grant, and Irene Tsu) hired to play harem girls. Wald's last theatrical motion picture *Dear Brigitte* (1965) featured her as the sexy wife of artist Charles Robinson, who likes to have his wife model nude for him on their houseboat. Wald's lack of attire is the film's running gag as the family of James Stewart (residing on the houseboat next door) is always trying to prevent their ten-year-old (Billy Mumy) from seeing her naked flesh. On television she turned up on *The Dick Van Dyke Show* in "Stacey Petrie, Part 2" playing an elegant love interest for Jerry Van Dyke as Dick's bungling brother and on *Batman* as a curvaceous bad girl who helps Cesar Romero's the Joker fake the kidnapping of a visiting maharajah in "The Joker Trumps an Ace" and "Batman Sets the Pace." Tired of being considered "a body," this glamour girl threw in the towel, so to speak, and quit acting in 1966, though columnists reported she was being considered for *Planet of the Apes*.

**The Beginning:** Jane Wald was born Jane Wolberg in Mount Vernon, New York. Her father was an international businessman and her mother an artist. As a young adult, she attended a few semesters at NYU before enrolling at the American Academy of Dramatic Arts. She began learning her acting craft while doing summer stock and supported herself by working as a model, appearing on billboards and in newspaper ads for Parliament cigarettes and Rheingold beer. Noticing her print ads, *Playboy* came a-calling three times but the modest Wald declined the offers to be a Playmate. Her first foray to Hollywood ended when the studio dropped her option and a dejected Wald flew to Europe to be with her parents. She decided to give acting one more try and returned, this time finding work due to her next door neighbor, actress Barbara Steele. Invited to lunch by the actress at the commissary at 20th Century–Fox, Wald was discovered by an independent producer.

**The '70s & Beyond:** Jane Wald married three times and has a number of children. Over the years she made half-hearted attempts to revive her career. In the mid–Seventies she turned up in the episode "Flight to Danger" on *Barnaby Jones* and in 1993 she co-starred with Deanna Lund and Liz Torres as college chums who look back on their university days while vacationing at a ski resort in *Girl Talk*, a sort of precursor to *Sex in the City*. Today, Jane Wald, now Antonoff, resides in Los Angeles and travels the world extensively.

# Jan Watson

She was known as "the girl with the perfect figure" so it is not unexpected that this brunette beauty, who resembled Deanna Lund, was scantily clad and the subject of double-entendres in most of her swinging Sixties movie roles. Her whole short career was one pinup photo session as she was invariably always chosen to pose for photos to help promote her movies even if she didn't even have a speaking part.

Perennial bikini girl Jan Watson (1965).

**You May Remember Her Most From:** the Matt Helm spy capers *The Silencers* (1966), *Murderers' Row* (1966), and *The Ambushers* (1967) as one of the beautiful young women, nicknamed Slaymates or Slaygirls, who hang around playboy agent-photographer Dean Martin.

**Her Groovy '60s Credits:** Jan Watson made her film debut as a bikini-clad robot in *Dr. Goldfoot and the Bikini Machine* (1965). Watson was next selected to play one of the original Slaygirls in *The Silencers* (1966) starring Dean Martin as the booze-swilling photographer-secret agent Matt Helm. Wearing a black bikini top and black lacy leotard with fishnet stockings, Jan appears in Helm's erotic dream. Though she is holding a fencing sword, the amorous Helm wants to make love not war as they begin kissing. During a tacked-on promo for the film's sequel *Murderers' Row*, Watson is snuggled up next to Martin on a rotating bed chock full of Slaygirls.

More bit roles followed for Jan in 1966. She appears briefly in *The Swinger* in an uncredited role as one of *Girl Lure* magazine's international models, introduced to reporters at an outdoor press reception by editor Tony Franciosa. As with *Dr. Goldfoot* and the Matt Helm movie, Watson was selected to help publicize the films by appearing in numerous pinup photos published in movie magazines worldwide, giving the illusion that her roles in the films were bigger than they actually were. She had more of a wardrobe and a line to recite as a whore in the western *Alvarez Kelly* (1966) starring William Holden and Richard Widmark. Watson looked nifty in her western garb (a bright emerald green gown). In *Murderers' Row* (1966) Jan was back as a Slaygirl and this time even got lines to recite! Chosen to be Miss July in the Slaymate calendar, she arrives early (wearing a very form-fitting floral pattern dress with blue gloves and picture hat) to her photo shoot with Dean Martin's Matt Helm, who tells her that they will be doing the Spirit of '76. The naïve Slaygirl retorts, "76? Are you kidding? I'm only a 44." Later she leads the other Slaygirls in a toast to Helm after believing that he was killed by a bomb planted by Corinne Cole's Miss January; she also appears in the film's finale wearing a velvet red, white and blue star-studded bikini and sapphires in her chestnut brown hair. 1967 continued to be a busy year for the glamour girl who began being billed as "Jann Watson," which she felt was more feminine. After playing a model in "A Piece of the Action" on *Batman*, she had a bit role in the teenage musical *The Cool Ones* and her pictures appeared in the May edition of *Stars and Stripes*. Watson immediately became a favorite pinup of the GIs in Vietnam. Her home address was listed, she received over 10,000 pieces of mail, and she publicly announced that she intended to answer each letter. She also made her third and final appearance as a Slaygirl in *The Ambushers*, which of all the Matt Helm films gave the most screen time to these delectable young ladies. After appearing with the other girls throughout the opening montage (clad in hip Sixties fashions) on the hunt for potential mates as the title tune is sung over the credits, Watson with her brown hair grown long is one of the Slaygirls at ICE's rehabilitation center, getting a refresher course on the newest gadgets developed by the spy organization. In a low-cut halter top with matching shorts, she rides up to Dean Martin's Matt Helm and offers him a ride on her Vespa. After he hops on, she quips, "I go pretty fast. Better find something to hang on to." With a nod to the audience, he reaches for her breasts as the scene fades out. Later she and the others are undercover at an Acapulco resort modeling fashions by Oleg Cassini. After playing a secretary in the serious secret agent thriller *Panic in the City* (1968), Watson married the much older director Henry Levin, whom she worked with on *Murderers' Row* and *The Ambushers*, on June 21, 1968. Following in the footsteps of many a Sixties glamour girl, she left acting to raise a family when her son Anthony J. Levin was born.

**The Beginning:** The daughter of hockey legend Phil Watson (who played for and later managed the New York Rangers), Watson was born Janet Helen Watson on December 17, 1942, in New York but raised in Los Angeles after her parents divorced. In 1961, she was crowned Miss Hollywood and later in the year placed first runner-up in the Miss California contest. She assumed the winner's duties when her predecessor forfeited the tiara by getting married. With an alluring smile and a figure measuring 36-23-35, it is no surprise movies beckoned for this beauty queen and she happily answered the call.

**The '70s & Beyond:** In 1972, Jan Watson divorced her husband Henry Levin and faded from the public eye. Today, her whereabouts are unknown.

---

# Carol Wayne

A platinum blonde beauty in the vein of Jayne Mansfield, she became extremely popular acting the bubble-headed ditz. But what made Wayne special was that she instilled a charming wide-eyed innocence into her characters, making them lovable and endearing rather than just the typical daffy buxom bimbo. Her ability to play sweet and naïve made her a fan favorite for years.

**You May Remember Her Most From:** her myriad appearances as the dumbfounded Matinee Lady on *The Tonight Show Starring Johnny Carson* during the Seventies.

**Her Groovy '60s Credits:** Carol Wayne made her television debut on *The Man from U.N.C.L.E.* in "The Super Colossal Affair" where she gave a very funny performance as bikini-clad Ginger LeVeer, a go-go girl, no-talent actress and girlfriend of a crime boss who gets her a part in a movie set in Las Vegas as a front to blow up the city. On *The Girl from U.N.C.L.E.* she was "Young Thing," an amorous dumb blonde in a tight gold lamé mini-dress who is immediately attracted to U.N.C.L.E. agent Noel Harrison as he goes undercover at a beatnik club in "The Faustus Affair." Wayne made her film debut playing the very minor part of a sexy blind date in Blake Edwards' *Gunn* (1967), the big-screen version of his popular TV series, *Peter Gunn*, starring Craig Stevens as the super-cool gumshoe. Edwards cast Wayne again in his comedy *The Party* (1967) starring Peter Sellers as a bungling Indian actor who is mistakenly invited to a big-time movie producer's A-list soiree. Wayne portrayed one of the guests—a Hollywood sexpot in a pink mini-dress with a plunging neckline that accentuated her 39-24-25 figure quite nicely. Though she doesn't utter a line of dialogue for the first 20 minutes she is on screen, audiences could not help but notice the platinum blonde in the background with the kewpie doll looks, bountiful bosom, and curvy body. When the guests all sit down to dine, Wayne finally has some comical interaction with Sellers before fading into the background right through the foamy finale. For unknown reasons, movies didn't beckon much for Wayne but she remained very active on television. She popped up on *I Spy* as an unhappy, ditzy starlet stranded in Spain in "The Trouble with Temple." Saddled with evil actor boyfriend Jack Cassidy (who is selling secret films of NATO maneuvers), Wayne is smarter than she looks and helps agent Robert Culp nab the creep. On *I Dream of Jeannie* she was the aptly named Bootsie Nightingale in "Here Comes Bootsie Nightingale"; *Bewitched* featured her as a rabbit accidentally transformed by warlock Paul Lynde into a sexy Playboy Bunny who falls for Darrin's client in "A Bunny for Tabitha."

**Carol Wayne (ca. 1968).**

**The Beginning:** Carol Wayne was born in Chicago, Illinois, on September 6, 1942. She and her younger sister Nina took up ice skating as teenagers on the advice of their doctor because they were sickly children. Highly skilled skaters, they were hired by the Ice Capades and left school. A few years later, a knee injury sidelined Wayne's career but after recuperating she joined her sister in Las Vegas and became a showgirl in the Folies Bergere while commuting between Vegas and Hollywood to take acting lessons with Jeff Corey.

**The '70s & Beyond:** Carol Wayne is best remembered for her 101 appearances on *The Tonight Show Starring Johnny Carson* beginning in 1971 playing the dippy but dazzling Matinee Lady to Carson's lecherous host Art Fern in the "Tea Time Movie" skits. Wayne wasn't the first actress to essay the role but once she did, the part was hers to keep. Its success was partly due to Wayne's caught-in-the headlights stare as she appeared not to understand Carson's bawdy jokes and double-entendres. She usually joined the guests on the couch after the skits and one of her most hilarious lines came when comedian Don Rickles mentioned to Johnny that his mother just moved to Miami. Wayne cooed in her little girl voice, "Oh, Miami Beach. That's God's little waiting room." Daytime fans were treated to Wayne's kooky quips as she appeared regularly on the women's talk show *Mantrap* in 1971, and the game shows *Celebrity Sweepstakes* and *The Hollywood Squares*. But acting roles were few and far between for Carol as she was becoming known for being more of a personality than actress. She had a supporting role in the forgettable battle-of-the-sexes TV-movie *Every Man Needs One* (1972) starring Ken Berry and Connie Stevens and landed dramatic guest star roles on *The Bold Ones: The Lawyers*, *Mannix*, and *Emergency!* In between she played various roles including distracting secretaries and love-starved women in six episodes of *Love, American Style*. When *The Tonight Show* was shortened to an hour in 1980, most of Carson's skits were jettisoned including the one with Carol Wayne. She returned to the big screen playing cameo roles in the comedy *Scavenger Hunt* (1979) and the obscure drama *Gypsy Angels* (1980) starring a pre–*Wheel of Fortune* Vanna White. Marriage to husband number three, Burt Sugerman, producer of the rock music TV show *The Midnight Special*, kept Wayne busy making a few appearances on the late night staple. During this time she let her natural hair color grow out and posed semi-nude in *Playboy* at age forty-two. After playing a mother (or as she told Johnny Carson "Annette Funicello all grown up") in the teen comedy *Surf II* (1984), Wayne won the best reviews of her career and proved she had acting talent when she was cast as an artist's kinky model (complete with garter belts and leather accessories) in *Heartbreakers* (1984) starring Peter Coyote and Nick Mancuso as two men in their thirties who have to finally face growing up. Wayne gave the film's most poignant performance when, after agreeing to a *ménage a trois*, she touchingly reveals her feelings about herself—from what she thinks of her body to her dreams that have passed her by. Some critics felt Wayne was confessing her own true thoughts about her life, giving the scene even more emotion. Unfortunately, Carol Wayne was never able to capitalize on the raves she received from *Heartbreakers*. On January 13, 1985, shortly after the movie was released, the newly divorced actress drowned while on vacation with a companion in Mexico. To this day, her death remains a mystery and foul play has long been suspected. She was survived by her sister Nina and son Alex from her second marriage to photographer Barry Feinstein.

# Nina Wayne

Sister of the more famous Carol Wayne, she was a dark-haired, 5-foot-9 beauty with the similar "little girl voice," big expressive eyes, bountiful bosom, and trademark innocence.

**Nina Wayne (1968).**

**You May Remember Her Most From:** the TV sitcom *Camp Runamuck* as a sweetly naïve camp counselor who drives all the male counselors and their charges wild with her looks and beauty.

**Her Groovy '60s Credits:** Accompanying Van Johnson onto *The Tonight Show*, showgirl Nina Wayne was spotted by producer David Swift, who was enchanted with her cooing style of speaking and comedic timing. Two days later she was in Hollywood playing a girls' summer camp counselor in the 1965 sitcom *Camp Runamuck*, the name of the boys' camp across the lake. The sexy Wayne turned a lot of heads amongst the male population, especially that of counselor Dave Madden who would shake uncontrollably every time she approached him. Airing on Friday night on NBC opposite CBS' *The Wild Wild West* and ABC's *The Flintstones*, this camp folded up its tent after only one season on the air. Even so, Nina received lots of press coverage and nice reviews for her performance. She resurfaced on *Bewitched* in "Disappearing Samantha" as a daffy bimbo groupie of witchcraft "expert" Osgood Rightmire (Bernard Fox). When she calls him "Mr. Rightmire," he replies, "Osgood." The amorous brunette coos, "Osgood too." Signed to a contract with Columbia, Nina made her film debut in the arty crime caper *Dead Heat on a Merry-Go-Round* (1966) starring James Coburn as a shifty parolee who plans to rob the bank at Los Angeles International Airport during the visit of a Russian premier and takes advantage of a number of people to aid him in his scheme including Wayne, giving an amusing performance as a bubble-headed maid. With her low-cut red blouse revealing ample cleavage, the babbling Wayne (who doesn't believe in names and only reads nonfiction) meets shoe salesman Coburn while buying regulation sneakers for her job. Pretending to be Swiss, he feigns interest in her and takes her to dinner only as a pretense to steal her key to her employer's townhouse, which he robs. When being questioned by a frustrated police detective trying to get Coburn's physical description, the daffy Wayne replies, "He was very shy."

In the farce *Luv* (1966) Wayne was cast in another dumb bimbo role as a buxom fitness nut and girlfriend of married Peter Falk, who decides neurotic friend Jack Lemmon is the perfect match for his unhappy wife Elaine May. When Falk's matchmaking scheme succeeds, he is free to marry Wayne but his life becomes even worse as the sexy blonde morphs into a hausfrau with curlers in her hair and nothing but complaints. Wayne's last theatrical motion picture was *The Comic* (1969) starring Dick Van Dyke as an egotistical silent film star loosely based on Buster Keaton. Nina is wonderful playing a wayward wife who breaks up Van Dyke's rocky marriage to Michele Lee. Wearing nothing but sneakers and holding a tennis racket, the sensuous brunette seduces the comic on a tennis court. It was around this time that Wayne's marriage to David Wheeler began to take precedence over her career, especially when she had a child.

**The Beginning:** Nina Wayne was born on September 13, 1943, in Chicago, Illinois. She and her sister Carol began ice skating as children to strengthen their weak ankles and skinny legs. They became so adept on the ice that they were signed to perform in the Ice Capades when Nina was fifteen. She left the ice show a few years later after her sibling was sidelined with an injury. Relocating to Las Vegas, the statuesque beauty found work as a showgirl. New York was her next move, working as a model by day and dancing in Van Johnson's act at the Latin Quarter by night.

**The '70s & Beyond:** Nina Wayne turned up in "Love and the Check" on *Love, American Style* in 1971 as a beautiful girl with a million dollar check written on her tummy. She was then off the small screen for two years. Her acting swan song was in an offbeat role as a blonde lesbian belly dancer called Charisma Beauty in the made-for TV movie *The Night Strangler* (1973) starring Darren McGavin as the nosy reporter of the macabre, Carl Kolchak. Despite being constantly accompanied by her older butch lover, Wayne becomes a victim of a madman on the loose in Seattle as he attacks her in her dressing room. Perhaps not having the drive to continue with her career and constantly being compared to her more famous sister Carol, Nina Wayne retired from show business and worked as a telephone operator. She had two children and remained married to David Wheeler until his death in 2001. She currently resides in Palm Springs, California.

# Delores Wells

A petite brunette beauty, she sported a knockout 36-20-36 figure, which was delectably on display in a handful of beach party movies.

**You May Remember Her Most From:** *Muscle Beach Party* (1964) and *Bikini Beach* (1964) as beach babe Annette Funicello's best gal pal Sniffles.

**Her Groovy '60s Credits:** As *Playboy*'s Miss June 1960, Delores Wells' pictorial featured her in a variety of hats including her centerfold lying on a beach blanket sans a bathing suit. Her ambition was "to do a Broadway show" and her turnoffs were "hypocrites and snobs." Signed to a two-year contract by *Playboy*, she traveled the country promoting the magazine and did a stint as a Bunny at the Chicago Playboy Club. In 1961, she began landing minor TV roles on the series *The New Bob Cummings Show*, *Thriller*, and *Burke's Law* before making her screen debut in *Beach Party* (1963) starring Frankie Avalon and Annette Funicello. She played Sue, one of Annette's bikini-clad girlfriends, who was paired with surfer John Ashley. When Annette dumps Frankie to be with the older Robert Cummings, Wells tries to be supportive but joins with the surfers to give "Old Pig Bristles" grief. AIP thought they had a new star in the making with Wells and featured her in several promotional layouts to promote *Beach Party*. In her next two beach movie appearances, Wells played a surfer chick nicknamed Sniffles and (unlike some of the other actresses hired to play beach bunnies) she had lines and received featured billing. She and the other girls compete for Frankie's attention though he has eyes only for Annette until Italian countess Luciana Paluzzi hits the sand in *Muscle Beach Party* (1964). In *Bikini Beach* (1964) Wells and the other beach bunnies flip their bouffants for singing sensation The Potato Bug to the chagrin of their surfer boyfriends. When the British pop star serenades the gals with a little ditty on the sand, Wells (whose shapely figure is hidden under a short blue beach wrap) drops to the sand in a frenzied state. It was Wells' last beach movie. In *The Time Travelers* (1964) Delores was cast as Reena, one of the last survivors of the human race living in an underground city in the year 2071. The producers were smart enough not to hide the curvaceous Playmate's body as she lies around topless at a spa of the future and tries to make time with goofy time traveler Steve Franken while the men folk construct a starship to escape from the mutant-run planet. She also appeared in a scene featuring the film's most impressive effects as she plays a spectacularly ornate organ which tosses up onto a screen perched atop it a Fantasia kaleidoscope of dancing galaxies.

After taking a brief hiatus from acting, Delores returned to the big screen in minor roles. Now with longer brown hair, she could be seen lounging around by the pool (bikini-

Former Playmate turned beach bunny Delores Wells (ca. 1965).

clad, of course) in the country club-set drama *Banning* (1967) and fleetingly glimpsed as one of the myriad of nubile attractive women tempting husband Walther Matthau to cheat on his wife in *A Guide for the Married Man* (1967).

**The Beginning:** Delores Wells was born on October 17, 1937, in Reading, Pennsylvania. She did some modeling before *Playboy* beckoned.

**The '70s & Beyond:** In the Seventies, she became the personal assistant to Linda

Lovelace for a period of time. She met the porn star at the Playboy Mansion in Los Angeles where Wells purportedly still resides.

# June Wilkinson

A busty British platinum blonde bombshell a la Jayne Mansfield and Mamie Van Doren, she had talent but couldn't shake the Amazonian roles and was forever typed as a glamour girl due to her many topless appearances in *Playboy* and other men's publications.

**You May Remember Her Most From:** the cult horror movie *Macumba Love* (1960) as a vacationing newlywed whose buxomness rattles even the zombies.

**Her Groovy '60s Credits:** June Wilkinson started off the decade in *Career Girl* (1960) playing a hopeful starlet out to make the big time in Hollywood. Exploiting Wilkinson's pinup past, the titillating ads proclaimed, "See what happens to girls who give up Hollywood careers to join a nudist camp!" The film received a lot of notoriety for June's nude dive into a swimming pool. The horror movie *Macumba Love* (1960), June's most infamous film, cast her as the honeymooning daughter of a scientist in Brazil who is out to prove that all that voodoo is nonsense. As the newly arrived newlywed, June loses her bikini top on the beach and almost loses husband William Wellman, Jr., who seems to have caught an early case of the seven-year-itch when he cozies up to sultry Ziva Rodann (who may or may not be a snake goddess). Minor roles followed in *The Private Lives of Adam and Eve* (1960) as one of the beautiful minions of Mickey Rooney's Devil, *Who's Got the Action?* (1962), and the Doris Day–Rock Hudson comedy *Lover Come Back* (1961) as a stripper (her scenes were excised).

John Cassavetes wanted Wilkinson for his leading lady in *Too Late Blues* (1962) but Paramount balked and June wound up with only a minor part as a sexy bar patron seen near the end of the movie. Her fans got to see a lot more of her 44D cup shimmying the night away in the low-budget musical *Twist All Night* (1962) where she played the girlfriend of musician Louis Prima, out to save the small nightclub he performs at by introducing the new dance craze, The Twist. Next, she worked with newcomer Francis Ford Coppola who was hired by Roger Corman to add additional color scenes to a black-and-white German sex comedy, which was re-titled *The Playgirls and the Bellboy* (1962). After journeying to Mexico to play a stripper in *La Rabia por dentro* (1963), she co-starred with Mamie Van Doren in the political sex farce *The Candidate* (1964), where she seduces politician Ted Knight. Tired of playing the sexpot in Grade Z productions, Wilkinson returned to the theatre. She had her biggest success with the racy sex farce *Pajama Tops* and brought the show to Broadway. As the sexy French mistress secretly wed to her lover's butler, June won decent reviews with one critic remarking that "Miss Wilkinson is a skyline all by herself." The show closed after only 52 performances but it was a hit on tour. Wilkinson soon became one of the highest paid actresses working on stage as she traveled the country starring in regional productions of *The Marriage-Go-Round* with Vivian Blaine and Louis Jour-

June "The Bosom" Wilkinson (ca. 1965).

dan, *Any Wednesday* with Tom Poston and Elaine Stritch, and *Come Blow Your Horn* with Sylvia Sidney. In between shows, June made a rare TV appearance in 1968 on *Batman* in "Nora Clavicle and Her Ladies' Crime Club," paired with Inga Neilsen as masked Amazonian bank robbers clad in tight-fitting gold Romanesque gowns. Incredibly, they are captured by decrepit Alfred the butler.

**The Beginning:** June Wilkinson was born on March 27, 1940, in Essex, England, began dancing ballet as a child and appeared in her first professional stage production, *Cinderella*, in 1952. After blossoming into a 44-23-36, 5-foot-6 beauty, she abandoned ballet and began performing the Can-Can and the Fan Dance at the Windmill Theater in London. At this time she also started modeling. In 1957 she accepted the offer of American Beacons, a plastics company, to do promotion for the firm and toured the U.S. as "Miss Plastic Houseware." She wound up also modeling fashions for Oleg Cassini and appeared on *The Today Show* where a talent scout from Seven Arts saw her and signed her to a movie contract. She also at this time took it upon herself to meet Hugh Hefner. He took one gander at her awesome 44-inch assets and dubbed her "The Bosom," rushing the underage teenager (who had parental approval) into the September 1958 issue though not as the monthly Playmate. June was so popular that over the next few years she posed for *Playboy* twice (including the August 1959 pictorial "The Bosom in Hollywood") as well as in the girlie magazines *Gent*, *Adam*, *Cavalier*, *Hi-Life*, *Modern Man*, and *Girl Watcher*. June's first film appearance featured her anonymous topless torso as she is standing at a window and pulls the shade down in the nudie flick *The Immoral Mr. Teas* (1959). It was directed by Russ Meyer, who had photographed the buxom blonde previously on numerous occasions and helped make her one of the top pinups of the late Fifties. She made her official acting debut in *Thunder in the Sun* (1959) in a minor role.

**The '70s & Beyond:** In 1970 June Wilkinson appeared as herself, talking about bikinis in the racy documentary *Hollywood Blue* (1970). Russ Meyer wanted her for the role of Ashley St. Ives in *Beyond the Valley of the Dolls* but 20th Century–Fox pushed contract player Edy Williams for the part. After a ten-year absence, "The Bosom" finally returned to the big screen in *The Florida Connection* (1974), a violent drug-smuggling tale where June played a pilot opposite her then-husband football player Dan Pastorini. After that marriage ended in 1982, the blonde bombshell appeared in a number of forgettable low-budget movies such as *Frankenstein's Great Aunt Tillie* (1984) and *Sno-Line* (1986). She went topless in *Talking Walls* (1987) and got to ham it up as a criminal mastermind who is executing mobster dons in the comedy *Keaton's Cop* (1988). In 1997, she posed once again for *Playboy* in a salute to "The Best of Glamour Girls: Then and Now." In 2005, Wilkinson came out of retirement to play a small role in the western *Three Bad Men* starring George Kennedy and Peter Brown. She resides in Los Angeles where she hosts a local cable show called *The Directors* where she interviews filmmakers. She is a fan favorite at celebrity autograph conventions throughout the nation.

# Edy Williams

She arguably had the most determination and drive of most Sixties glamour girls to become another Raquel Welch. Standing 5-foot-7 with dark brown hair and brown-green eyes, she had a curvaceous 39-26-37 body, breathy voice, and captivating personality that men drool over. Loving the camera, Edy posed bikini-clad for numerous cheesecake and

**Edy Williams (ca. 1967).**

pinup photos. She turned every public appearance into a media event and undeniably became a sex goddess of the Glamazonian kind. What she lacked was that one breakout role (a la Raquel's *One Million Years B.C.*) to propel her to international stardom.

**You May Remember Her Most From:** *Beyond the Valley of the Dolls* (1970) as the voraciously man-hungry starlet Ashley St. Ives.

**Her Groovy '60s Credits:** Edy Williams began her acting career with bit roles in a few movies including *For Love or Money* (1963) before getting noticed playing call girls in *A House Is Not a Home* (1964) and more memorably in Sam Fuller's film noir *The Naked Kiss* (1964) as one of Madam Candy's "Bon-Bons," nicknamed "Hatrack." As with her contemporaries, she also landed minor roles on TV including episodes of *Burke's Law*, *The Beverly Hillbillies* as a gold digger in "Jethro's Pad," and *The Man from U.N.C.L.E.* as a sultry lab technician in an almost skintight yellow uniform in "The Hula Doll Affair." The ravishing beauty then signed a contract with 20th Century–Fox but whereas that studio's Raquel Welch landed big movie roles Edy toiled on television making appearances on *Batman* as a bagpipe-playing bad girl in cahoots with evil Liberace in "The Devil's Fingers" and "The Dead Ringers," and *Lost in Space* as a lizard-type alien on the lam with her gang of thieves who morphs into a seductive blonde humanoid pretending to be a vacationer in "Two Weeks in Space." Edy was voted a Hollywood Deb Star for 1965 but still was only landing bit parts on the big screen in *Nevada Smith* (1965), *Red Line 7000* (1965), and *Paradise, Hawaiian Style* (1966) where she competed with Ann Morell and China Lee to become Elvis Presley's secretary. She was simply delectable in her first film role of note, *The Pad (and How to Use It)* (1966), playing one of playboy James Farentino's girlfriends, but went right back to bit parts in the awful Sonny and Cher musical *Good Times* (1967) playing one of mogul George Sanders' three secretaries.

It was at this point that Williams went blonde and had one of her best roles in *The Secret Life of an American Wife* (1968) as the "dumb but well-stacked" suburban neighbor of Anne Jackson who imagines Edy as this sexy siren who can seduce any man. After playing one of sailor Gardner McKay's shapely shipmates in *I Sailed to Tahiti with an All-Girl Crew* (1969) and a Vegas showgirl who is sent by casino owner David Janssen to seduce his son (Robert Drivas) who he suspects of being gay in *Where's It At?* (1969), Williams landed her most notorious role in *Beyond the Valley of the Dolls* (1970), directed by Russ Meyer. Edy, now with chestnut brown hair with blonde highlights, played Ashley St. Ives, a porn star who covets young David Gurian. Meeting him at a wild happening, the amorous mini-skirted vixen tells the shocked lad, "You're a groovy boy—I'd like to strap you on sometime." When his rock star girlfriend Dolly Read jilts him for a matinee idol, Gurian gives in to the seductive Edy and they have sex in the backseat of her Rolls-Royce as she squeals in delight, "There's nothing like a Rolls... nothing... not even a Bentley!" After an aborted tryst on the beach where Gurian can't get it up, Williams mocks him and calls him "a fag" before finding another boy toy to take his place and disappointingly disappears from the rest of the movie. Edy Williams goes all-out as Ashley and steals the film, giving an outrageously amusing performance. The movie typed her as a sex star though Williams surprisingly kept her clothes on, unlike the other starlets in it.

**The Beginning:** Edy Williams was born Edwina Beth Williams on July 9, 1942, in Salt Lake City, Utah, and grew up in California's San Fernando Valley where her next door neighbor was Johnny Carson. After graduating from Van Nuys High School, she attended Valley State College for three semesters. As a teenager she worked as a model and became a local beauty queen. She was crowned "Miss California Bikini" and "Miss Tarzana" in 1963, followed by "Miss Sherman Oaks" in 1964, the year she began acting.

**The '70s & Beyond:** After completing *Beyond the Valley of the Dolls*, Edy Williams wed her director Russ Meyer. He then cast her as a rich bitch who disapproves that her fiancé Wayne Maunder is representing an author in a censorship case in his deadly dull melodrama *The Seven Minutes* (1971). The Meyer-Williams marriage was rocky from the get-go; the couple split, and in 1974 Williams began her annual trek to the Cannes Film Festival where she removed her clothes for the eager paparazzi and then landed a lead role in the sexy Italian movie, *Peccati in famiglia* a.k.a. *Scandal in the Family* (1975). Back in Hollywood she became an annual fixture on the red carpet at the Academy Awards though there her dress stayed on... barely. By this time Hollywood considered her to be a joke and for the remainder of her career she was required to disrobe in practically every low-budget exploitation movie she appeared in. Audiences had to suspend disbelief to accept her as a physician in *Dr. Minx* (1975) and a college professor in *The Happy Hooker Goes to Hollywood* (1977). She landed one good film, Paul Mazursky's *Willie and Phil* (1980), but she had only a very minor role in it. It seemed Edy was more comfortable on camera undraped and looked like she was having a ball playing an over-sexed sexpot in *Hollywood Hot Tubs* (1984) and an aspiring starlet who willingly heads for the casting couch in *Nudity Required* (1988). In between, she played a convict in two women-in-prison films from the same screenwriter—*Chained Heat* (1984) where Edy with her hair dyed red has a full frontal nude shower scene and *Hellhole* (1985) whose highlight is her topless brawl. On TV, she appeared as herself parodying her on-screen persona during a dream sequence in a 1987 episode ("They Call Me Mr. Trunk") of the cult sitcom, *Sledge Hammer!* By the Nineties, Williams' career had so completely dried up she was forced to accept a role in the X-rated *Snatch Masters 6* (1995). Today, Edy Williams still looks gorgeous; she made an appearance on the red carpet of the 2006 Academy Awards but for the most part was ignored by the press. She is active on the autograph circuit and was interviewed for the TV documentary *The Award Show Awards Show*. She has shunned all inquiries regarding her ex-husband Russ Meyer and, disappointingly, she did not participate in the release of the deluxe DVD edition of *Beyond the Valley of the Dolls*.

# Francine York

Similar in looks and figure to Julie Newmar, this glamourous brunette was usually cast as sophisticated ladies in major productions or in bigger-than-life Amazonian roles on TV and in low-budget fantasy and sci-fi movies. But a la Edy Williams she never scored that one movie role that would progress her to more accomplished fare. Nevertheless, York could never be accused of giving a lazy performance no matter if she was tackling a minor role or the female lead and approached all her projects with a professionalism and enthusiasm some of them probably did not deserve. "I always thought I was better than the picture," she once quipped. The critics usually agreed.

**You May Remember Her Most From:** TV's *Batman* as the Bookworm's accomplice Lydia Limpet or *Lost in Space* as the noble Amazonian warrior Niolani who imprisons the Robinson family, making the men her slaves.

**Her Groovy '60s Credits:** Though it was not released until 1962, Francine York's first feature *Secret File: Hollywood* lensed in 1960. She was perfectly cast as the unscrupulous head of a scandal sheet a la *Confidential*. She followed this with an uncredited role in *The Right Approach* (1961) and then played a supporting part as a WAC in the low-budget military comedy, *The Sergeant Was a Lady* (1961). This was the beginning of a pattern that can be traced throughout York's career: Minor roles in major studio productions followed by leads or second leads in B-movies. In 1962, Francine starred in *Wild Ones on Wheels* playing the philandering wife of an ex-con who owns a greasy spoon in the desert where they are abducted by his vengeful former motorcycle buddies. Then it was back to a bit as the "Sexy Girl" in the Jerry Lewis comedy *It's Only Money*. York is memorable in this for her 45-second kiss with actor Jesse White. Lewis so liked Francine that he cast her in a few of his Sixties comedies. She played a college coed in *The Nutty Professor* (1963), a nurse in *The Disorderly Orderly* (1964), and a flight attendant in *The Family Jewels* (1965). All of these roles were fleeting and are a basically a waste of York's assets.

Francine (along with a number of other stylish model-type starlets) turned up in the Paul Newman–Joanne Woodward comedy *A New Kind of Love* (1963) which spoofed the fashion industry but she did not receive screen credit. York's first standout role was playing a gorgeous Italian girl (clad in a tight red dress that accentuated her lusty figure) who meets scoundrel Marlon Brando on the train in *Bedtime Story* (1964). Television offered Francine much better and bigger parts on *The Gallant Men, Burke's Law, Bob Hope Chrysler Theatre, My Favorite Martian*, and *Hazel*. Returning to the big screen, it was back to decorating the background for York in the Elvis Presley flick *Tickle Me* (1965). She was one of a bevy of beauties (along with Diane Bond, Linda Rogers, Eve Bruce, and Ann Morell) playing actresses and models who go gaga over the King as a singing rodeo cowboy moonlighting as handyman at a beauty spa. Possessing an authoritative quality and sophisticated poise, York found the studios shying away from giving her larger roles, possibly due to the insecurities of its leading men. Grade-Z movie producers however were not so timid but misused her in a series of drab sci-fi and monster flicks. She was cast as astronauts in *Mutiny in Outer Space* (1965), where the crew has to fight off a lunar fungus, and the made-for-TV *Space Monster* (1965) as the first female in orbit; she had the rare role of the innocent heroine, married to a mad doctor experimenting on the locals deep in the bayous of Louisiana in *Curse of the Swamp Creature* (1966). Though Francine looks great in her green outfit and tries to act the helpless female, she is miscast, especially in scenes where the Glamazon is slapped around by four-eyed nerd Jeff Alexander as her husband and she does not strike back.

For York it was the small screen that really gave her roles with some bite. She camped it up playing the Bookworm's moll Lydia Limpet who gets bat-gassed in "The Bookworm Turns" and "While Gotham City Burns" on *Batman* and the Amazonian alien leader noble Niolani who enslaves the Robinson men in "The Colonists" on *Lost in Space*. Back on the big screen, Francine was wasted playing the mayor's wife in the western *Ride to Hangman's Tree* (1967) but fared much better as a fiery belly dancer in *Cannon for Cordoba* (1970) opposite George Peppard. York finally received the attention she deserved but it was not for her performance but for her brief nude scene (photos found their way into the pages of *Playboy* magazine to the delight of her male admirers). In between she turned up on such mega-popular TV shows as *It Takes a Thief* in a few early episodes as Robert Wagner's sexy parole officer, *Green Acres* as a shapely coed sent to Hooterville in "The Agricultural Student," *The Wild Wild West* as a doctor working at a prison in "The Night of the Pelican," *Ironside* as a radical college student in "Not with a Whimper, But a Bang," *Love,*

Francine York strikes a pose as the Bookworm's nefarious moll Lydia Limpet in *Batman* (20th Century–Fox Television, 1966).

*American Style* as a wife who swings in "Love and the Wild Party," and *The Courtship of Eddie's Father* as Brandon Cruz'a Auntie Mame-ish Aunt Kate in "Who Pulled the Blues Right Out of the Horn?"

**The Beginning:** Francine York was born Francine Yerich on August 26, 1938, in Aurora, Minnesota. She was performing from the time she was a toddler and appeared in all her school plays. Winning a local beauty contest led to the Miss Minnesota pageant where she placed first runner-up. A career as a model came next as she toured the country sporting sweaters for Jane Richards Sportswear. York settled in San Francisco, where she was represented by the House of Charm Modeling Agency. After she had stints as a beauty queen (Miss San Francisco), a department store model, and showgirl at the famed nightclub Bimbo's, Hollywood finally beckoned to Francine and, boy, did she answer the call!

**The '70s & Beyond:** Back on TV, a new crop of teenage boys enjoyed Francine York's appearances on *Land of the Giants* as a mini-skirted scientist in "Doomsday" and *Bewitched* as a breathtaking Venus de Milo come to life in "Bewitched, Bothered and Baldoni." York rode her wave of notoriety to play an adulterous wife who has a brief affair with a biker in *Welcome Home, Soldier Boys!* (1972), the leader of an all-girl commando unit in *The Doll Squad* (1973), and a photographer's shapely assistant who meets a nasty end while showering in *The Centerfold Girls* (1974). *Flood* (1976), Irwin Allen's first made-for-TV disaster movie, gave Francine her first real girl-next-door role as a heroic nurse and love interest of Robert Culp's hotshot helicopter pilot who comes to the rescue of the waterlogged townspeople. She also played trashy ex-hooker Lorraine Temple on the soap opera *Days of Our Lives* in 1978 and co-starred with Jerry Lewis again in the comedy *Cracking Up* (1982). The latter gave Francine a wonderful part in the film's 15th-century France sketch as a fractured French-speaking, buxom woman who encounters Lewis' ancestor while she is being carted around in her horse-drawn coach. During the Eighties and Nineties York stayed active on television appearing on *Mama's Family*, *Mr. Belvedere*, *Matlock*, and *Burke's Law*, and in low-budget movies that went direct to VHS or DVD. One of the oddest was *Marilyn Alive and Behind Bars* (1992) where York channeled Marilyn Monroe, who was being held prisoner in a mental ward after her death was faked by a mysterious powerful businessman. In 2000, York had a memorable comedic role as Nicolas Cage's mother-in-law in the comedy fantasy *Family Man* (2000) and continues to act to this day. She was perfectly cast as Hera, the mother of all goddesses, in the short film *Hercules in Hollywood* (2005), Michael Parks' wife in the well-received family western *Miracle at Sage Creek* (2006), and as randy seniors on TV's *The King of Queens* and *Las Vegas*. Like the Energizer Bunny, York keeps on going and going and going...

# *Bibliography*

Abbott, Jon. *Irwin Allen Television Productions, 1964–1970: A Critical History.* Jefferson, North Carolina: McFarland, 2006.

Betrock, Alan. *The I Was a Teenage Juvenile Delinquent Rock 'n' Roll Horror Beach Party Movie Book.* New York: St. Martin's Press, 1986.

Castleman, Harry, and Walter J. Podrazik. *Harry and Wally's Favorite TV Shows.* New York: Prentice Hall, 1989.

*Classic TV Archive, The.* http://www.geocities.com/TelevisionCity/Stage/2950.

Craig, Yvonne. *From Ballet to the Batcave and Beyond.* Venice, California: Kudu Press, 2000.

Doll, Susan. *The Films of Elvis Presley.* Lincolnwood, Illinois: Publications International, 1991.

Dougherty, Joseph. *Comfort and Joi.* New York: iUniverse, 2005.

Gerani, Gary, and Paul H. Schulman. *Fantastic Television.* New York: Harmony Books, 1977.

Handy, Aaron, III. *The Monkees Film & TV Vault.* http://members.tripod.com/~ahiii/monkeesfilmTV.html.

*Headquarters of Wildwest2-L—The Wildest Netfolk in the West.* http://www.wildwildwest.org.

Howe, Michael. *The Unofficial Fanpage of Village of the Giants.* http://www.angelfire.com/weird2/villageoftheg.

Inman, David M. *Television Variety Shows: Histories and Episode Guides to 57 Programs.* Jefferson, North Carolina: McFarland, 2006.

Internet Movie Database. www.imdb.com.

Klossner, Michael. *Prehistoric Humans in Film and Television: 581 Dramas, Comedies and Documentaries, 1905–2004.* Jefferson, North Carolina: McFarland, 2006.

Koenig, Bill. *The Man from U.N.C.L.E. Episode Guide.* http://members.aol.com/Wmkoenig/unclepg.htm.

Krafsur, Richard P., ed. *The American Film Institute Catalog of Motion Pictures: Feature Films 1961–1970.* New York & London: R.R. Bowker, 1976.

Lance, Steven. *Written Out of Television: A TV Lover's Guide to Cast Changes 1945–1994.* Lanham, Maryland: Madison Books, 1996.

Lisanti, Tom. *Drive-in Dream Girls: A Galaxy of B-Movie Starlets of the Sixties.* Jefferson, North Carolina: McFarland, 2003.

_____. *Fantasy Femmes of Sixties Cinema: Interviews with 20 Actresses from Biker, Beach, and Elvis Movies.* Jefferson, North Carolina: McFarland, 2001.

Lisanti, Tom, and Louis Paul. *Femme Fatales: Women in Espionage Films and Television, 1962–1973.* Jefferson, North Carolina: McFarland, 2002.

McDonough, Jimmy. *Big Bosoms and Square Jaws: The Biography of Russ Meyer, King of the Sex Film.* New York: Crown, 2005.

Monush, Barry. *Screen World Presents the Encyclopedia of Hollywood Film Actors: From the Silent Era to 1965.* New York: Applause Theatre & Cinema Books, 2003.

Http://www.newspaperarchive.com

Palmer, Randy. *Herschell Gordon Lewis, Godfather of Gore: The Films.* Jefferson, North Carolina: McFarland, 2006.

*Playboy Online.* http://www.playboy.com/.

Rotter, C. Robert. *Glamour Girls of the Silver Screen.* http://www.glamourgirlsofthesilverscreen.com.

Slifkin, Irv. *VideoHound's Groovy Movies: Far-Out Films of the Psychedelic Era.* Detroit: Invisible Ink Press, 2004.

Stidworthy, David. *High on the Hogs: A Biker Filmography.* Jefferson, North Carolina: McFarland, 2003.

Strodder, Chris. *Swingin' Chicks of the '60s.* San Rafael, California: Cedco Publishing, 2000.

*TV.com.* http://www.tv.com/.

Walker, Brian J. *Brian's Drive-in Theater.* http://briansdriveintheater.com/beach.html.

Weldon, Michael. *The Psychotronic Encyclopedia of Film.* New York: Ballantine, 1983.

_____. *The Psychotronic Video Guide.* New York: St. Martin's Griffin, 1996.

Whipple, Blair. "Beauties of *The Beverly Hill-*

billies." *Polar Blair's Den.* http://www.polarblairsden.com/home.html.

*Wikipedia, The Free Encyclopedia.* http://en.wikipedia.org/wiki/Main_Page.

*WOm! WAm! Women Doing Things to Men.* http://www.womwam.net/index.html.

Wooley, John, and Michael H. Price. *The Big Book of Biker Flicks: 40 of the Best Motorcycle Movies of All Time.* Tulsa, Oklahoma: Hawk Publishing, 2005.

# *Index*

Aberg, Sivi 5–8
Adams, Beverly 8–11
Adamson, Al 142
*The Adventures of Ozzie & Harriet* 51, 121
*Airport* 89
Albertson, Jack 135
Alda, Alan 107
*Alice* 36
Allen, Gracie 198
Allen, Woody 116, 153
*The Ambushers* 151
Andress, Ursula 21
Andrews, Julie 54
Ann-Margret 52, 56, 165
Arden, Don 32
Arnaz, Desi 141
Arness, James 21, 22
*The Art of Love* 34
Arthur, Maureen 4, 11–13
*As the World Turns* 136
Asher, William 199
Austin, Pamela 4, 14–16
Avalon, Frankie 181
Axelrod, George 121, 123

Baer, Max, Jr. 37
Ball, Lucille 141
Barry, Gene 198
Bartlett, Hall 181
Bartold, Norman 168
*Batman* 199, 235
*Beach Ball* 114
*Beach Blanket Bingo* 137
*Beach Party* 181, 182
*Bedtime Story* 67
Bell, Michael 36
*Ben Casey* 19
Benedict, Richard 182
Benton, Barbie 167
Berg, Dick 105
Berghof, Herbert 197
Berle, Milton 199
*The Beverly Hillbillies* 37, 199
*Bewitched* 199
*Beyond the Valley of the Dolls* 171

*The Big Mouth* 52
*Bikini Beach* 155
Bishop, Joey 51
Bixby, Bill 34
*Black Bart* 105
*The Bob Hope Chrysler Theatre* 105
Boetticher, Budd 165, 166
Bond, Diane 169
*Boxcar Bertha* 143
*Bracken's World* 46
*Branded* 143
Brando, Marlon 67
Brandt, Christopher 22
Brandt, Thordis vii, 4, 16–25, 152
Brenna, Bettina 22–24, 152
Bridges, Beau 107, 121–123, 166
Bridges, Jeff 123
Bridges, Lloyd 123
Brolin, James 47
Brooks, Mel 133, 135, 153
Brown, Dale 210
Bruce, Eve 24–26
Brutsche, Jerry 184
Bundy, Brooke 47
Burgess, Barbara 208, 210
*Burke's Law* 198
Burnett, Carol 153
Burns, George 135, 198
Buttons, Red 198

Caan, James 107
Cannon, Dyan 55, 56
*Caprice* 196
*The Caretakers* 181
Carey, Michele 4, 26–29
*The Carol Burnett Show* 152
*The Carpetbaggers* 198
Carroll, Bob, Jr. 38
Carroll, Victoria vii, 4, 29–38
Cassavetes, John 165
Cassidy, Ted 55
*Cauliflower Cupid* 135
Chabot, Amedee 4, 38–40, 210
Chaney, Lon, Jr. 142
Charles, Arlene 4, 40–42
*Charlie's Angels* 167

Charny, Suzanne vii, 4, 42–47
Chase, Barrie 45
*Cher* 168
*The Christian Licorice Store* 166
*The Cincinnati Kid* 142
Clary, Robert 34
Clavell, James 19
Coburn, James 20, 151, 169
Cole, Corinne vii, 47–56
Coleman, Cy 34
Collins, Jo 4, 56–58
*The Comeback* 38
*The Comedy of Terrors* 181
Connors, Chuck 143
*Coogan's Bluff* 105, 106
Cook, Luci Ann 210
*Cool Hand Luke* 87
Cooper, Jackie 19
Corey, Jeff 19, 51
Corman, Roger 143
Craig, Yvonne 4, 58–61
Crane, Bob 34
Crawford, Joan 181
Crawford, Johnny 122
Crichton, Michael 167
Cukor, George 32–34
Cummings, Robert 181
Curran, Pamela 61–64
Curtis, Tony 67
Czar, Nancy 182, 183

Davis, Bill 166, 168
Davis, Madelyn 38
Davis, Phyllis 4, 70–72
Davis, Sammy, Jr. 51
Dawson, Richard 34
Day, Doris 142
*Days of Our Lives* 35, 166
*Days of Wine and Roses* 52
*The Dean Martin Show* 149
De Carlo, Yvonne 105
De Metz, Danielle 54
Demy, Jacques 165
Denberg, Susan 72–74
*Desire Under the Elms* 197
D'Hondt, Danica vii, 4, 64–70

*Divorce Court* 167
Douglas, Donna 199
Douglas, Gordon 20
Douglas, Kirk 68
*Dracula vs. Frankenstein* 142
Dreyfuss, Richard 134, 135
Duffy, Dee 210
Duryea, Dan 105

Eastwood, Clint 105, 106
Ebsen, Buddy 199
Edgington, Lyn 74–77
Edwards, Blake 52–54
Eilsey, Anthony 21
*Electra Glide in Blue* 174
Entratter, Jack 50–52, 54–56
*Everything You Wanted to Know About Sex\* But Were Afraid to Ask* 153

Fabian 197
Faith, Dolores 77–79
*Fantastic Voyage* 199
Farentino, James 105
Farrington, Kay 169
Farrow, Mia 51, 52, 165
*Faster, Pussycat! Kill! Kill!* 186
*The Fastest Guitar Alive* 35
Feldman, Marty 153
Ferrer, Jose 189
Fife, Allen 184
Finch, Peter 20
*Force of Impulse* 99
Ford, Anitra 167
Ford, Virginia Ann 23, 152
Fosse, Bob 45, 46
Foster, Linda 79–82
Franciosa, Tony 152
Frank, Mel 149, 150
Franken, Steve 53
Frankenheimer, John 68
Frawley, James 166
Fredericks, Dean 78
Funicello, Annette 181
*Funny Girl* 20–23, 108, 151–153
*Funny Lady* 153
*A Funny Thing Happened on the Way to the Forum* 149–151

Gaba, Marianne 57, 82, 83
Gabriel, John 165
*Gaily, Gaily* 106
*The Gallant Men* 198
*Garden of the Dead* 47
Gardner, Ava 68
Gavin, Erica 171
*General Hospital* 166
George, Lynda Day 21
Gerber, Gail vii; *see also* Gilmore, Gail
*Gilligan's Island* 67
Gilmore, Gail 86, 121–123
*The Girl from U.N.C.L.E.* 19
*Girl Happy* 123

*The Girls on the Beach* 129
Gordon, Bert I. 122, 123
Gordon, Marianne 167
Grant, Cary 46
*Grave of the Vampire* 153
Graziano, Rocky 135
*The Green Hornet* 19
Groag, Lillian 38
The Groundlings 32, 36, 38
*Gunsmoke* 21

*Hail to the Chief* 135
Hale, Jean 20, 151, 169
Hamilton, Sue 57, 83–85
Harmon, Joy 4, 85–88, 121–123
Harris, Jack 68
Harrison, Noel 19
Harrison, Rex 33
Hart, Susan 101
Hartley, Mariette 36
Hartman, Ena 4, 88–90
Hartman, Phil 36
Hartoch, Lynn 210
Harvey, Bob 184
Hathaway, Henry 51
Hawks, Howard 142
Hay, Alexandra 4, 91–93
*Hee Haw* 166, 167
Heffron, Robert 55
Hefner, Hugh 50, 141, 164, 167
Hefner, Kimberly 164
*Hello Dolly* 151
*Hello, Down There* 134, 135
*Hell's Bloody Devils* 165
Helm, Anne 68, 69
Hepburn, Audrey 33
Hershey, Barbara 143
Hill, Benny 136
Hill, Marianna 4, 93–96
*Hogan's Heroes* 34
Holloway, Susan 96–98, 209
Hope, Teri 98–100
Horten, Rena 210
Horton, Edward Everett 199
*A House Is Not a Home* 67, 149, 194, 198
*How to Stuff a Wild Bikini* 34, 57, 184
Howe, Bones 107
Hudson, Rock 182
Hughes, Mary 57, 100–102, 210
*Hullabaloo* 45
Hunter, Ross 34
Hyer, Martha 21

*I Love Lucy* 38
*In Like Flint* 20, 150, 151, 169
*The Incredible Hulk* 34
Ishimoto, Fred 19
*It Takes a Thief* 142

Jewison, Norman 106, 107
*John Goldfarb, Please Come Home* 142

Johnson, Melodie vii, 4, 103–107
Johnston, Alena 107–109, 152
Jory, Victor 19

Karlson, Phil 150
Keith, Brian 107
Kelly, Gene 151
Kelly, Grace 21
Kersh, Kathy 66
Kessler, Bruce 54
Kilcher, Q'Orianka 200, 201
Kilcher, Saskia 200
Kincaid, Aron vii
Kirk, Tommy 68, 69, 123
*Kissin' Cousins* 159
*Kolchak: The Night Stalker* 47
Korman, Harvey 67
Kotto, Yaphet 55
Kovack, Nancy 52
Kudrow, Lisa 38

Laine, Lari *see* Cole, Corinne
LaMotta, Jake 135
Lancaster, Burt 68
*Land of the Giants* 127
Lane, Jocelyn 142, 182
Lansing, Joi 4, 109–113
Lapp, Richard 165
Lavelle, Anna 113, 114
Lawford, Peter 51
Lee, Bruce 20
Lee, China 4, 115–117
Lee, Harriet 53
Lembeck, Harvey 155, 181
Lennon, John 182
Lester, Mark L. 55
Lester, Richard 151
Levene, Sam 135
Levin, Henry 52
Lewis, Herschell Gordon 67, 68
Lewis, Jerry 52
Liberace 66
Liberace, George 66, 67
*The Limit* 55
Lincoln, Abby 47
Lindsay, Lara 117–119
Lipton, Peggy 164
*Little Fauss and Big Halsy* 191
*Live a Little, Love a Little* 16, 21
*Living Venus* 66, 67
Lockwood, Gary 165
London, Vicki vii, 119–123
Longet, Claudine 53
Lord, Jack 105
*Lord Love a Duck* 121
Lorre, Peter 181
Louise, Tina 67
*Love in a Goldfish Bowl* 197
Lovett, Lee 153
Lucht, Darlene 123–125
*The Lucifer Complex* 55
Luna, BarBara vii
Lund, Deanna 125–128
Lupino, Ida 69

Macchia, Jerry 184
MacLaine, Shirley 142
*The Maltese Bippy* 176
*The Man from U.N.C.L.E.* 1, 19, 66, 68, 80
*Man-Trap* 197
Mangler, Mary Jane 23, 152, 208, 210
Mann, Paul 195
*Marilyn, Remembered* 68
Marshall, Linda 128–130
Martin, Dean 51–53, 150, 208
Martin, Dick 176
Martin, Steve 168
Mason, Jackie 135
Matthau, Walter 135
McBain, Diane 181
McBroom, Marcia 171
McCallum, David 19, 66, 68
McCrea, Jody 182
McDowall, Roddy 123, 134
McEachin, James 47
McElwaine, Guy 141
McGoohan, Patrick 107
McQueen, Steve 142
Mehta, Zubin 52
Mercouri, Melina 107
Meredith, Lee vii, 4, 130–136
Merman, Ethel 34
Michael, Mary 169
Michelle, Donna 4, 136–139
Miller, Denny 54
Mirisch, David 144
Mitchell, Cameron 35
Mitchell, Don 47
*The Mod Squad* 164
*The Model Shop* 165
The Monkees 54
*The Monkees* 54
Montgomery, Elizabeth 199
*The Moonshine War* 107
Moorehead, Agnes 199
Morell, Ann vii, 5, 139–144
Mostel, Zero 133, 151
*Mother Goose a-Go-Go* 65, 68, 69
*Murderers' Row* 52, 53, 210
Murphy, Audie 165, 166
Musante, Tony 47
*My Fair Lady* 32
Myers, Cynthia 144–146, 171

Naish, J. Carrol 142
Neilsen, Inga vii, 4, 20, 146–153, 169
Nelson, Alberta 154–156, 184
Nelson, David 51
Nelson, Harriet 50, 51
Nelson, Margie 209
Nelson, Ozzie 50, 51
Nelson, Ricky 51
*The New World* 201
Newmar, Julie 68, 149
*Nightmare in Wax* 31, 35, 36
*North to Alaska* 51

O'Brien, Edmund 197
O'Connor, Donald 135
*Oh! What a Lovely War* 69
*One of Our Spies Is Missing* 60
Opie, Linda 57
Orbison, Roy 35
Orr, Richard 149
Ott, Warrene 21, 156–158

*Pajama Party* 101, 182
*Paradise Pictures* 200
*The Party* 52–54
Peckinpah, Sam 142
Peppard, George 198
*Petticoat Junction* 120
*The Phantom Planet* 78
*The Phynx* 143
Pidgeon, Walter 20
Platler, James, Dr. vii, 75
Polanski, Roman 165
Poulsen, Patty 89
Powers, Beverly 158–161
Powers, Sefanie 19
Presley, Elvis 21, 34, 35, 123, 141, 142, 159, 182
Price, Vincent 181
*The Producers* 131, 133

*Rabbit, Run* 107
Rackin, Marty 197
Rain, Jeramie 135
Raines, Christina 167
Randall, Anne vii, 4, 161–168
Randall, Tony 134
Random, Bob 123
Rapp, Paul 143
Ray, Aldo 55
Ray, Jacki 4, 168–170
Read, Dolly 170–172
*Red Line 7000* 142
Reiner, Carl 198
Reubens, Paul 36
Reynolds, Burt 143, 165
Richards, Rudy 32
*The Ride to Hangman's Tree* 104, 105
Riley, Jeannine 173–175
*The Road Hustlers* 35
Rodgers, Pamela 175–177
Roeg, Nicholas 151
Rogers, Kenny 167
Rogers, Linda vii, 4, 178–183
Rogers, Steve 129
Roland, Gilbert 198
Romano, Andy 155, 184
Rooney, Mickey 105
Rooney, Mickey, Jr. 123
*Rosemary's Baby* 165
Ross, Herb 151, 152
Ross, Merrie Lynn 55
Ross, Myrna 183–185
Rowley, Jeremy 38
Ryan, Irene 199

Ryan, Jack 198
Ryder, Mitch 133

Sabich, Spider 53
Sachse, Salli 57
Sands, Tommy 197
Satana, Tura 185–187
Savage, Peter 135
Schmidtmer, Christiane 187–190
Schreiber, Avery 151
Scorsese, Martin 143
Scott, Linda Gaye 190–193
Scott, Sandra 198
Seagram, Lisa vii, 4, 193–201
Sebring, Jay 199
Sellers, Peter 25, 53
*Seven Days in May* 68
Sharma, Barbara 45
Shaw, Bobbi 4, 201–203
Shear, Barry 46, 47
Sher, Jack 197
*Ship of Fools* 189
*Short Walk to Daylight* 45–47
Sidaris, Andy 167
Sidney, George 50–52, 54–56
Siegel, Don 105
*The Silencers* 52, 147, 150, 209
*Silent Movie* 153
Silvers, Phil 151
Sinatra, Frank 51, 52, 54, 121
Sinatra, Frank, Jr. 120, 123
Sinatra, Tina 105
Six, Eva 203–205
Smith, Roger 165
Smith, William 153
Spang, Laurette 47
Spillane, Mickey 136
*Stacey* 167
Stark, Ray 20
Sterling, Tisha 121–123
Stevens, Connie 142
Stevens, Stella 3, 4
*The Stoolie* 135
Strasberg, Susan 47
Streisand, Barbra 20, 23, 151, 152
*The Sunshine Boys* 134, 135
*Sweet Charity* 43–46
*The Swinger* 52

Taka, Miiko 34
Tamblyn, Russ 142
*Tarzan* 69
Tate, Sharon 4, 66, 68, 165, 199, 205–208
Taurog, Norman 182
Tayback, Vic 36
Taylor, Robert 68
*A Teaspoon Every Four Hours* 135
Teele, Margaret 208, 209
Tenzer, Bert 199
Terry-Thomas 199
*That Girl* 46
Thomas, Larri 208

# Index

Thomas, Marlo 46, 142
*Tickle Me* 141, 182
*A Time for Dying* 165, 166
Tindall, Marilyn 4, 208–211
*Toma* 47
Townsend, Bud 35
Trinka, Paul 186
*Truck Stop Women* 55
Tsopei, Corinna 211–213
Tsu, Irene 19
*2000 Years Later* 199

*The Unkissed Bride* see *Mother Goose a-Go-Go*

*Valley of the Dolls* 199
Vaughn, Robert 19, 55, 68, 80
Verdon, Gwen 45, 46
Vetri, Victoria 4, 213–216
Villere, Dawn 34
*Village of the Giants* 121–123

*Viva Las Vegas* 142
Vogel, Ron 50

Wagner, Robert 142
Wald, Jane vii, 216–218
Watson, Jan 4, 151, 208, 210, 218–221
Wayne, Carol 4, 54, 221–223
Wayne, John 51
Wayne, Nina 223–226
Welch, Raquel 1, 2, 21, 35, 56, 67, 106, 149, 183, 198, 199
*Welcome to the Club* 135
Weld, Tuesday 123
Welles, Meri 198
Wellman, William, Jr. 182
Wells, Carole 153
Wells, Delores 4, 226–228
*Wendy and Me* 198
West, Adam 199
*Westworld* 163, 167, 168

*What's Up, Tiger Lilly?* 116
*When Dinosaurs Ruled the Earth* 215
*Where Does It Hurt?* 25
Widmark, Richard 107
*Wild and Wonderful* 67
Wilkinson, June 4, 228–230
Williams, Edy 4, 105, 198, 230–233
Williams, Van 19
*Winter a-Go-Go* 179, 182
Winters, David 45
Winters, Shelley 67, 198
*The Witchmaker* 21
Wright, Ben 68
Wyler, William 20

York, Dick 199
York, Francine 4, 182, 233–236

Zanuck, Darryl 51

www.ingramcontent.com/pod-product-compliance
Ingram Content Group UK Ltd.
Pitfield, Milton Keynes, MK11 3LW, UK
UKHW050534150426
5217IPUK00026B/1937